RHETORIC IN HUMAN RIGHTS ADVOCACY

RHETORIC IN HUMAN RIGHTS ADVOCACY

A Study of Exemplars

Richard K. Ghere

LEXINGTON BOOKS
Lanham • Boulder • New York • London

Published by Lexington Books
An imprint of The Rowman & Littlefield Publishing Group, Inc.
4501 Forbes Boulevard, Suite 200, Lanham, Maryland 20706
www.rowman.com

Unit A, Whitacre Mews, 26-34 Stannary Street, London SE11 4AB

British Library Cataloguing in Publication Information Available

Library of Congress Cataloging-in-Publication Data

Ghere, Richard K., 1945-
Rhetoric in human rights advocacy : a study of exemplars / Richard K. Ghere.
pages cm
Includes bibliographical references and index.
ISBN 978-0-7391-9393-8 (cloth : alk. paper) -- ISBN 978-0-7391-9394-5 (electronic)
1. Human rights advocacy. 2. Rhetoric. I. Title.
JC571.G448 2015
323.01'4--dc23
2015002887

∞ ™ The paper used in this publication meets the minimum requirements of American National Standard for Information Sciences Permanence of Paper for Printed Library Materials, ANSI/NISO Z39.48-1992.

Printed in the United States of America

CONTENTS

PREFACE

On a chilly winter afternoon in 1981, a window display at a bookstore near Boston University caught my attention as I walked toward Marsh Chapel on the other side of Commonwealth Avenue. Specifically, I spotted two light-blue sweatshirts, both with facial silhouettes of famous duos on their fronts. One featured "Steve and Idi" with representations of a well-known vocalist of the 1960s and the third president of Uganda. The other displayed "Ike and Tina" with the thirty-fourth President of the United States and an entertainer sometimes called "the queen of rock." Why I did not cross the street to purchase one or both, I cannot recall—whether a case of a lack of cash (as often the case at that time) or of initiative.

That window display flashed back in my mind some twelve years later when I came across a terrific book on public ethics that offered comparisons of some public servants whose careers exemplified the loftiest of ethical standards with others of lesser scruples. Through their novel format, Terry Cooper and Dale Wright—editors of *Exemplars in Public Administration* (1992)—invited readers to evaluate how exemplars approached their public callings, some with ferocious integrity and others with quite less. Cooper and Wright challenged me to discern how ethical character makes a qualitative difference in public service; but beyond that, they prodded their readers to determine how contextual circumstances surrounding these public officials impinged upon their actions. In this respect, strong character and principles are to be celebrated, so long as individuals can persevere over the long haul to tackle the complexities and frustrations of their work. Suffice it to say that I am grateful to both Terry and Dale for their book that now provides a cogent model to characterize human rights advocacy *in praxis*, especially in terms of the rhetoric and narratives that particular rights exemplars employ to support their appeals.

A number of events over the past few years have coincided to extend my work at the University of Dayton to teaching and research in the area of human rights. Specifically, the University of Dayton has instituted an interdisciplinary human rights undergraduate major intended on one hand to prepare some students for human rights–related vocations but on the other to articulate what it means to be human and to advocate for human dignity in *any* chosen career. The University has also established a Human Rights Center that draws upon its faculty members from various disciplinary backgrounds to share their expertise in researching human rights.

The Center prioritizes research and programming efforts directed to what it calls *the social practice of human rights* that, among other concerns, focuses upon *advocacy* as a craft if not an *art*. As one involved with Human Rights Center research, I grapple both with what the *practice of rights advocacy* actually entails and exactly *who qualifies* as a human rights advocate. As for the first, our emphasis upon advocacy implies that an understanding of the human rights movements extends beyond concerns about global standards and mechanisms of protection to direct attention to *people* who champion the causes of *other people* who suffer indignity and deprivation. Somehow we need to reconcile mixed messages that on one hand convey absolutist resolve to "denounce injustice" (reminiscent of the late cartoonist Doug Marlette's character Will B. Dunn) but on the other call for pragmatic collaboration that brings diverse stakeholders to the table.

In our passions to breathe life into the Center, we colleagues continue our dialogues about what *human rights* specifically encompasses. True to our moorings in the social sciences, we tend to proceed along the reductionist road of the *"isn'ts"*—*human rights isn't humanitarianism, isn't peace-keeping,* and so forth—to endorse a precise identity for it as a legitimate academic pursuit. Such a stringent road would effectively disqualify some exemplars included in the book (as examples, Mary B. Anderson and Daniel Barenboim) as bona fide human rights advocates.

An alternative, expansionist path wanders through human experience circuitously. It meanders, for example, from future to past and present (as the sixteenth-century painter Titian did in his *Allegory of Prudence*) as well as from any number of cultural settings—some with their own track records of human deprivation—to the value systems of international organizations that advocate for universal human rights. Nonetheless travelers on this path can be fairly sure that rights advocacy has predated university programs such as ours through the works of those who have cared about the human condition—whether parliamentarians such as William Wilberforce, writers such as Dostoyevsky, composers such as Verdi (with compassion for an Egyptian slave girl), or an observer who framed didactic narratives to goad the pretentious.

In this book I explore the latter road in reaching out to exemplars who (have) dedicate(d) much of themselves to advancing the human condition, and also to others with no such intentions, both in the current frame and the recent past. Reliance upon rhetorical inquiry expands the study of human rights beyond the positivist foci of "*is*" and "*isn'ts*" to the plausible "*could be's*" and retrospective "*could have been's.*" In particular, "the could have been's" reassess familiar historical episodes such as Lyndon Johnson's 1964 Gulf of Tonkin Resolution and the 1989 Tiananmen Square killings as human rights conundrums that remain embedded in national identities.

More recently, the US Senate Intelligence Committee's late-2014 release of its report on the CIA torture program (in the aftermath of the 9/11 terrorist attack) led some to speculate on the "could have been's." "'Imagine if we didn't go down that road. Imagine. We played into the enemy's hand,' said Ali H. Soufan, a former FBI agent who clashed with the CIA over its interrogation tactics. 'Now we have American hostages in orange jumpsuits because we put people in orange jumpsuits'" (Apuzzo and Risen 2014, A1). Regarding plausible "could have been's," the authors of *The New Rhetoric* (1969) make the case that argumentation reaches beyond the self-evident and rationally verifiable to the "that of the credible, the plausible, and the probable [that eludes] the certainty of calculation" (Perelman and Olbrechts-Tyteca 1969, 1) with a good measure of indignant commentary on 'he positivist's insistence upon proof.

Along the expansionist road, rhetorical inquiry offers an especially perceptive ear for what a culture "sounds like" in terms of what Gerald Hauser calls "the language of lived experience" (2008, 445), particularly as it supports rights ideals or condones abuses. Presumably artists have as perceptive ears and eyes on culture as do researchers who follow positivist traditions. For example, in his recent book *Hallelujah Junction: Composing an American Life* (2012), composer John C. Adams reviews his musical projects (e.g., scores and operas) that essentially amount to political and cultural interpretation conveyed through the rhetoric of music.

In a chapter about his efforts shaping the opera *Nixon in China*, Adams refers to his collaborator Alice Goodman, who captured a piece of 1970s American culture in the libretto she wrote for the Pat Nixon character:

> Pat Nixon, dressed in the traditional First Lady's fire-engine red coat, is the quintessence of middle-American womanhood, obedient and submissive, bowing to the historical imperative of her husband's ego. . . . It was part of Alice's genius to be able to handle images of Americana—so routinely abused in magazines and television advertising—in a way the recaptured their virgin essence, making them, when Pat Nixon sings them, not clichés at all but statements of deeply felt, non-conflicted belief. (137–138)

Moving to his chapter "Singing Terrorists," Adams speaks of his own agony amid the vitriolic condemnation of his opera *The Death of Klinghoffer* about the 1985 murder of a disabled Jewish American on the cruise ship *Achille Lauro* by Palestinian terrorists: "The unforgivable transgression of this opera [according to one critic] was that it made the intolerable mistake of going beyond the condemnation of terrorism to question the motivation of those perpetuating it" (169). It is refreshing that artists such as Adams with eyes and ears on culture recognize their work for *what it is, interpretation*. Their observations should matter in the study of human rights.

Rhetorical inquiry opens the possibility of *hope* for deliberation, often in the midst of the shrill rhetoric of *fear* conveyed by speakers who capitalize upon self-evident "certainty" and "necessity." As apparent in various case studies in this book, those who articulate a rhetoric of hope undertake a substantial burden in the face of adversaries who exploit fear. Perhaps some of the cases herein can inform those who struggle for hope.

Permit me to express my gratitude to those who have supported my work on this book. In addition to my colleagues in the Department of

Political Science at the University of Dayton, I would like to thank Provost Paul Benson, Interim Dean of Arts and Sciences Jason Pierce, and Center Research Director Mark Ensalaco for their encouragement. I have depended heavily upon Youssef Farhat, who collaborated in drafting the Iqbal Masih sketch in chapter 4, for his assistance and resourcefulness. At Rowman and Littlefield, Justin Race's enthusiasm for this project, Kate Tafelski's guidance, and an anonymous reviewer's candor offered valued motivation and direction. Lisa Ellison (my spouse) provided editorial help in proofreading text and critiquing ideas. Lastly, I am indebted to long-time personal friends who assist me in exploring dimensions of thick moral vernacular, especially in travels to Moorhead and while there, that offer up much for rhetorical inquiry.

Hopefully readers will not attribute my interests in history and the arts to pretentiousness on my part; in college my performance was little more than adequate as a history major and less impressive as an English minor. Regarding the latter, I dedicate this book to the memory of an English professor, Walther C. Prausnitz, with whom I was neither that close nor distant. A Juilliard-trained cellist, Prausnitz was home on the range at our small college on the Minnesota–North Dakota border. His narrative of *the artist as priest* helps me understand praxis, particularly as it relates to human rights advocacy.

I

INTRODUCTION
Rhetoric and Human Rights Advocacy

Wild grass grows in particular areas unaffected by chemicals that "reputable" lawn services administer to keep lawns appearing well manicured, typically in affluent neighborhoods and subdivisions. "Responsible" neighbors (not all of us) presumably abide by an implicit norm to have their lawns rid of unsightly dandelions, "wild grass," and other weeds that compromise the aesthetics of outdoor space.

For some "wild grass" serves as a metaphor for human rights activity that "sprouts up" from particular soil, or cultural contexts, wherein people have been deprived of rights through the policies and actions of particular social institutions. Journalist Ian Johnson drew upon his experiences as a *Wall Street Journal* correspondent posted for several years in China during the late 1990s to illustrate three particular human rights episodes in that nation in his book *Wild Grass* (2004). More recently, Johnson wrote an article entitled "A Toppled Spire Points to a Church-State Clash in China" that appeared in the May 30, 2014, *New York Times*. As Johnson describes the situation in the first two paragraphs, attendees of the Sanjiang Church confront a conundrum that infringes upon their rights as individuals:

> For nearly a year, the Sanjiang Church was the pride of this city's growing Christian population. A landmark in the fast-developing northern suburbs, its 180-foot spire rose dramatically against a rocky promontory. Wenzhou, called "China's Jerusalem" for the churches

dotting the cityscape, was known for its relaxed ties between church and state, and local officials lauded the church as a model project.

Late last month, however, the government ordered it torn down, saying it violated zoning regulations. After fruitless negotiations and a failed effort by the congregation to occupy the church, on April 28 backhoes and bulldozers knocked down the walls and sent the spire toppling to the ground. (2014, A4)

Nonetheless, Johnson's initial description here focuses on some typical themes found in "wild grass" human rights stories: *individuals* (perhaps) with cause to claim their rights; a *context*—a fast-growing suburb that commands particular attention on the part of local officials; and *institutions*, including governmental bureaucracies that could be viewed as "rights-withholders" as well as the church itself. If Ian Johnson's story does in fact take on significance as a human rights problem, it is one unlikely to be settled in international fora. Although *The Universal Declaration of Human Rights* attests to "freedom of religion," it is doubtful that Sanjiang Church members would depend on that international norm as the crux of their claim or that government officials would acquiesce if confronted by such a claim. Rather, it seems more likely that "wild grass" rights-claims depend upon how locals argue their case *within the context.*

The congregation based its rights-claim on an agreement "signed by the congregation and by the local bureau of religious affairs, representing the government." In fact church members assert that they were told, "This will be your last church for twenty years, so make it big." Although it appears the church might have a case to litigate on the basis of that statement, it turns out that the provincial government arrested its own bureaucrats who made those accommodating statements. Johnson comments, "An official in the city's religious affairs bureau acknowledged that 'officials said it could be bigger, but perhaps this was a mistake.'" So much for the provincial court as a venue for rights-claiming.

WHY A STUDY OF RHETORICAL EXEMPLARS? THE ARGUMENT AND APPROACH

This book examines the rhetoric of various "exemplars" who advocate for causes and actions pertaining to human rights in particular contexts. Although some of these exemplars champion human rights, others are indeed "exemplars, but not of morality" (see Cooper and Doig 1992, 110) or of human rights. Simply put, the argument here is that concern for how particular individuals *advocate* for human rights causes—as well as how *antagonists* obstruct such initiatives—adds significant value to understanding the successes and failures of human rights efforts in particular cultural and national contexts. On one hand, we can grasp how specific international organizations and actors function to *develop* norms (for example, the rights of the child) and how rights are subsequently articulated in universal declarations and formal codes. But on the other, it becomes apparent that the *actual meanings* of those rights mutate when "accepted" within particular cultures.

For example, an advocate for gender equality in the Arab world relates, "I am a 47-year-old Egyptian woman. And I am among the fortunate few of my countrywomen whose genitals have not been cut in the name of 'purity' and the control of our sexuality." Mona Eltahawy proceeds to explain that although Egypt had banned female genital mutilation (FGM) in 1959, that ban was subsequently lifted. A more recent law again outlawed the practice, but it nonetheless permitted cutting under the "care" of medical professionals:

> "Medicalized" cutting is at 77 percent—up from 55 percent 20 years ago. When I interviewed a 53-year-old survivor of the practice in Cairo for a BBC radio documentary about women in the Middle East, she told me, "It must be carried out, because that's the way to maintain the purity of girls, to make sure that the girl is not out of control. We don't care if it's against the law or if they're trying to stop it. We know doctors who are willing to continue and have done so." (2014, A23)

So as Eltahawy attests, "Laws aren't enough" to advance girls' and women's rights not to be mutilated in this cultural setting. She points to successes in Senegal, where the practice has been curtailed through the efforts of the non-governmental organization (NGO) Tostan (discussed in chapter 2) that raised women's awareness about the severity of injury inflicted upon daughters through the practice.

Returning to our argument, rights advocates such as Tostan's educators involve themselves in *praxis* or *the practice* of rights advocacy. Focusing upon human rights advocacy as *praxis*, it follows that *how* individuals engage in conversations within a culture about a particular right is at least as critical as how the right evolved from its normative foundation or how it is articulated as a universal standard. Furthermore, the praxis orientation heightens our sensitivity as to how a proposed human right could be interpreted as an assault on "cultural purity," as Eltahawy's interviewee claims in the above quote. The praxis perspective informs us that the conversation about the rights issue (in this case, about FGM) may sound substantially *different* in a particular setting than that in the international human rights community.

Therefore, rights advocates who engage in practice need to act as interpreters between the discourses of the culture and the rights community. As explained later in this chapter, the art of praxis requires one to be an accomplished pragma-dialectician (Johnson 2013) who can demonstrate competency in advancing dialogue between communities that hold distinctly different, perhaps opposing, views about an issue (for example, the societal benefits or harms of FGM). Thus, the study of exemplars in this book allows readers to evaluate particular rights advocates *in praxis*.

A complementary facet of this argument relates to the centrality of *rhetoric* in observing how rights advocates function in praxis. Although more will be said of rhetoric in subsequent sections of this chapter, suffice it here to suggest that rhetoric focuses upon the *art of argumentation* and the various strategies and techniques enlisted therein. In that much of the "reality" surrounding human rights (from the standpoints of advocates and antagonists alike) is fundamentally *interpretive*, rhetorical (or argumentative) skill is of vital importance for advocates as competent pragma-dialecticians in presenting the case that a rights ideal can enhance life in a culture predisposed to reject that ideal. As will become apparent in subsequent chapters, some rights advocates (e.g., Mary B. Anderson and Daniel Barenboim) exhibit stronger rhetorical skills than others (e.g., Julian Assange); but it is also the case that some exemplars exercise their rhetorical capabilities as *antagonists* of rights-causes (e.g., Joe Arpaio and Geert Wilders) in justifying actions that (however implicitly) dismiss human rights ideals. Thus, readers would do well to assess the strengths and weaknesses of the exemplars discussed in chapters 3 through 6 in terms of their rhetorical skills in advancing arguments that either support or obstruct human rights initiatives.

In summary, the thrust of this book rests upon the argument that human rights are realized through the difficult work of advocates in praxis. In large part, these "rights practitioners" need to advance rights ideals that are formulated in the discourse (or "language") of the human rights community into that of particular societies that may regard those ideas as threats to their culture. The study of particular human rights advocates *and* antagonists as *rhetorical exemplars* adds to a general understanding of human rights by comparing the argumentative skills of those who advocate *for* and *against* human rights initiatives.

As for *approach*, the book searches for meaningful comparisons among the exemplars examined, particularly in reference to the natures of rhetorical argumentation they employ. Specifically, inquiry follows three general concerns: (1) the extent of similarity or difference in rhetorical character of argumentation concerning rights issues, (2) the extent to which advocacy rhetoric is affected by cultural and institutional factors, and (3) whether exemplars (appear to) follow particular ethical orientations (such as deontological principle, consequentialism, or virtue) in pursuit of their advocacy for or against human rights ideals.

In chapter 7, readers will proceed to elaborate discussions of three general conclusions drawn from comparisons of rhetorical exemplars in this book. To summarize the first conclusion related to *rhetorical character*, it can be said that

- *The exemplars, whether human rights advocates or antagonists, appear more similar than different in regard to the character of rhetorical argumentation.*

In particular, most exemplars seek adherence from *diverse audiences*, engage in *dialogic* discourses (that is, seek out interaction with audiences), and speak both to the *universal rights community* and to *specific societal contexts*. However, human rights advocates in this study (all of them) appear more apt to engage in discourses directed toward *the future* as compared with antagonists—some of whom focus more on the past and present.

The second, concerning how advocacy rhetoric relates to *cultural* and *institutional* matters, reveals that

- *Rights antagonists are more inclined to engage discourses of "cultural purity" in their arguments than are advocates*

and that

- *Antagonists, more so than rights advocates, argue in support of "opening" institutional boundaries to permit dominant societal discourses to affect policy.*

In the first case, rights antagonists engage in discourses that place themselves as protectors of cultural values and defenders of the established social order. With the latter, rights antagonists appear inclined to build narratives that encourage cultural influences to permeate institutional boundaries, whereas advocates often depend on those boundaries to safeguard rights protections.

The third, relating to the *ethical orientation* of human rights advocates, uncovers evidence that

- *Human rights advocates respond both to the deontological principles embedded within notions of universal human rights and virtue ethics in pursuit of rights within specific societal contexts.*

Explained more fully in chapter 7, this mix of ethical orientations corresponds to the praxis work of advocates. Specifically, their professions call them to uphold rights principles to the extent possible in confronting particular challenges and obstacles "on the ground." Virtues such as optimism and perseverance provide ethical anchors for such difficult endeavors.

The bulleted generalizations above offer readers glimpses of what can be learned about the nature of human rights advocacy by evaluating the character of an advocate's (or rights antagonist's) rhetoric. In that comparative analysis assesses similarities and differences of time as well as space, it is instructive to compare the rhetoric of a few historical figures (e.g., President Lyndon Johnson as well as various elites involved in the Kent State University and Tiananmen Square tragedies) with that of more contemporary actors. However, some readers (perhaps undergraduate students) may find it helpful to focus specifically on the rhetoric of contemporary speakers; thus, the following comparisons of contemporary exemplars raise significant questions about the nature of discourses related to human rights:

- *Iqbal Masih and Pussy Riot.* Although these exemplars appear aptly characterized as human rights advocates, Iqbal frames narratives that justify actions in terms of legitimacy while Pussy Riot appeals to its *illegitimacy*. Are each of these narratives effective within their respective contexts? Are the members of Pussy Riot *fools*, or do they exercise practical wisdom in their rights advocacy as did Iqbal?

- *Iqbal Masih and Julian Assange*. Both exemplars appeal to their respective cultures as human rights advocates—Iqbal advocates for children's liberation from bonded labor and Assange for government transparency in its collection of personal data. From the standpoint of rhetorical strategy, which exemplar is more effective? What do Assange's self-deliberative narratives reveal about himself in regard to his (in)capacity to engage in praxis as a human rights advocate?

- *Joe Arpaio and Daniel Barenboim*. Maestro Barenboim actively pursues human rights advancement through his professional calling, but Sheriff Arpaio . . . well, not so much. In that rhetoric centers upon speakers and audiences, it is fitting to compare how each of these exemplars "play to their audiences." If (as asserted in chapter 6) Joe Arpaio can be aptly characterized as *an entrepreneur*, can the same be said of Daniel Barenboim? How do each of these speakers characterize the nature of *human empowerment* within their respective narratives?

- *Geert Wilders* and the Muslim women (whom Wilders provokes). Perhaps not so familiar to readers, Geert Wilders is a populist Dutch legislator who presumably qualifies as a human rights antagonist by virtue of his virulent rhetoric against Muslim immigrants. The sketch about Wilders (in chapter 5) details how Wilders's inflammatory rhetoric and actions provoked a number of Muslim women to post YouTube videos in which they articulated their voices in affirming their identities as devoted Dutch citizens and followers of their faith. Readers can compare Wilders's narratives within his rhetoric of fear with those within the women's rhetoric of hope.

The balance of this chapter addresses the nature of rhetoric as it relates to contemporary societies and rights-related issues therein. Particularly, attention is directed to "speakers" and their mode(s) of expressions, "audiences" as understood from various perspectives, the "status" of rhetorical analysis (or lack thereof) in empirical inquiry, and the connections between rhetorical analysis and human rights advocacy. Whether readers opt for the "contemporary track" (delineated by the above comparisons) or for each of the twelve sketches, it is advisable to peruse both the next section on contemporary rhetoric and the discussions in chapter 2 that relate to "thick and thin" ethics and institutional vernaculars.

RHETORIC

From the outset, our proposition that rhetorical analysis can generate powerful insights about human rights advocacy confronts the canonical problem of determining what modes of expression and action qualify as *rhetoric*. Used often as an authoritative reference in the chapters to follow, Perelman and Olbrechts-Tyteca's seminal work *The New Rhetoric* (TNR 1969) in large measure corresponds with Aristotle's classification scheme that distinguishes among three types of oratory: deliberative, legal, and epidictic (or emotive). Nonetheless, at various points in their extensive compilation of argumentative techniques and strategies, these rhetoricians "open the canon" that Aristotle introduced in his *Rhetoric*. In so doing, they encourage readers to utilize rhetorical study in ways that can ground discursive argumentation (that is, argumentation through *language*) in contemporary terms. At one point, Perelman and Olbrechts-Tyteca expand Aristotle's principal focus on public oratory to include written text as well (1969, 6, 135–136). Elsewhere they elevate the status of epidictic speech (showpieces of "artistic virtuosity" as in a funeral oration), discounted by Aristotle in classical rhetoric, as significant argumentation on a par with the legal and deliberative (47). In still another discussion, Perelman and Olbrechts-Tyteca update Aristotle's broad notion of "dialectic"—as the art of formal logic debate—what they call a "rapprochement" with rhetoric to accommodate a more specific, contemporary conception of struggle between contradictory assertions (5; Kennedy 1991, 14).

Perhaps Perelman and Olbrechts-Tyteca's most significant departure from the classical orientation toward rhetoric lies in their insistence that concern about rhetoric should not be confined to the "upper crust," students aspiring to become governing elites in the civic sphere. Rather, rhetorical attention should extend as well to argumentation in the everyday lives of ordinary people (1969, 7–8). Nevertheless, Perelman and Olbrechts-Tyteca maintain some boundaries on rhetoric that limit its use in analyzing expression pertinent to human rights advocacy, particularly in view of Gerald Hauser's interest in moral vernaculars. First and especially troublesome is the rhetoricians' limitation to consider only discursive argumentation (using formal language), ironically *not as a matter of principle* but instead as an expedient to garner political legitimacy (TNR 1969, 8).

But if human rights advocacy can do no more, it *must* renegotiate the boundaries of legitimacy particularly when those boundaries reinforce status quos. Referring to Polish graffiti that symbolized the Catholic Church's defiance toward the Communist state, Hauser asserts,

> Such uses of vernacular rhetoric have specific salience to human rights because they are the way discourse communities of the disempowered sustain their sense of identity and moral empowerment to resist oppression. Their moral vernacular stands apart from the political language provided by human rights covenants. . . . [T]heir appeals for solidarity and support were expressed in a *language of lived experience* specific to their community. (2008, 445; italics added)

Moreover, Perelman and Olbrechts-Tyteca's move to disqualify dramatic presentations as rhetorical argumentation berates "the language of lived experience" which animates the vernacular of the disempowered. An expert on the American theater illustrates how four black sisters as Vaudeville performers during the 1920s were able to negotiate "the politics of performance and management" through their stage performances in ways that re-oriented the audience's attitudes toward race, gender, and class:

> [T]he Whitman sisters were able to use their color to their advantage . . . that is, to go back and forth between black and white identities, while remaining popular with both black and white audiences. Granted, as women they did not pose the same perceived threat to white women [as two white female entertainers passing from white to black], but their act of passing threatened the hegemony nonetheless. (George-Graves 2000, 68)

George-Graves's numerous examples of how the Whitman sisters conserved their own cultural heritage while improvising in ways that altered existing cultural orientations powerfully affirm Perelman and Olbrechts-Tyteca's statement (quoted above): *"[W]e are firmly convinced that the most solid beliefs are those that are not only admitted without proof, but very often are not even made explicit*" (italics added). They also demonstrate why performative rhetoric constitutes an essential element of Hauser's moral vernacular, and as such it warrants particular attention as argumentation that can either support or obstruct human rights advocacy.

Another of Perelman and Olbrechts-Tyteca's boundary restrictions appears reasonable from an ethical standpoint, but it unduly constrains rhetorical analysis in matters of human rights nonetheless. Specifically the rhetoricians disqualify coercive statements as rhetoric (8). Yet one might expect to uncover instances when argumentation laced with unspoken dire consequences sets the tone within particular contexts of rights-deprivation. It would appear then that efforts to assess these veiled threats *as argumentation* would serve to advance an understanding of antagonistic environments surrounding human rights advocacy.

The concern about veiled threats and implied promises become more problematic as the rhetoricians include references to supernatural influences as coercion: "There are yet other cases—for example, blessing and cursing—in which language is utilized as a direct, magical means of action and not as a means of communication unless the framework is integrated into the framework of argumentation." (8) Hauser's conception of vernacular appears to do just that, as he illustrates how religious faith led to solidarity in opposing the Communist regime in Poland. With regard to cursing, George-Graves comments upon the symbolic sensitivities of certain dances on the Vaudeville stage:

> The Ring Shout did not allow the dancer to cross his or her legs and feet, because the Voodoo tradition at the root of this dance held that anything crossed would keep the "saints" away. As long as the feet did not cross, the movement was not considered sinful dancing and was allowed as a form of religious expression. (2000, 31)

Black performers such as the Whitman sisters could be effective in re-orienting cultural attitudes so long as they took care not to offend mainstream religious sensibilities. Beyond that, the Ring Shout example demonstrates how a particular mode of expression not customarily accepted as "legitimate rhetoric" assumes particular salience as perfomative discourse in the framework of the moral vernacular.

At this point, this discussion about rhetoric focuses upon two specific issues: (1) the speaker and modes of expression and (2) conceptions of the audience.

The Speaker and Expressive Modes

For practical purposes here, it is helpful to categorize "speakers" as public orators, authors, and performers (not to exclude others outside these schemes) who seek *adherence* (defined below) from their audience(s). The initial pages of Perelman and Olbrechts-Tyteca's *The New Rhetoric* outline specific tasks required of speakers and characteristics of rhetoric that speakers should grasp. First, it becomes incumbent on the speaker to either develop or rely upon a common language (which they specify as *formal, discursive language*) while others such as Hauser expand this to include the "language" of lived (or common) experience. For Perelman and Olbrechts-Tyteca, Alice offers an example of a speaker initiating language in her attempts to initiate conversation with Wonderland's creatures. When she encounters the caterpillar, Alice asserts, "'I think you should tell me who you are.' . . . [He responds] 'Why?'" (1969, 14 quoting Carroll 1960, 41)

The caterpillar's response underscores the speaker's obligation to demonstrate relevance in order to establish the "contact of minds" between herself and the audience. Beyond this, speakers need to "size up" their audience by anticipating how unified or diverse it may be in terms of its attributes and opinions and what it might expect from the speech or text. A religionist elaborates on expectations in focusing on a readership's "felt needs"; Tim Beal asserts that Bible publishing is a lucrative business because editions purchased previously fail to meet consumers' felt need to feel sufficiently holy (2011, 29–40). In another context, audiences may expect clarity, perhaps in the face of a highly ambiguous circumstance. Speakers do well to compare their own value orientations—for example, toward value monism or pluralism—with those of the audience. If differences exist, prudence would incline the speaker toward tactical adjustments that re-orient how members of the audience approach the topic. A noted literary theorist and legal scholar advises pluralists to "give their neighbor's value monism a fair shake" (Fish 1982, 501, quoting his colleague Wayne Booth).

In terms of text (either in print or digital form), authors exercise certain options or may be unconsciously drawn to them by virtue of their ideologies. As implied above, authors can characterize their expression as monistic and monologic (in essence as the "final," authoritative answer) or as pluralistic dialogue that invites readers either to draw their own conclusions or to carry on the debate indefinitely. In terms of the latter, Tim Beal understands sacred text *not* as imparting definitive answers but rather as providing a "library of questions" that spur on the faithful to socially construct applications appropriate to their particular times and contexts as they see fit (2011, 146–183). Such a perspective, one that stresses "doing" the Gospel within the situation, is strongly endorsed by contextualists such as Stanley Fish, who argue that "universal" principles do not and cannot exist outside of context (1982).

Stated differently, authors can frame their texts as open or closed canons; dialogic texts generally open discussion to divergent views of the past, present, and future, while closed texts follow a monologic intent to authoritatively settle a problem for all times and circumstances. In this Internet age, the dialogic text can be readily understood as analogous to a digital document containing multiple hypertexts that connect to other past or present speakers and texts. Although such intertexuality occurs digitally, its print analogies are easily recognized as standard footnotes and internal references to other speakers or texts (as examples, Aristotle referring to Plato or Moses to Abraham).

In a social or political sense, performers speak indirectly through their efforts to apply their talents toward goals beyond basking in applause and making money. One rhetorical grounding for a performer's "social" speech can be found in an "argumentation [against] waste" (see TNR, 279–281), an imperative *not* to squander *opportunities* afforded her by virtue of given talent. In an intriguing twist on conventional thinking related to human rights, Nadine George-Graves argues convincingly that minstrelsy (minstrel shows long regarded as patently racist) afforded black entertainers the opportunity to ply their trade so as to develop race, gender, and class consciousness in the minds of their audiences (2000, 59–60).

Finally in terms of human rights advocacy, some attention should be devoted to speakers who reside within institutions such as government bureaucracies, established religious bodies, cultural formations, and other pertinent organizations. Concerning audience adherence, it is worth noting that these "institutional speakers" have previously populated an audience addressed by speakers—such as mentors, in-service trainers, and other agents of socialization. These rhetors convey what the institution recognizes as fundamental regime or organization values (see Rohr 1989, 59–96) that account for a contextual logic of "ethics" within the institution. In essence, the expression of this logic constitutes the moral vernacular of the institution. By virtue of training, formal preparation, and depth of experience, institutional speakers can claim a "position of privilege" (see Fish 1982, 497) above those outside the institution (for example, citizens, refugees, and the stateless, among other groupings). Thus, they maintain the boundaries of institutional competence and authority.

Such privilege can justify the institutional speaker's prerogative to exercise discretion in "interpreting" what fundamental values, derivative laws, and "facts" mean as applied to particular contexts as well as in assigning priorities among values and laws. Perelman and Olbrects-Tyteca suggest that an institutional speaker's discretion to prioritize values in essence justifies the legitimacy of her institutional hierarchy as well as her authority to speak for it (1969; 80). To the extent to that values, laws, and norms derive from revered texts (as examples, the Bible or Koran, national constitutions, or even the Universal Declaration of Human Rights), institutional speakers may be situated to manipulate the iconic power of these cherished documents. In summary, these individuals rely upon institutional authority to legitimize speech.

Audiences

For Perelman and Olbrechts-Tyteca, the *new* rhetoric signifies a fundamental departure from the *old*—the new recognizes the *audience* rather than the *speaker* as central within rhetoric (TNR, 6–14). This difference in perspective, in its emphasis on the agency of individuals in the audience, implies that the audience exercises power through its dialogical participation in discourse. Illustrating the contrast between the old and new rhetoric, communications scholar Michael Leff cites others who comment upon the power asymmetry embedded in traditional understandings of "heroic" oratory: Traditional rhetoric

- "[regarded] the speaker as active and the audience as passive. (Scott 1975, 440),
- [placed] the speaker at the center of the transaction. . . . From [the classical literature] to the thrust of many twentieth-century textbooks in public speaking, the rhetorical transaction has been seen as one in which a speaker seeks to have his way with an audience both to achieve an immediate end and to achieve power or glory as a respected member of society. (Brockreide 1971, 124–25), and

- was unidirectional thereby vesting those with authority the power to impart information to inferiors, and its goal was to manipulate and exploit (Byham 1979, 22)." (Leff 2003, 136).

It follows then that the new rhetoric regards arguers *not* as cultural heroes but as ordinary individuals, themselves members of the audience, who engage dialogical (interactive) conversation within a particular context—or, in Hauser's terminology, a moral vernacular (2008).

Although Perelman and Olbrechts-Tyteca offer a number of insights about the audience as central to rhetoric—e.g., "the audience as a construction of the speaker" (TNR, 19–23) and "adaption of the speaker to the audience" (23–26), they leave much about the nature of the audience in the new tradition for others to work out—concerning such questions as those raised by logician Ralph Johnson:

1. How are we to define an audience?
2. What are the various types of audiences? and
3. How does the type of audience affect the arguer's ability to know it? (2013, 538)

In redirecting Johnson's first question of definition to one of *audience identity*, it is possible "to consider the ways in which audiences receive arguments and to develop better understandings of the nature of audiences" (2013, 509). Tindale relates that people are by nature "primed to receive"; they are socialized within their cultural tradition to listen to others' messages and perhaps "operate as an arguer because we fully live the condition of being *an* audience" (2013, 510; italics in original). Although expressed in the context of public affairs, Patrick Dobel's notions of "traditions" relate as well to particular audiences and their moral vernaculars:

> Traditions develop over time as people work with the practices, norms, meaning, and rituals that have been collectively developed by a community to address fundamental problems. Traditions accumulate knowledge and practice by empirically and reflectively engaging reality and adopting to it in incremental and collective ways. . . . Traditions exist because they provide answers, practices, and ways of conceptualizing the world that help solve basic and enduring problems for people. Workable answers and knowledge gain authority, which can

be reinforced by individuals or schools of knowledge that deepen, expand, or adapt the tradition to new challenges. (2001, 168)

Applied to rhetorical exchanges, Dobel's comments complement James Crosswhite's assertion that what Perelmen and Olbrechts-Tyteca call "adherence" actually amounts to an internal negotiation process whereby audience members "evaluate one another's arguments in a way that ensures that the most worthy argument will be the most effective one" (1989, 159). This suggests that audiences assume the function of updating and clarifying their traditions. It also implies that any evaluative standard for argumentation derives from *within* the audience and not from some external "God's-eye view" (see Tindale 2013, 516).

Another way to understand "adherence" in *new* rhetoric is to distinguish it from the general notion of "compliance"; the former involves give-and-take negotiation within the tradition while the latter connotes obedient acceptance. Further, the process of negotiating adherence becomes all the more critical in what Perelman and Olbrechts-Tyteca call *composite audiences*, explaining, "It often happens that an orator must persuade a composite audience, embracing people differing in character, loyalties, and functions. To win over different elements of the audience, the orator will have to use a multiplicity of arguments" (1969, 21–22). Tindale adds,

At any particular time, we deliberate about facets of our identity in deciding what to foreground and what to background. Our citizenship, residence, place of origin, class, race, gender, education, occupations, family relations, cultural pursuits, religious interests, and so on, form a web of belonging from which we emerge and within which we understand ourselves. (2013, 513)

Reference to a multiplicity of arguments implies that various issues of concern are complementary and inter-related. But more important, the typical diversity of the audience underscores the relevance of negotiation among its members.

Related to Ralph Johnson's second question (stated above)—*what are the various types of audiences*, Perelman and Olbrechts-Tyteca specify four particular categories: audience before a single hearer, self, particular audiences, and universal audiences. The rhetoricians devote specific attention to "argumentation before a single hearer" (35–40) and "self-deliberating" (40–45) as particular frameworks of argumentation. "Particular audiences" refers to argumentation within a cultural tradition (most of the discussion above has focused on the particular audience). Perelman and Olbrechts-Tyteca establish a framework as well for "the universal audience" (31–35), in which the speaker can find unanimity. However, much of their discussion appears equivocal in implying that such unanimity may only reside in the speaker's mind. Thus, concern about "the universal audience" persists as a cogent topic for discussion.

For example James Crosswhite concludes that, instead of recognizing the existence of the "universal audience," Perelman and Olbrechts-Tyteca merely recommend techniques for constructing one. If this interpretation is accurate, it follows that "pure" universal audiences do not exist but that synthetic ones can be cobbled together through political negotiations that seek "adherence" from several audiences. Put another way, even if universal assent to a given argument can be achieved, it is likely that the various parties reach that consensus through justifications, rationales, and agendas *specific* to their cultural outlooks. Nonetheless, even a "cobbled together" universal audience offers utility as a reference point for discussion among and within particular audiences by encouraging criticism in order to move consensus forward (Crosswhite 1989, 164–168).

Ralph Johnson's third question—"*How does the type of audience affect the arguer's ability to know it?*"—presumes that speakers prepare arguments before they study their audiences. For Johnson, the speaker's conundrum is much like an academician's anxiety in drafting a paper for a professional conference; he worries: *What kind of people will attend the session, how will it "go over," who (if anyone) will care,* and *what criticisms might surface?* So how can speakers cope with such uncertainty? Johnson asserts that the speaker can work through this uncertainty by thinking in terms of a *dialectical environment* that places the core of her argument against likely objections and feasible responses she might offer in response to them (2013, 540–41). In pursuing this strategy, the speaker becomes what Johnson calls a *pragma-dialectician* prepared to negotiate the significant disagreements and objections that arise within the audience. Such an approach inclines the speaker toward a nuanced interpretation of "adherence" and encourages her to think in terms of more realistic goals such as raising awareness or simply making an impact.

Johnson comments that if unanimous adherence "to the conclusion is the aim I am attempting to achieve, well, my goose is cooked. I might as well take it out of the oven or, rather, not even have bothered to put it in in the first place" (2013, 544). Thus, in casting it as the centerpiece in discourse, the *new* rhetoric characterizes audiences of various types as problematic, complex entities that exercise power in redirecting the speaker's logic or challenging her assertions.

RHETORICAL ANALYSIS AND EMPIRICAL INQUIRY

In common parlance, the term *rhetoric* is often belittled as "talk" or opinion without much substance. A more charitable view may recognize it as the study of public oratory that concerned Aristotle, Cicero, and others in classical times but largely discount it as irrelevant to empirical endeavor today. Occasionally issues of rhetoric in relation to scientific inquiry do surface about the "scientific" claims of doctrinal narratives on natural or physical phenomena (e.g., the origins of biological life) and to an assertion that the practice of science incorporates its own rhetoric. Concerning the latter, the editor of *The Journal of Theory Construction and Testing* points out that Charles Darwin laid out his ideas of evolution in *Origin of Species* as rhetorical argumentation; this prompts Charles Walker to include the following limerick in his editorial comments (2010, 31):

> *There was a young fellow named Darwin*
> *Whose theory folks found alarmin'*
> *He said that our species*
> *Descended from trees-zeese*
> *With rhetoric most disarmin'.*

Our concern however extends beyond ideological debates with science and the rhetoric of science (however poetic) to assess whether rhetorical analysis qualifies as legitimate empirical inquiry. The case made here— that rhetorical analysis *indeed* embodies and advances empirical in- quiry—rests primarily on two complementary assertions. First, if under- stood broadly as associated with "narrative framing" and "social con- struction," rhetorical analysis adds to the social scientist's repertoire of methodological tools; it can be especially useful in recognizing enact- ment processes whereby human volition accounts for objectified social realities. Second, and extending the first argument, rhetorical analysis can follow the cognitive processes that determine what "makes sense" within social institutions and in turn how that "sense-making" is conveyed and acted upon in political communities.

First Perelman and Olbrects-Tyteca make the case that (consistent with Aristotle's interest in dialectical oratory *in addition to* the deliberative) argumentation reaches beyond the self-evident and rationally verifiable to the "that of the credible, the plausible, and the probable [that eludes] the certainty of calculation" (1969, 1). Indeed the first few pages of *The New Rhetoric* present an indignant critique of the positivist position that knowledge must be validated by formal calculation. In his efforts to theorize on the rhetoric of "publicness," Gerald Hauser argues that researchers can assume an "empirical attitude" toward the study of rhetoric, rhetorical environments, and moral vernaculars. He explains, "By *empirical* I mean that the framework draws its inferences about publics, public spheres, and public opinions from actual social practices of discourse. . . . The evidentiary requirements of the framework, therefore, ultimately are tied to statements social actors advance on public problems" (1999, 275).

Moreover, some experts in social science research stress the desirability of incorporating the studies of narratives, rhetoric, and social construction into the methodological tool box to accommodate "the postmodern critique" or reaction against "modern" social science inquiry that insists upon experimental analysis or statistical inference. For example, Brewer and Hunter argue:

> [The] central argument, that there is no best singular way to the truth and that a variety of different methods should be considered in its pursuit, both antedates and resonates with many of the postpositivist critiques. In this light, multimethod research calls for a "soft" postmodern revision of more extreme versions of positivistic, scientistic modernity; and yet, at the same time, it is a postpositivist critique that still retains modernity's ultimate goal of a meaningful pursuit of scientific truth. (2006, 152)

As for rhetorical analysis in particular, Brewer and Hunter's further comments appear especially germane concerning the study of advocacy: "We suggest rhetoric's major contribution lies in seeing the process of research . . . as a concern for the variety of tools that might be employed to better convince other reasonable people of the truth of one's assertions. . . . From a rhetorician's point of view, the more arguments (methods), the better" (157).

Second, rhetorical analysis not only offers empirical inquiry a wider array of social research methodologies but also centers upon human expression's critical roles in explaining

1. the formation of institutional structures and systems,
2. the bonding of social groups that negotiate what is taken as institutional "knowledge," and
3. the outward utilization of that sense-making "knowledge" (i.e., "what everybody knows"; Berger and Luckmann 1966, 61) in institutional operations, especially as it affects people outside the institution.

Rhetorical analysis's contribution in elucidating this nexus is especially significant because it emphasizes what is so often overlooked in studying institutions (such as government bureaucracies, ecclesiastical hierarchies, NGOs, etc.)—that what *appear* as inanimate, machine-like institutional "objects" (organization structures, spans of control, regulations, procedures, and so forth) materialize from human efforts to "make sense" out of the ambiguities that surround them.

Institutional sense-making can be utilized to affect individuals in the broader political community in myriad ways, as Ian Johnson's account of the Sanjiang Church (discussed earlier) demonstrates. At a more general level, it can be said that human expression supports logics of institutional legitimacy, along with the "privileged positions" of speakers within the institution, that in turn condition the thinking and expectations of those in the community. Berger and Luckmann explain:

> Language provides the fundamental superimposition of logic on the objectified social world. The edifice of legitimization is built upon language and uses language as its principal instrumentality. The "logic" this attributed to the institutional order is part of the socially available stock of knowledge and taken for granted as such. Since the well-socialized individual "knows" that his social world is a consistent whole, he will be constrained to explain both its functioning and malfunctioning in terms of this "knowledge. It is very easy, as a result, for the observer of any society to assume that its institutions do indeed function and integrate as they are "supposed to." (1966, 60–61)

In this manner, individuals are socialized or conditioned to accept the "facts" and values articulated by the regime as determinations of "truth" and standards for honorable conduct.

In summary, the arguments unfolded here assert that rhetorical analysis supports empirical inquiry in the social sciences, particularly as it addresses postmodern concerns about the significance of discourses as expressions of power and vehicles of persuasion. In addition, rhetorical analysis offers an especially valuable lens for investigating the cognitive processes in social institutions, specifically those that account for institutional sense-making "logics" and how those logics are operationally utilized.

RHETORICAL ANALYSIS AND HUMAN RIGHTS ADVOCACY: A CONCLUSION AND INTRODUCTION

This chapter began by referencing Ian Johnson's report on an encounter between rather "ordinary" people, members of the Sanjiang Church in Wenzhou (China), and ordinary bureaucrats of Zhejiang Province. By no means does this episode about government efforts to demolish a church constitute a "life-or-death" matter, but it *does* assume the shape of a human rights problem of institutional abuse that compromises individual agency and freedom. It is noteworthy that, at least for a time, church members were able to mount arguments that bureaucrats could understand and accept—until their provincial superiors had them arrested. However, the local setting of Johnson's story, along with the verbal exchanges that made sense in that local setting, speak to the local, particularistic nature of many instances of human rights abuse. To paraphrase former US House of Representative speaker Tip O'Neill, most if not all human rights abuses appear to be *local*—that is, they occur within particular situations and contexts rather than as universal abstractions.

The Sanjiang Church episode offers a setting that distinguishes human rights "talk" about universal principles, often derived from intergovernmental organizations and international development agencies, from what Gerald Hauser calls particularistic moral vernaculars—the "lived language" of those claiming rights within their tradition. Hauser asserts:

[Moral particularism] assumes the primacy of its value system's maxims and rules of action, which are validated by tradition. It argues that fundamental values are culturally specific and that the communal group—whatever that might be (tribe, village, or kinship), and not the individual—is the basic social unit. If human rights are meaningful only in a frame specific to a cultural or political system, then there is no higher good that makes the specific claim meaningful beyond the benediction of being good because it is desired. (2008, 451)

Consistent with Perelman and Olbrechts-Tyteca's ideas on a viable framework of argumentation, this chapter then proceeded to discuss the speaker and audience, in terms of both characteristics and functions. As explained above, the freshness of *The New Rhetoric* lies in its understanding of audiences exerting power in the rhetorical exchange and of the speaker's place *within* the audience. This new thinking about rhetoric (as compared with classical assumptions that exalted the speaker in heroic terms) connects well with Hauser's moral vernaculars within traditions. To be effective, speakers need to advance dialogic arguments in order to reach *not compliance* but rather some sort of negotiated "adherence" with their fellow members of the tradition.

Michael Leff (mentioned earlier) argues that *tradition* can be used to intercede on behalf of human rights advances, likening the speaker as advocate to a jazz saxophonist who introduces improvisations to a traditional "theme" that are met with audience approval. Leff comments,

This fluid relationship between individual and community also seems to describe the conception of agency implicit within humanistic rhetoric. Like the jazz artist, the orator leads the community by merging with it, and identifies the self not as a still, isolated essence but as something realized in and through public performance. The individual and the collective . . . interact in relationships of collaboration. (2003, 141)

Perhaps Leff's analogy can be stretched further in suggesting that the jazz artist could lace her improvisations with other cultural idioms that may resonate with the audience. In other words, outside (international or "universal") vernaculars might be introduced, at least as points of reference, whereby the speaker could introduce new "wrinkles" to re-conceptualize issues within the tradition. In this way, the advocate's awareness of the universalism/particularism divide (Hauser 2007, 448) affords her the strategic opportunity to negotiate the various moral vernaculars (particularly the universal with the local) as improvisations on recognizable themes that will meet with audience approval or, in Perelman and Olbrechts-Tyteca's terminology, *adherence*. Presumably, such a skilled speaker takes on the role of pragma-dialectician that Ralph Johnson introduces above.

Chapter 2 expands on the notions of particularistic and universalistic moral vernaculars by associating each with corresponding interpretations of ethics and morality (used interchangeably here). Specifically, particularistic vernaculars incorporate a "thick" morality animated by "memory" (and historicity) within the tradition. By contrast, the universal vernacular involves a "thin" morality of universally abstract, categorical principles. Chapter 2 offers brief case studies to illustrate how vernaculars and moralities intertwine and to suggest how rights advocates might work through them dialectically. It also poses dialectical criteria for comparing the various advocate exemplars treated in chapters 3 through 6.

2

ADVOCACY RHETORIC THROUGH THICK AND THIN

A Conceptual Backdrop

Three young boys are at play. For whatever reason, one of the boys begins to blink his right eyelid; in response, the second boy starts winking, and then the third follows suit. Did the first intend to wink, or did he involuntarily twitch because of some irritation to the eye? Maybe a speck of dust landed on his cornea. Or perhaps he sought the attention of one friend to conspire against the other. Conceivably the other two could have mimicked the first attempting to placate him, or they may have been mean-spirited in mocking his "weird" gesture.

Noted anthropologist Clifford Geertz presents this hypothetical to explain what ethnographic research is all about and to convey what cultural anthropologists "do" in pursuit of their ethnographic work. Ethnographically then, "what is going on" with these boys? Thinly described, the situation could be cast simply as the three "clowning around" as kids typically do. But the cultural anthropologist, according to Geertz, probes beyond *thin description* to unearth *thick explanation*; the latter requires *interpretation* of expression and behavior—in this case what "winks upon winks upon winks" (1973, 9) could mean in the contexts of the boys' personalities and past behaviors.

Presumably Gerald Hauser delves into cultural ethnography when he elaborates on the idea of "vernacular rhetoric and [its] public influence" as it applies to human rights advocacy (2008, 443). As in superficially accounting for the boys' behaviors simply as "clowning around," we can thinly describe what is said in the Universal Declaration of Human Rights. But it is quite another matter to interpret how it may actually apply in what op ed. columnist David Brooks (an accomplished lay ethnographer in his own right) calls "the republic of fear," a different emotional landscape where one perpetually worries "that somebody is going to slash [his] throat, or that a gang will invade [his] house come dinnertime, carrying away [his] kin and property" (2014, A27). Human rights conventions notwithstanding, Brooks's thick description appears foreboding.

Moreover, David Brooks's reference to "a republic of fear" alludes to what Michael Mulkay calls a "rhetoric of fear" (in stark contrast to that of "hope") expressed by authoritative figures who defend particular *cultural categories* in a moral vernacular against those who would violate them. In particular, Mulkay associates "the rhetoric of fear" with British parliamentarians and church officials who opposed the "new reproductive technologies" (NRTs) in an extended debate in the House of Commons about the status of the human embryo and the (im)morality of its use in medical research (1995). The rhetoric of fear imposes certain boundaries that, if violated, would cause cultural upheaval. Management scholars Bloomfield and Vurdubakis elaborate upon how these opposing discourses relate to moral categories in a particular society:

> Mulkay suggests that the rhetoric of fear is associated with the violation of basic cultural categories and moral values. For us, the notion of "violation" is a particularly interesting one, and provides the key to what is to follow. Both Hope and Fear, we suggest, tend to derive their evocative powers from the notion of boundaries as the means through which cultural categories and moral values are upheld. Boundary talk can in this sense be understood as providing a key discursive register for formulating issues pertaining to new technologies in ways that imply either threat or reassurance. (1995, 535)

Generalized beyond the context of NRTs in Britain, Bloomfield and Vurdubakis's ideas of cultural boundaries and categories (interpreted from Mulkey's analysis) add texture to Gerald Hauser's moral vernaculars in a manner that resonates with cultural anthropologists such as Mary Douglas. In particular, she associates these categories as domains of authoritative "purity" that warrant protection from "pollution" or "dirt" (1966/

2002). Chapter 7 elaborates relationships between cultural categories implicit in particular vernaculars and the discourses of fear and hope; for now there is reason to expect those rhetorical exemplars designated as rights *advocates* in this study with the rhetoric of hope and *antagonists* with the rhetoric of fear.

This study of rhetorical exemplars who (for better or worse) affect human rights calls us to investigate *advocacy upon argumentative strategy upon moral vernaculars upon particular cultures*. Thus more often than not, the impact of human rights advocacy (or in the negative, antagonism) raises questions of thick interpretation *even if* the substance of that argument can be expressed in thin descriptive terms. This chapter offers a conceptual backdrop that traces the inter-relationships among Gerald Hauser's "thick" (particularistic) and "thin" (universal) moral vernaculars, conceptions of "thin" and "thick" ethics, and "thin" and "thick" institutional discourses, which together can support subsequent examinations of exemplars' advocacy rhetoric in chapters 3 through 6.

The next two sections in this chapter present (respectively) distinctions between thin and thick ethics and thin and thick institutional rhetoric. Following those discussions, two cases studies related to international development illustrate how thin and thick moral vernaculars characterize human rights initiatives to empower women. The last two sections explain the logic of this book's organization and identify five analytical questions to guide comparisons of the rhetorical exemplars examined in this study.

THIN MORALITY AND THICK ETHICS

As Hauser implies, thin moral vernaculars of human rights are typically supported by universal ethics of abstract principles that may not resonate as legitimate within particular traditions. As shown below, alternative ideas of "thicker" ethics associated with particular cultures and their histories reveal a far more nuanced view of ethical rights and obligations than do the thin conventional ethics of universal abstractions. [1]

Thin Morality

Thin conceptions of morality (or ethics) generally reduce ethical considerations to a minimal set of obligations required of the individual. Fundamentally, these obligatory principles are expressed in terms of what is "good" or "bad" and what "can" or "ought" to be done, regardless of the context. In his discussion of Emmanuel Kant's theory of "rule deontology"—a prime example of "thin ethics" that focuses on duties to rules, ethicist William Frankena uses Kant's words to demonstrate the universalistic character of the theory:

> We must confine our discussion to what he calls the first form of the categorical imperative, "Act only on that maxim which you at the same time will to be a universal law." In this dictum, Kant is taking a principle . . . and offering it as the necessary and sufficient criterion for determining what more concrete maxims or rules we should live by. (1973, 30)

It can be said that thin morality regards the individual as an autonomous decision-maker whose identity exists apart from community and tradition. Jewish philosopher Avishai Margalit argues,

> Caring . . . in the context of morality, can be a thin, ad hoc notion, which may nevertheless be very demanding on the occasion it is exercised. Still, having paid the inn-keeper to look after the wounded man, the Good Samaritan is free to leave the inn, thereby terminating his accidental relationship with the injured Jew. (2002, 46)

Thin ethics may obligate one to some basic responsibility of care, but that duty requires no enduring commitments to the community.

Thick Ethics

Margalit articulates a thick understanding of ethics that corresponds to Gerald Hauser's notion of particularistic moral vernaculars. Margalit is especially concerned with the ethics of community, and of memory *in* community, as they elucidate members' obligations to each other. For him, ethical obligations are understood as a "thick" texture of caring relationships within community. This is not to suggest that "thin" morality is discounted. Rather, he argues, "[a]gainst the claim that caring belongs to morality and even constitutes its core, I would like to present a counterclaim, according to which we need morality precisely because we do *not* care" (2002, 32; italics his), inferring that we only care within the specific contextual relationships of families, communities, and other significant groups.

Posing the difference another way, Margalit asserts that "[thin] morality is long on geography [extending toward the universal or "whole of humanity"] and short on memory [a community's cultural *"knowledge from the* past]" (2002, 14). He anticipates that some might contest his terminology, particularly those who believe that "morality, properly understood, can handle all thick relations as well as thin ones" (45). Although he concedes that this point has merit, Margalit nonetheless suggests that these quarrels generally amount to "quibbling about the word *morality.*"

Margalit's thick ethics of memory appears especially germane to the rhetoric of human rights advocacy for two reasons. First, the Western conception of "rights" is most often understood in terms of "thin" abstractions (see Dubnick and O'Kelly 2005, 150), as explicitly stated in authoritative texts, even though the actual exercise of those rights are mitigated by contextual circumstances (e.g., one cannot shout "fire" in a crowded theater). So by inference, Margalit reminds us that rights are "thicker" and more circumstantial than may be recognized. Second, Margalit's attributes thick ethics to a community of memory, or a *tradition*, rather than to a politically defined society (i.e., a nation). His thick ethics therefore calls attention to rights and obligations in the context of a tradition's history that incorporates the emotions of ancestors as a basis of cultural legitimacy. Margalit compares Western democracies with other cultural traditions as follows:

> But do *democratic* regimes also need to recruit memory in order to secure their legitimacy? A democratic regime, so it seems to me, anchors its legitimacy not in the remote past but in the current election. It would seem, therefore, that liberal democracies are exempt from an orientation to the past and rest their power on the vision on the future . . . [but that] is by no means the whole truth. Constitutional democracies anchor the source of their legitimacy not only in the current election but also in a document from the past. A constitution is a constitutive part of the community's shared memory. (2002, 11–12)

Thus, Margalit's thick ethics of memory subjects rights vernaculars to the scrutiny of past and present audiences within the community.

THIN AND THICK INSTITUTIONAL VERNACULARS

Both thin and thick vernaculars abound in institutions such as government bureaucracies, non-governmental organizations (NGOs), and corporate entities, often colliding with each other and sometimes affecting human rights. More often associated with (universal conceptions of) "rights," thin discourses concerning a particular issue (as examples, "accountability" and "performance"; see Dubnick and O'Kelly 2005) typically rise above particular contexts and situations (in organization scholar Charles Perrow's words, to "purge particularism"; 1986, 6–9) as the fundamental purpose of Max Weber's "rational bureaucracy." Thus, thin discourses within institutions generally reinforce a "one-size-fits-all" management mentality limited to standard operating procedures (see Kearns 2013). By contrast, thick discourses—to extend Margalit's "ethics of caring" to institutional contexts—relate to matters of loyalty, trust, and value-sharing *within particular organizations*, such that what "performance" or "accountability" amount to in the US Marine Corps may differ markedly from that in the US Centers for Disease Control.

In distinguishing between thin and thick vernaculars in institutions, the intent here is to first identify (in a bullet format) a sample of bureaucratic concerns that are typically understood in terms of thin descriptions. Second, discussion turns to some particular contextual circumstances (also presented as bullets) that lead to a "thicker" understanding of such bureaucratic issues.

Thin Institutional Vernaculars

Rhetoric within bureaucratic institutions and about them in public audiences frequently addresses evaluative criteria in the form of thin description, as the following summaries of discourses of legal parameters, accountability, ethics, professionalism, performance, and management systems each illustrate:

- *Legal Discourses.* Bureaucratic leaders frequently stress the formality of their legal mandates (i.e., the "letter of the law") as justifications for their decisions. In some cases, this thin vernacular reflects risk-aversion—in the case of public bureaucracies, fear of litigation (Roth, Sitkin, and House 1994) and in international development and humanitarian NGOs, of recrimination by host regimes (see Hashemi 1996; Karim 1996).
- *Accountability Discourses.* Bureaucracies are usually expected to "account" for their decisions and outcomes in narrow terms of "answerability" restricted to compliant reporting. This thin discourse discourages initiatives to provide more elaborate (or "thicker") explanations to mitigate circumstances or to reframe the issue in a more pertinent fashion (see Dubnick 2005). "Account receivers" demanding accountability *as answerability* typically include elected officials and constituents in the case of government bureaucracies and donors with regard to NGOs.
- *Ethics Discourses.* Thin ethics conversations typically impose behavior standards that can be readily incorporated into laws or codes of conduct (i.e., prohibitions against accepting gratuities and bribes) or can be easily defined in terms of parity (as opposed to issues of "fairness" as contextual questions).
- *Professional Discourses.* Those serving in professional capacities within institutions frequently subscribe to "best practices" endorsed by professional organizations (for example, social work protocols for dealing with troubled families). By following such "industry accepted" rules-of-thumb, bureaucrats can become emotionally detached from the clientele served. In reference to international aid agencies, development expert (and critic) Robert Chambers directs a penetrating question to professional experts in the field—*Whose Reality Counts* (1997)? That of the professional or of the community served?
- *Performance Metric Discourses.* The double entendre in Robert Chambers' book title about "reality *counting*" speaks to an institutional preoccupation with metrics (quantitative indicators) to document program success. Institutional missions are thus understood as "production processes" as one organization scholar comments in caricaturizing the metric vernacular: "(1) anything 'good' (say, humanitarian efforts to assist displaced refugees) must be 'worth

something' in terms of dollars and cents; (2) thus, there is a need to *count* how many people 'do good' and how much 'good' they do" (Meyer 1994, 127).

- *Management Systems Discourses.* Much of the operational logics in government bureaucracies are articulated in management systems conversations surrounding concepts surrounding strategic planning, implementation, and evaluation. In development NGOs, the logical framework (or logframe) document embodies the connection between programming and planning and subsequently offers the evaluative criteria for monitoring project success. For example, a project to improve children's health in a rural (poor) local village might link various development objectives (e.g., "Children or estate laborers in X district enjoy better health than earlier."), indicators (e.g., "frequency of treatment of relevant diseases, health personnel's statements, mothers' statements"), and indicators for evaluation (e.g., "height, weight/age, frequency of diarrhea") (Dale 2003, 63).

Thick Institutional Vernaculars

Institutional discourses "thicken" when particular circumstances intervene in ways that justify (1) an organization's particular sense of institutional integrity (Selznick 1957; Frederickson 1996) and belief systems (Goodsell 2010); (2) its shared interpretations about what constitutes "knowledge" and "expertise" (Davenport and Prusak 1998; Cox and Piakyural 2011); and (3) other particular circumstances relating to the needs of those served (Chambers 1997; Payne 2005; Frederickson 2010). In view of the multitude of circumstances that could justify thick descriptions of "unique" situations, attention is directed to three particular circumstantial issues: contexts of class, race, and ethnicity; interpretations of knowledge and expertise; and enduring commitments to institutional integrity.

- *In Contexts of Class, Race, or Ethnicity.* Some public institutions have engaged themselves in the thick discourses of attending to social equity not only in terms of individual parity but also between significant racial and ethnic groups (Frederickson 1996; 2010). As a US school administrator, Ruby Payne urges her colleagues to become conversant in the vernacular of their students who contend with poverty and to value the strategic skills that equip those students to survive in poverty environments (for example, "*how to live without electricity or a phone*" and "*how to get by without a car;*" 1996, 38). An increasing number of local governments in the United States are currently engaging in accommodating and constructive conversations with undocumented populations in contradiction to the thin rhetoric of immigration law (see Ghere 2013). In regard to international development, Robert Chambers advocates for participatory strategies that "that put first last," that is, subordinate professional mores and discourses to the vernaculars of traditional cultures (1997, 210–237).

- *In Interpretations of Knowledge and Expertise.* In their book on knowledge management, business experts Thomas Davenport and Laurence Prusak argue that "knowledge derives from minds at work" (1998, 5). This implies that, in the midst of a technical age wherein data and information abound, socially bonded work groups collectively select what they regard as "tacit," actionable knowledge in preference to other available "thin" information. Often guided by colleagues with considerable experience working within the institutional setting, these socially endorsed reservoirs of favored knowledge drive discretionary decisions (Cox and Pyakural 2013). Administrative theorists Melvin Dubnick and Ciarán O'Kelly explain how, during the run-up to the Iraq War, highly experienced personnel within the British intelligence community held to the view that Saddam Hussein had "weapons of mass destruction" despite the lack of tangible evidence to support their position (2005).
- *In Enduring Commitments to Institutional Integrity.* Particularly strong commitments to particular missions and values typically associate with "thick" normative cultures shared within the institution. Such commitments oblige leaders to take care in conserving their missions and values in the midst of pressures to compromise them—perhaps in efforts to accommodate "thin" discourses of "accountability as answerability" or performance metrics (see March and Olsen 1989; Terry 1995). Some scholars of public bureaucracy elaborate on a "spirit of public administration" (Frederickson 1996) and a "mission mystique" (Goodsell 2010); these commitments as-

sociate public service with a higher calling of care for citizen well-being than typically found in more generic discourses on administrative processes.

Although the above offers only a sampling of thin and thick discourses within institutions, it presumably substantiates the case that Gerald Hauser's notions of alternative moral vernaculars can be found within institutions as well as in society. The next section illustrates how divergent institutional vernaculars related to human rights emerge in two case studies in international development.

HUMAN RIGHTS VERNACULARS IN TWO INTERNATIONAL DEVELOPMENT INITIATIVES

So far, much has been said about two significant but rather abstract topics central to this study of advocacy rhetoric, alternative moral vernaculars (as characterized by Gerald Hauser 2008), thick and thin ethics, and the dialectics of argumentation (by Ralph Johnson 2013). Perhaps these abstractions become more sharply focused when presented in a case study format. Readers are encouraged to identify and compare alternative human rights vernaculars that surface in two cases below that relate to international development efforts to empower women.

Case I: Microfinance for Silk-Reeling in Rural India

Fiona Leach and Shashikala Sitaram describe the efforts of an (unidentified) NGO in implementing a microfinance program intended to empower lower-caste Indian women to become entrepreneurs in the silk-reeling industry. This project involving twenty women in Karnataka State in South India was undertaken as part of a four-country initiative (along with comparable projects in Ethiopia, Peru, and Sudan), funded by the UK Department for International Development (DFID) during 1997 and 1998.

The project objectives focused upon "develop[ing] the women's skills and confidence in managing all aspects of silk-reeling and enabl[ing] them as entrepreneurs to earn three to four times their present income" (Leach and Sitaram 2002, 577). As could be expected, the program logics and management protocols in the Bank's micro-lending initiative was expressed in the thin bureaucratic vernacular of linear cause-and-effect sequencing and expected outcomes at various milestones. For example, the women were required to participate within microfinance groups that would provide them access to loaned working capital to purchase reeling units for their homes and silk cocoons to be processed. The NGO required the women to attend an intensive 28-day training course that emphasized motivation and self-confidence and included visits to various industry sites such as the silk exchange in Bangalore.

On one occasion, the NGO invited husbands or male relatives to participate in discussions about the project rationale, family changes to be expected, and ways they could contribute to project success; most appeared supportive of the project. Nonetheless, the Bank's discourse with the men conveyed the program's logic in a monological manner (although it *did* apprise the men of family-related impacts and disruptions they might expect.) Subsequently, the women followed a production process in their work groups that involved rotation among specific functions such as buying at the cocoon market, reeling the silk at home, and selling the finished product on the Bangalore Silk Exchange.

Ranging in age between twenty and forty, the women (each non-literate and all but two married) had engaged in silk-reeling as hired laborers as a means of supporting their families. Leach and Sitaram relate that these women were expected not only to provide for household expenses but also to subsidize their husbands' indulgences (tobacco, alcohol, and so forth). In most of these extremely poor households, men worked sporadically if at all, and families contended with significant indebtedness.

Early on, the women's participation in the microfinance program affected their lives both positively and negatively. In large part, the women perceived themselves as "business people"; some had in fact become employers (having hired their own laborers) and as having gained economic and social status within the community (Leach and Sitaram 2002, 580–581). But on the downside, they became frustrated by the excessive work of combining vocation with family responsibilities and by husbands' complaints about having to escort them to the cocoon market and Silk Exchange and about their long and frequent absences from the household. In rhetorical terms, the women were very understandably ill-prepared to negotiate the thin vernacular of business enterprise with the thick vernacular of their tradition, especially as the latter related to power dynamics in the family system.

Over the longer term, the NGO's training sessions did not provide the women sufficient entrepreneurial know-how to weather the precipitous decline in the price of silk on the volatile Silk Exchange. Leach and Sitaram detail the women's "descent into despair" that occurred two months into the project when it became increasingly difficult to generate proceeds needed to cover the working-group's financial obligations to the NGO as lender. In response, the NGO demanded that husbands sign over house deeds, thus fueling spouses' animosities toward the women's participation in a program that led them further into debt. The authors characterize the program's effects on marital relationships as follows:

> The men continually interfered with the [working-] group's activities by assembling outside the meeting place, encouraging the women to fight among themselves, and participating in the women's arguments when they arose. One woman reported being beaten by her husband, who was trying to convince her to withdraw from the scheme, although she was now president of the group. More ominously, another woman said that her husband had tried to drown her by plunging her head in the water tank. (2002, 582)

Returning to Karnataka State three years later, one of the authors (Leach) found that all of the women except one (who continued trading on the Silk Exchange) had returned to casual labor working for others in the silk industry. For the most part, life reverted to as it had been prior to program involvement, except for the heightened indignation of their spouses, or in the authors' words, "[t]he men blamed the women for what they saw as a disastrous experiment and clearly did not intend to let them forget it" (Leach and Sitaram 2002, 584).

CASE 2: ADULT EDUCATION AND LITERACY PROGRAMMING IN SENEGAL

As external evaluators of an educational and community development initiative in Senegal, Peter Easton and his colleagues chronicle the efforts of Tostan (an in-country NGO) in leveraging adult education to promote the formulation of social policy "from the bottom up." Tostan—meaning "breaking through" or "coming out of the egg" in the indigenous Wolof language (2003, 446)—commits to development that evolves through grassroots dialog and that generally resists thin planning vernaculars. Regarding its efforts in Senegal, Easton et al. explain, "[t]he initiative got underway in the late 1980s as an attempt to develop non-formal education and literacy programming for Senegalese women grounded in their own perception of problems and based on their own learning styles" (446).

Tostan targeted its literacy initiatives toward women in specific Wolof-speaking, agricultural villages in Senegal (and also in Pulaar-speaking communities in Gambia) and invited men to participate as well. Consistent with Tostan's problem-solving approach, program participants were called upon to design a curriculum that met their needs and that was "anchored . . . in a Senegalese version of women's ways of knowing" (Easton et al. 2003, 447) in workshop settings. Thus, the Tostan curriculum was collaboratively designed as an 18-month study consisting of six modules: hygiene, oral re-hydration, immunization, leadership skills, feasibility studies for local projects, and project management techniques; literacy instruction in the native language was interwoven within each of these modules.

Easton et al. relate that the six-module program proved so popular that participants requested further continuing education after the 18-month study concluded. In response, participants and the Tostan staff developed four subsequent modules of local interest: human rights, women's health, early childhood development, and sustainable natural resources management. Discussions relating to the first two broached issues of women's sexuality that had been taboo and thus generated record attendance at the sessions; awareness of these activities spread by word-of-mouth within the villages. Especially sensitive discussions arose concerning the oppressive experiences endured through the ritual of female genital cutting (FGC). As Easton et al. report,

> [T]he concept of human rights and the evidence of its international endorsement seem to have struck a chord with a rural population quite aware of its disadvantage compared to urban areas and the industrial world and not far removed from a history of oppression. Programme designers realized that the human rights component provided a means for addressing health issues as well and of fostering consciousness-raising, empowering experiences that allowed women to open up for the first time about topics that had been traditionally taboo and created

a platform for involving both women and men in social problem solv-
ing. (2003, 448)

Further, the authors suggest that male participants were especially curious
about human rights and their implications for themselves, so men's attendance increased as well.

Tostan officials were then caught off-guard by the direction of discussion in the follow-up sessions concerning "what to do" as a basis for
community action—the obvious course of action for participants was to
publicly renounce the practice of FGC and to lobby local officials to do
the same. Easton et al. relate that the group assembled twenty Senegalese
journalists to convey their demand to abandon FGC, and that message in
turn was transmitted via television and other media. Although space limitations here preclude a full account of the group's mobilizing efforts, two
events merit particular attention. First, the Tostan participants successfully co-opted a woman—a traditional "cutter" having depended upon the
ritual for her livelihood—who was moved to offer public testimony of the
abuse inflicted upon girls that she had witnessed first-hand. The cutter
comments: "In the past, women did not dare to express their opinions
publically. If today we know our human rights and responsibilities, it is
thanks to the Tostan education program. We learned that everybody has
the human right life, health, education, land, and to be protected, and to
express one's thoughts and opinions." (In the interest of full disclosure,
note that this quote, as well as the other two below, were taken from a
Tostan-produced video.[2])

Second, the group negotiated with a much-respected imam who had
come forward to protest its actions. Tostan participants heeded the religious leader's appeal to conduct their efforts in a more diplomatic fashion,
to reference FGC more generally as "the custom," and to avoid outright
condemnation of those performing it. The group was receptive to the
imam's prudence in these matters because "the custom" was so closely
associated with "marriageability" and therefore had to be dealt with deli-
cately to avoid families' hostilities on behalf of their daughters' futures.
The imam reflects,

> For years we knew from experts about the harmful effects of FGC. But
> we did not want to believe them. Finally we all came to the conclusion
> that many of the health problems of our girls came from FGC. We
> were determined to end this source of our problems and improve the

overall health of the community. Today we can say we know more than our ancestors. The world does not stand still. It is forever evolving.

Easton et al.'s account of development assistance through education leading to social action characterizes the power of bottom-up participation given the number of villages in Senegal and elsewhere that abandoned "the custom." Tostan Executive Director Molly Melching sums up Totstan's efforts as follows:

> When Tostan allowed people themselves to look at some of these issues to reflect on what happened and find out what was happening to their children and what the consequences of that were, but always in relation to the vision of where they want to be in the future . . . , they said "no longer, we will not do this any longer."

Nonetheless, Tostan was left to grapple with two unintended consequences of its successes. First, spurred on by Tostan's accomplishments, Senegal's Assemble Nationale adopted a law prohibiting the practice of FGC and meting out severe punishments on violators. Although many NGOs would likely celebrate their advocacy forged into public law, this was not the case with Tostan that had in fact testified *against* this thin, top-down legislation as inimical to its bottom-up mission to motivate community action through program participation. Second, Tostan's successes attracted the attention of several donor agencies eager to have the NGO scale-up (or replicate) its efforts elsewhere, *provided* that it could develop thin, cost-effective implementation vernaculars.

How might an accomplished pragma-dialectician assess the "human rights" vernaculars that emerge in each of these cases? Figures 2.1 and 2.2 adapt Ralph Johnson's diagrammatic representation of the dialectical argument surrounding a particular theological argument (2013, 541), by stretching his context a bit, and can help us to examine rhetoric in development strategies. After identifying the *issue*, Johnson encapsulates what he calls the argument's *illative core*, which our figures refer to as the "inferential core." After that, his sketch calls first for ordering the "dialectical tier" that spells out the logic of means to ends implied in the vernacular argument and second for anticipating the critical "responses" that each logic could elicit from particular audiences (in his theological example, from atheistic and agnostic audiences). Finally, Johnson's diagram arrives at "criticisms," the crux of the dialectical issue.

As shown in Figure 2.1, the issue at hand is whether the Grameen Bank's micro-lending program can empower poor women in rural India who worked as casual labors in the silk-reeling industry by providing them the business acumen to serve as entrepreneurs. The "inferential core" of program logic is fairly straightforward—a 28-day program of instruction and field trips can provide that background, and micro-loans can provide capital for investment in a home silk reel. The "dialectical tier" shows two (out of perhaps several other) program "logics" that could elicit dialectical opposition, the first dealing with the (in)adequacy of the training program and the second with the (in)effectiveness of the Bank's outreach to male spouses. Presumably, the Bank could not (or did not care to) work through the local vernacular and integrate it into the implementation the micro-loan initiative; thus, Grameen Bank officials deserve low marks in "Pragma-Dialectics 101."

Figure 2.2 depicts a dialectical environment around Tostan's efforts to empower Senegalese village women by raising consciousness through

Issue *(Does a Grameen Bank micro-lending program empower poor silk-reeling women in Rural India?)*

Argument: Inferential Core
By increasing income, program will lead to "virtuous cycle" of gender empowerment
PROGRAM → GENDER EMPOWERMENT

Argument: Dialectical Tier
OBJECTIONS:
28-day training program cannot provide sufficient business acumen ← **RESPONSES** *(Perhaps these women don't have "what it takes.")*
Session with husbands does not garner their support ← **RESPONSES** *(. . . "what else could be said?")*

Alternate Positions:
Male spouses ← **RESPONSES** *How can Grameen Bank help without exploiting us and our tradition?*
Women participants ← **RESPONSES** *How can we benefit without offending each other and disrupting our families?*

CRITICISMS:
Grameen bank is "tone deaf" to the tradition's vernacular ← **RESPONSE** *We need to be profitable or else the program is unsustainable.*

Figure 2.1. Sketch of Case I Dialectical Environment.
Adapted with permission from Ralph H. Johnson, "The Role of Audience in Argumentation: From the Perspective of Informal Logic." *Philosophy and Rhetoric 46* (2013): 541.

adult education. Although this diagram presents the "inferential core" as a linear chain of causal events, Tostan likely understands them as a "messier" cluster of interrelated impacts. The dialectical tier of arguments largely focusing on whether the Tostan approach of serendipitous learning and community action can be packaged for replication in other places and supported by donors who expect a more conventional prospectus written in a global business vernacular. Even considering these "alternative positions," there is reason to assume that Tostan workers would ace "Pragma-Dialectics 101."

The rhetorical exemplars in this study will be judged according to their pragma-dialectical skills among other criteria. The next section explains what is (and is not) meant by the term "exemplar," particularly in reference to an existing comparison of moral exemplars in public administration that serves as a template for this book's organization.

RHETORICAL EXEMPLARS IN THIS STUDY

As mentioned in chapter 1, an exemplary book about exemplary public servants stimulated imagination leading to this effort to focus on the rhetoric of exemplars who have impacted human rights causes for better or worse. Terry Cooper and Dale Wright's edited volume *Exemplary*

Issue *(Can NGO-sponsored adult education program empower women in Senegalese villages?)*

Argument: Inferential Core
(By encouraging participant leadership, education can empower women self-defined as relevant to their tradition.)
PROGRAM → PARTICIPANT LEADERSHIP → BUY-IN → GENDER EMPOWERMENT

Argument: Dialectical Tier
OBJECTIONS:
Program lacks suitable planning and business models to be replicable ← **RESPONSES** *It spread throughout Africa*
Alternate Positions:
Needs to adapt program logics to attract conventional donors ← **RESPONSES** *We'll seek out small "venture" donors looking for new ideas*

CRITICISMS:
                                                                ??? ← **RESPONSE** *???*

Figure 2.2.   Sketch of Case 2 Dialectical Environment.
Adapted with permission from Johnson (2013, 541).

Public Administrators (1992) primarily focuses on the moral virtues (or in some cases, lack thereof) of thirteen US public administrators who served in various governmental capacities during the twentieth century—as examples, George C. Marshal, William D. Ruckelshaus, and C. Everett Koop. For Cooper and Wright as editors (as well as for David Hart, who provided the conceptual chapter), Alasdair MacIntyre's virtues of excellent practice serve as an appropriate criterion for assessing the moral dimensions of exemplars' works. In his preface, Cooper explains,

> The project is . . . not intended to identify the *most exemplary* practitioners; it does not list our nominees for "the top ten" ethical administrators. Rather, it contains a treatment of *some* exemplars. The book we set out to produce was intended to provide an initial exploration of how virtue is embodied in the work of public administrators—some famous, others rather obscure—and how such embodiment can become examples for the field. (1992, xiii; italics in original)

MacIntyre's virtues of excellent practice support the study of human rights exemplars as well but in a different manner. A critical question posed herein (addressed in chapter 7) is whether human rights advocates bear certain ethical responsibilities that may be characterized in terms of virtues. However at this point, it appears less than obvious that effective rights advocates necessarily *need* to be paragons of ethical virtue. Twentieth-century journalist Mignon McLaughlin once remarked, "Every society honors its living conformists and its dead troublemakers." Issues of ethics and morality related to human rights are often best understood in terms of tensions between how local and universal vernaculars characterize "appropriate" behaviors and beliefs.

In his conceptual chapter "The Moral Exemplar in an Organizational Society," (Chapter 1 in *Exemplary Public Administrators*), David Hart discusses a rhetorical problem associated with laudable public service, specifically "the 'expressive obligation' as the paradox of publicity" (1992, 18). In essence, he suggests that "honorable works" invite scrutiny when they are widely advertised as such:

> When moral actions proceed from genuine qualities of character, they are exemplary. But their impact upon others is made clear, is heightened, and becomes more inspirational when graced by a seeming gesture, enhanced by eloquent word or framed by a noble setting. This

bring us to the "expressive obligation." . . . The expressive obligation must *never* be false or self-aggrandizing but must flow honestly from one's unique moral character. (1992, 19; italics in original)

Hart's concern here appears directly pertinent to Perelman and Olbrecht-Tyteca's move to re-position the *audience* as the centerpiece of argumentation to take the place of Aristotle's eloquent rhetor. Affirming their *new* rhetoric, Michael Leff in fact argues that less-eloquent speakers, fearful of their oratorical limitations, may prove more authentic in persuading audiences than others more polished (2003, 139). Perhaps the Old Testament Moses was such a meek and modest speaker, as a preeminent administrative theorist characterizes: "Moses has reason to be modest. If meek means imposed upon, Moses certainly qualifies. If meek means admitting mistakes, Moses does. Coming closer to the matter at issue, there is a meekness born of recognizing one's own faults sufficiently to intervene for others who are also weak" (Wildavsky 1984, 176–177). Perhaps some human rights advocates can speak effectively for others from their own limitations.

Later in his chapter, Hart justifies a typology for classifying exemplary public administrators—one that I follow for grouping rhetorical exemplars in chapters 3 through 6 of this book. Aware that "not all moral actions are equivalent" (1992, 21), Hart first categorizes circumstances calling for virtue as either "moral episodes" or "moral processes," the former concerning experiences of relatively short duration while the latter continues over the course of one's career. He then subdivides "episodes" as "moral crises" and "moral confrontations" and breaks down "processes" into "moral projects" and "moral work."

Generally, these four types of moral circumstance make sense as fitting topical themes (respectively in chapters 3 through 6) in grouping our twelve sketches of rhetorical exemplars. One departure from the logic in *Exemplary Public Administrators* (1992) warrants particular comment: Hart casts the "moral hero" as the subject of "crisis" episodes such as Danish bureaucrats who resisted World War II–era Nazi occupation (see Frederickson and Hart 1985) and Freedom Riders who participated in the 1960s US civil rights struggles. But in the extreme circumstances of human rights deprivation (often involving armed conflict), self-preservation might militate against the "paradox of publicity" that calls attention to "heroes." Moreover, as mentioned previously, the *new* rhetoric characterizes speakers as ordinary members of audiences who seek adherence through give-and-take negotiation. Thus ordinary people who explain themselves admirably in crisis situations *do* exist, perhaps in great numbers, but they are not inclined to seek out notoriety. Rather, moral antagonists appear easier to identify, likely because for them publicity offers more opportunities than paradoxes.

ANALYTICAL QUESTIONS FOR COMPARING RHETORICAL EXEMPLARS

Comparisons of the rhetorical exemplars (whether rights *advocates* or *antagonists*) included herein can promote learning about human rights advocacy so long as the criteria for comparisons make sense. The task here is to rework previous discussions related to argumentation—such as

- how speakers relate to audiences,
- narratives constructed and strategies adopted to secure audience adherence,
- particularistic moral vernaculars, and
- dialectical skills to mediate contradiction and opposition—

to formulate viable questions that coax out cogent insights. Thus, the topics listed above are condensed into the following five questions.

I. Among the various types of audience, from which does the rhetorical exemplar seek adherence?

In establishing various frameworks for argumentation, Perelman and Ol-brechts-Tyteca either explicitly or implicitly speak of four different types of audience: the self, another individual ("a single hearer"), "the universal audience," and a particular (in essence, their default) audience. They argue that self-deliberation need not take the form of soliloquy since "discussion with someone else is [often] simply a means we use to see things more clearly ourselves" (TNR, 41). The rhetoricians' attention to the universal audience is largely directed to text (even though it could relate to oratory as well). As previously mentioned, contemporary scholars of rhetoric (e.g., James Crosswhite) doubt that purely universal audiences exist, implying that they are actually composites of various particular audiences, that find consensus (perhaps for differing reasons and motives). Although their arguments may be pitched toward a particular group, it can be expected that the rhetorical exemplars seek adherence from multiple audiences.

2. Is the rhetorical exemplar's argumentation monologic or dialogic in nature?

As suggested in the previous chapter, dialogic persuasion engages the reader or listener in interactive discourse while monologic expression expects a passive audience to accept the appeal as an authoritative "once and for all" answer. It follows that rhetors who speak monologically would encounter particular difficulties in seeking adherence from composite or diverse audiences, more the norm than the exception. Thus, it is reasonable to expect rhetorical exemplars in this study to craft their arguments in a dialogic manner.

3. Does the rhetorical exemplar incorporate a "thick" ethics of memory or a "thin" morality of universality within her or his argumentation?

Generally, the terms "morality" and "ethics" are used interchangeably, usually in reference to standards or principles that apply universally. However Gerald Hauser's distinction between particular (or local) and universal moral vernaculars, especially as they relate to human rights questions, suggests that the expectations of moral (or ethical) behavior are understood differently *within particular traditions* than as universal abstractions as discussed above. Israeli philosopher Avishai Margalit explores the normative contours of his own particular tradition and its moral vernacular in considering whether there *is* such a thing as "an ethic of memory" and if so, exactly what it requires of those within that tradition (2002, 6–7). Similarly some speakers within institutions (e.g., whistle-blowers in government bureaucracies) may appeal to "thin" universally accepted standards such as transparency or equitability while others justify the "thick" institutional norms relating to precedence, expertise, and procedures (see Dubnick and O'Kelly 2005). It is logical to expect at least some of the rhetorical exemplars examined to express their arguments as normative appeals—whether to (in Margalit's characterizations) "thin" universal morality or a "thick" ethics within a particular tradition.

4. How (if at all) do Hauser's two types of moral vernacular affect antagonists' vis-à-vis advocates' discourses?

In his book *Human Rights as Politics and Idolatry*, Michael Ignatieff argues that the "language" of human rights can be spoken only in reference to individual (rather than collective or communitarian) concerns, typically associated with the singular voices of a rights-holder (2001, 67). Thus for Ignatieff the notion of a cultural or societal vernacular from which particular interpretations of human rights could emerge makes little sense. In his discussion of the "moral vernacular of human rights," Gerald Hauser challenges Ignatieff's position, arguing instead that two particular types of moral vernacular—the "thin" universal vernacular of individual rights found in formal documents such as the Universal Declaration of Human Rights and the "thick" moral vernacular "constituted performatively" within cultural traditions—coexist or alternatively challenge each other in human rights conversation.

Following Hauser's logic, it appears that these two vernacular types may account for varying distinctions in discourses among antagonist exemplars as compared with variations among advocates. For example, antagonists may vary in terms of those who justify their arguments or actions on a "thin" official vernacular as compared with others who (explicitly or implicitly) base their justifications on "thick" cultural expectations. On the other hand, some advocates may base their rights discourses upon their actual "thick" experience of having *personally suffered* rights abuse *within* the particular culture as distinct from having not suffered but who base their rights discourses on "thin" (perhaps universal) discourses.

5. Does the rhetorical exemplar address the future or merely the past and/or present?

Rhetoric associated with human rights, particularly as it pertains to people's agency in controlling their own circumstances, can be expected to address better futures. By contrast, justifications for the political and social status quo may be grounded in the present or past; thus, hypothetical futures could be cast in dire, threatening terms (i.e., *"If we don't take countermeasures, watch out!*). Since dialogic expression invites audience interaction (sometimes well into the future, particularly in the case of text), the temporal orientation of arguments advanced by rhetorical exemplars in the study appears significant.

CONCLUSION

A *new rhetoric* has emerged in contemporary societies in ways that appear quite different from the rhetoric of the eloquent orator in Aristotle's classical times. Now the critical issues do not relate so much to the speaker's articulation, fluency, and charisma but more so to the audience and its receptivity to arguments conveyed. The new rhetoric's implications for human rights causes appear profound; the "speaker" or text specifying what human rights entail may not be taken as relevant, empowering, or for that matter *legitimate* by the audience, in its "language of living" of particular moral vernaculars (Hauser 2008). The human rights dialectic that Gerald Hauser poses pits alternative vernaculars (often universally articulated human rights norms) against local ways of living. From his rhetorical dialectic it becomes apparent that effective human rights advocates need to negotiate seemingly contradictory discourses. In other words, there is cause to evaluate human rights advocates, as well as antagonists, in terms of their capabilities as pragma-dialecticians (to use Ralph Johnson's term; 2013).

The implicit thread woven through chapter 2 ties rhetorical analysis with the ethnographic pursuit as Clifford Geertz describes it as interpreting the meaning of "winks upon winks upon winks" (1973). For the skillful human rights advocate as a pragma-dialectician, this thread underscores the importance of interpretation in order to grasp how human rights matters are understood and expressed in thick (local) vernaculars because situations of abuse and deprivation typically unfold within them. Thus, attentiveness to "thin versus thick" vernaculars, ethics, and institutional discourses supports the advocate's effectiveness as a pragma-dialectician.

NOTES

1. Avishai Margalit specifically uses the terms "thin morality" and "thick" ethics to distinguish between universal categorical imperatives and his ethics of memory and caring. Presumably, the terms "thin ethics" and "thick ethics" (or "thin"/"thick" moralities) could be used as well, since the key distinction here is between thin and thick description (rather than between "ethics" and "morality").

2. *Tostan: Empowering Communities to Abandon Female Genital Cutting*, http://www.youtube.com/watch?v=JcX32btTU48. Accessed June 24, 2014.

3

RHETORIC IN MORAL CRISES

A moral crisis involves a circumstance "that carries with it real danger for individuals who act rightly. The exemplar in a moral crisis is a *moral hero*" (Hart 1992, 23; italics in original). Looking back historically, Joan of Arc stands out as a fifteenth-century hero, both as a very young woman who unhesitatingly "spoke truth to power" and as a fighter in the Hundred Years War on behalf of King Charles VII of France. When Charles VII's armies were overcome by the combined efforts of English and French Burgundian forces, Joan was captured and convicted of heresy in a politically charged church trial. Her claims of having received divine guidance from the voices of departed saints were used against her by prosecutors who characterized her as a demented witch.

Playwright George Bernard Shaw characterizes Joan's moral heroism in the final act of *Saint Joan*, taking place in the courtroom as she is sentenced to death:

> *D'Estivet [the church prosecutor]*: Assuredly, if you are in the hands of the Church, and you wilfully take yourself out of its hands, you are deserting the Church; and that is heresy.

> *Joan*: It is great nonsense. Nobody could be such a fool as to think that.

> *D'Estivet*: You hear, my lord, how I am reviled in the execution of my duty by this woman. [He sits down indignantly].

Cauchon [the church judge]:I have warned you before, Joan, that you are doing yourself no good by these pert answers.

Joan: But you will not talk sense to me. I am reasonable if you will be reasonable . . .

Courcelles [a young priest]: My lord: she should be put to the torture.

The Inquisitor: You hear, Joan? That is what happens to the obdurate. Think before you answer. Has she been shewn the instruments?

The Executioner: They are ready, my lord. She has seen them.

Joan: If you tear me limb from limb until you separate my soul from my body you will get nothing out of me beyond what I have told you. What more is there to tell that you could understand? Besides, I cannot bear to be hurt; and if you hurt me I will say anything you like to stop the pain. But I will take it all back afterwards; so what is the use of it?

As explained in the previous chapter, moral heroes may well emerge in contemporary contexts of humanitarian crises, but prudence may dictate that they remain "below the radar" for reasons of self-preservation; in other words, publicity and notoriety do not serve them well. In that regard, none of the sketches in this chapter relate to particular individuals that have exhibited heroism on a par with Joan of Arc. The first sketch focuses on Mary B. Anderson, a humanitarian who has led peace-building efforts on the ground in deadly situations of international conflict.

In stark contrast to sketches in chapters 4 through 6, the next two sketches center *not* upon a particular individual. One of these discussions concerns Rwandan "hate radio" that encouraged ordinary Hutu citizens to kill Tutsis in the run-up to the genocide in 1994. The final sketch compares the roles of four individuals—two American and two Chinese actors—associated with government crackdowns against student protesters (respectively) at Kent State University in May of 1970 and Tiananmen Square in Beijing in June of 1989.

MARY B. ANDERSON, ADVOCATE FOR PEACE-MAKING AMID STRIFE

In February 2012, peace advocate Mary B. Anderson[1] delivered a public lecture, titled "The Listening Project: How Recipients Judge International Assistance," at the Joan B. Kroc Institute for Peace and Justice (on the University of San Diego campus), where she served as scholar-in-residence. The introduction to her address included the following statement:

> Four years ago, Mary B. Anderson launched an international effort to explore how and why [human abuse] occurs by listening to the analyses and judgments of people who live in societies on the recipient end of international aid efforts. . . . Teams of "listeners" have engaged thousands of people in 20 countries around the world in open-ended conversations exploring how they experience the cumulative impacts of aid. By listening to these people—from the fishermen on the beach to government ministerial staff—the teams' intent was to gain their perspectives on the cumulative impacts of international aid. (Kroc Institute 2012)

Anderson's lecture predated the release of *The Learning Project* (which she co-authored with Dayna Brown and Isabella Jean) cited in the sketch below. Anderson has worked with the International Relief/Development Project at Harvard University. In 1985 she founded Collaborative for Development Action, Inc., a small consulting firm based in Cambridge, Massachusetts, and served as its executive director until her retirement in 2009. The following sketch characterizes Anderson as (1) a "collaborative learner and (lay) social psychologist," (2) an ethicist, and (3) a bridge builder.

COLLABORATIVE LEARNER AND SOCIAL PSYCHOLOGIST

If experience is a good teacher, an advocacy community learns best by sharing its experiences in collaborative settings wherein participants openly acknowledge their past errors and mistaken assumptions. Mary B. Anderson has dedicated her career to assisting communities of humanitarians working in conflict; such violent conditions often call for humanitarian action on the part of outsiders with limited knowledge of the communities they assist.

From a rhetorical standpoint, much of Anderson's work involves speaking to an audience of other speakers, those who advocate both for immediate relief in the midst of strife and for subsequent human development over the long term. As a "coach" or an adviser to her humanitarian colleagues, Anderson advances a rhetoric of listening and reflection that acknowledges that humanitarian aid and action *can* do far more harm than good to recipient communities and that even successful efforts cannot stop or prevent conflicts. Anderson's leadership in facilitating reflective discourse assumes particular resonance in professional conversations that typically address fundamental dilemmas—for example, difficult choices such as "whether (or not) to enter" a new emergency location, "whether to stay or leave," and "whether to be quiet or speak out" regarding the actions of authorities in troubled situations (2007).

Her advocacy of listening extends as well to surmounting barriers of understanding between donors of international aid as "hearers of people on the receiving end" of those funds. This advocacy discourse culminated in "The Listening Project," established in 2005, "the product of over 6,000 people who were willing to tell their stories and reflect on the patterns they had observed in how aid benefits, or fails to benefit, their societies." (Anderson, Brown, and Jean 2012, i–ii). A sample of responses to "The Listening Project" include:

- *The donors never take the time to consult with and listen to the beneficiaries. This is the first time I have seen that!* (Female president of an association, Mali);
- *All this while, organizations came only to take a head-count. You are the only people who have come and listened to our problems* (Elderly man, Sri Lanka); and
- *Thank you for listening to us and allowing us to tell you what we would like to tell those who have power over us this great power that is international cooperation* (Afro-Ecuadorian women, Ecuador). (2012, 15)

Anderson's collaborative learning focuses upon errors and shortcomings in individual or organizational experiences rather than upon successes that can be disseminated as "best practices" to be replicated in other contexts. Some experts on professional learning differentiate such a concern for error as "double-loop learning" from more conventional "single-loop" approaches to evaluation. For example, Chris Argyris suggests that double-loop learning is especially powerful in its emphasis on embracing error:

> *Single-loop learning* occurs when errors are corrected without altering the underlying governing values. For example, the thermostat is programmed to turn on if the temperature in the room is cold, or turn off the heat if the room becomes too hot. *Double-loop learning* occurs when errors are corrected by changing the governing values and then the actions. A thermostat is double-loop learning if it questions why it is programmed to measure temperature, and then adjusts the temperature itself. (2002, 206; italics his)

Organization learning therefore occurs in a questioning (rather than defensive) atmosphere in which all participants (including leaders) "say what they know yet fear to say" and advocate their ideas "in a way that invites inquiry into them" (Argyris, 217). In large part, double-loop learning involves what rhetoricians describe as "self-deliberation." In *The New Rhetoric*, Perelman and Olbrechts-Tyteca discuss self-deliberation as a particular kind of argumentation such that "discussion with someone else is simply a means which we use to see things more clearly ourselves. . . . Accordingly, from our point of view, it is by analyzing argumentation addressed to others that we can best understand self-deliberation, and not vice versa" (1969, 41).

In the context of collaborative learning among humanitarian workers "embracing errors" in their past work, a program officer with the World-Vision Sudan Program recounts how that non-governmental organization (NGO) inadvertently depended on the military to recruit in-country aid workers, which in turn exacerbated conflict. She then discusses WorldVision's subsequent participation in the Local Capacities for Peace Project (LCPP), a collaborative effort among several large NGOs created "to investigate the relationship between aid and conflict" (Riak 2000, 501). Earlier in her analysis, Riak briefly outlines how the LCPP emerged under Anderson's leadership:

> [T]he Local Capacities for Peace Project (LCPP) was launched to investigate the relationship between aid and conflict. The Project is a

collaborative effort involving international and local NGOs: the International Federation of Red Cross and Red Crescent Societies, Catholic Relief Services, World Vision, UN agencies, and European and American donor agencies. Spearheaded by Mary B. Anderson of the Collaborative for Development Action, the LCPP set out to answer the following question: how can humanitarian or development assistance be given in conflict situations in ways that, rather than feeding into and exacerbating the conflict, help local people to disengage and establish alternative systems for dealing with the underlying problems? (501)

Thus, a collaborative assessment of World Vision's inadvertent missteps offered valued insight for the larger community of humanitarian advocates.

To the extent that she leads conversation about prior humanitarian experiences, Mary B. Anderson becomes a social psychologist of sorts who encourages her audience to take responsibility for their individual and collective actions so that authentic learning is possible. Not only is it important for humanitarians to critically analyze their rationales and justifications for actions taken—as well- (or ill-) founded as they may be—but also for them to acknowledge their "blind spots," what they do not know or understand (see e.g., Tavris and Aronson 2007, 40–67). For example in *Do No Harm*, Anderson relates the critical reflection of one particular LCPP participant who recognizes her own blind spot:

In a . . . workshop in Sarajevo, one aid worker looked up with a rueful smile. "Every time I relax with my local staff, I ask them to tell me about their war experiences. The more horrible the story, the more riveted my attention. I commiserate, and together we relive the horrors of war. What if I asked them instead to tell me about their relationships with the "other side" before the war? What if we spent more time talking about people they like and trust from the other side? . . . I just realized that I am reinforcing their negative experiences and attitudes with my questions. . . . What kind of example am I setting? (1999, 62)

It is especially crucial that groups intending to develop harmonious relations between warring ethnic or religious factions practice tolerance in their approaches to peace-making. Anderson reports on the efforts of a Jesuit community of Catholic priests in Ahmedabad, India, that was successful in alleviating urban violence between Hindus and Muslims by involving both groups in activities such as establishing schools as safe havens for children from both groups, facilitating "myth-busting" communication, and directing street plays that recount the historical events leading up to conflict from the perspectives of both religious groups (1999, 119–127). It is noteworthy that these Jesuits pursued an even-handed approach that gained the trust of two altogether different religious factions. Their commendable example contrasts with that of another case cited by two social psychologists in their book *Mistakes Were Made (but not by me)*.

> [At the Museum of Tolerance in Los Angeles] you watch a video on a vast array of prejudices, designed to convince you that everyone has at least a few. And then you are invited to enter the museum proper through one of two doors: one marked PREJUDICED, the other marked UNPREJUDICED. The latter door is locked, in case anyone misses the point, but some occasionally do. When we were visiting the museum one afternoon, we were treated to the sight of four Hasidic Jews pounding angrily on the Unprejudiced door, demanding to be let in. (Tavris and Aronson 2007, 41)

Presumably, reflective learning can guide fallible humans serving in humanitarian causes (as well as the rest of us) to approach work through the appropriate door.

Social psychologists assert that matters of war and peace—whether between spouses in marital disputes or ethnic groups in civil wars—are typically perpetuated by alternative historical narratives that "make sense" to victims who claim the moral high ground and alleged perpetrators who cling to justifications for their actions (Tavris and Aronson 1999, 185–197). In other words, conflicts are often prolonged by "dueling" selective accounts of history. In her discussion of "mixed motives" in *Do No Harm*, Anderson applies this tenet of social psychology to war in general and ongoing civil strife within Afghanistan in particular: "Some people cite lofty purposes and root causes as the reasons for every war. 'Leaders' always claim a high purpose. Conflicts often embody elements of both principle and self-aggrandizement. Sometimes the initial purposefulness of war changes, and the war itself becomes the reason for future fighting" (1999, 10).

But then she refers to an Afghan colleague whose reflective (or double-loop) learning enables him to advance beyond the moral justifications of belligerents to understand protracted conflict in terms of stages that account for changing versions (or narratives) of victimhood and aggressor justifications. Anderson concludes:

> Continuing tensions in [various locales] retain some of the historical purpose that originally motivated them. In each of these cases, however, local analysts report that violent incidents are often perpetrated by groups of bandits who lay claim to familiar ideological positions to "appear" to have a purpose other than their own enrichment. . . . Thus, our experiences, combined with what we have heard from many local people in conflict areas in recent years, lead us to conclude that wars are not entirely fought to address root causes. . . . Often there is at best a tenuous link between war and justice as its motive. (10–11)

Psychologists Tavris and Aronson convey a similar idea in the context of US history: "There is nothing united about us Southerners and you damned Yankees; we'll keep flying our Confederate flag, thank you, that's *our* history. Slavery may be gone with the wind, but grudges aren't. That is why history is written by the victors, but it's victims who write the memoirs" (2007, 197; italics in original).

Ethicist

On an explicit level, humanitarians may appear justified in claiming the high ground of ethical virtue as providers of vital relief in the forms of security, food, and shelter to those trapped by deadly conflict. However Anderson, consistent with her advocacy for counter-intuitive learning, largely deflates such professional hubris in alerting her audience of humanitarians to contemplate the *implicit* messages they send to those they serve:

> Many aid professionals believe the explicit messages are so clear that they are always understood by aid recipients and others in society. Unfortunately, because aid also conveys implicit messages often unrecognized by providers, the messages many recipients receive are ambiguous. Some of these dilemmas aid workers face are better understood when these ethical messages are clarified. (1999, 55)

The "implicit ethical messages" that Anderson reveals in *Do No Harm* lend themselves to further discussions about the fundamental ethical theories embedded within them as well as the rhetorical qualities of those messages. For example, Anderson argues that humanitarian organizations send the implicit message that "*it is legitimate for arms to determine who gains access to food or medical supplies and that security and safety is derived from weapons*" (1999, 56) if they in fact hire their own armed guards. At the core of this message is the commonly applied theory of *act-utilitarianism* which "appeals directly to the principle of utility by trying to see which of the [possible alternatives] is likely to produce…the greater good over evil. One typically asks 'what good over evil?', *not* 'What effect will *everyone's* doing this kind of situation have on the general balance of good over evil?'" (Frankena 1973, 35)

To the extent that (perceived) utility translates into pragmatism, rhetoricians may be more inclined toward leniency toward such motives than some ethicists and Anderson herself. In particular, Perelman and Olbrechts-Tyteca observe that "the pragmatic argument is criticized by those who believe in an absolutist or formalist conception of values and, especially, of morals" (1969, 269). In the words of two ethnographic researchers, "Humanitarians are not heroes. Neither are they selfish vultures. Nor indeed do they correspond to any other stereotype concocted by friends or foes. Accounts of everyday NGO practices and dilemmas correct blind expectations, expose uncritical admiration, and put unrealistic critiques into perspective" (Fernando and Hilhorst 2006, 301). But it is within the contexts of these "everyday practices" that Anderson's concern about "arms and power" as (un)justifiable means to humanitarian ends become morally instructive in a professional community committed to collaborative learning.

Further, Anderson relates that aid workers send another ominous message when they relieve their stress working in dangerous circumstances through pleasure-seeking social behaviors. "They have few outlets for recreation. The pressure of their work can lead to physical exhaustion and emotional burnout. . . . They may have parties in the aid compound with beer, music, and good food, even though the people they are there to assist have little food or joy" (1999, 56–57). Anderson offers the following case:

> An aid worker recounted that he and his fellow staff had worked very hard in an emergency situation. . . . When he returned home and had his film developed, however, he noted how many pictures showed him and his colleagues enjoying a meal together, leaning on their cars drinking beer, or lounging under a tree with food and drink. He was

both amazed and amused. He concluded that the atmosphere of constant pressure was in part a mind-set rather than a full reality. He declared that he would never again claim there was "no time" to think, discuss, plan, and consider options. (57)

The message, according to Anderson, is not only about discontinuity from humanitarian concern but also that one can use resources "for personal purposes and pleasure. Accountability is unnecessary" (57).

Since Aristotle, ethicists have studied self-justification as *psychological egoism*, the argument that it is human nature to act in ways that advance one's own well-being either as a general rule or relative to particular contexts (Frankena 1973, 20). But to claim that occasional excesses in socializing suggests that these workers are *egoists* under the premise that "all rational interests may be traced ultimately to self-interests" (Burks 1966, 400) may be unwarranted. Although Anderson's concern that this behavior appears contrary to efforts to maintain "common ground" with those served has its merits, a case can be made that humans are by nature social beings (see Dewey 1960); as such, "mind and self are [for Dewey] products of social interaction" (Burks 1966, 416). From a strictly rhetorical standpoint, gregarious social behavior could be considered as discourse among members of a group (in this case, those working in a challenging environment) and as a means of "working through burnout" (see Parkinson 2013, 160–162). Nonetheless Anderson's point is instructive: loud partying by aid workers sends ominous messages to recipients of humanitarian efforts.

At another point, Anderson counsels her audiences to recognize how their expressions of *powerlessness* directed toward particular conundrums could be interpreted by those whom they serve:

> Field-based aid staff often assert their powerlessness over events around them: "I can't do anything to change this. . . Because I am not in charge and cannot control everything that affects me, I am not responsible for the impact of my limited actions. The implicit message of powerlessness . . . is clear. If aid workers, with all of their resources and apparent power, feel unable to change things or that they are not responsible for the impacts of their choices, then no one need feel differently. (1999, 58)

Presumably an aid worker's claim of powerlessness carries with it attitudes of fatalism and determinism (a predominance of forces external to the person) that undercut a virtue ethic devoted to service and works.

From an ethical perspective, it follows that the general notion of individual morality in society largely depends upon the premises that "human beings are free to do as they choose" and that there is sufficient freedom in the society to do so (Frankena 1973, 77)—in essence, no freedom, no morality. In this vein it appears that Anderson articulates a straightforward, rhetorical argument that stresses a virtue ethic that connects "the person and [her] acts." In Perelman and Olbrechts-Tyteca's words, Anderson regards the humanitarian as "the author of . . . acts and judgments as a durable being, around whom is grouped a whole series of phenomena to which [s]he gives cohesion and significance" (1969, 295). Yet the rhetorical strategy of evading moral responsibility through a surrender to determinism is, in essence, to "compartmentalize" or dissociate oneself from (non-)action (411–415). Anderson recognizes dissociation in her complaint against those who claim powerlessness: "For many, it is someone else's job to change things, to take responsibility, to improve the situation, to make peace. Bad actions are explained as the fault of someone else's decision, order, or pressure" (58–59).

Another category of implicit (non-)ethical messages that relief workers send relates to ethical virtue, or lack thereof, within dangerous contexts that trigger emotions of stress and fear. Specifically, Anderson cautions aid workers to recognize how their emotions of *belligerence, tension, and suspicion* may lead to a "vicious cycle" whereby adversaries whom aid workers fear could become even more threatening. She relates, for example, that

> fieldworkers tell of their apprehensions as they approach checkpoints manned by soldiers. One reaction is to be assertive and belligerent, to expect the worst and assume a defensive posture against it "you have no right to stop this truck. Don't you see the name of our aid agency on the door? You must let me pass." One message is "I have the power here and not you." . . . Another is, "You are mean and untrustworthy. I know that you only understand toughness. I am interacting with you in the only way you'll understand." It can reinforce the likelihood that the worst will happen. (59)

From an ethical standpoint, Anderson appeals to her audience to take courage in stressful situations so as to avoid creating their own self-fulfilling prophecies.

Referring to a trait-based theory of virtue ethics (that he prefers over others), ethicist William Frankena identifies seven cardinal virtues in the Christian tradition: faith, hope, love, wisdom, courage, temperance, and justice (1973, 64). From a rhetorical lens, some associate discourses of fear with attempts to create monsters of adversaries. For example, in his book *At Stake: Monsters and the Rhetoric of Fear in Public Culture*, Edward Ingebretsen elucidates a "monster narrative" whereby those causing anxiety are demonized in the name of civility—"the discourse, gestures, and disciplinary techniques by which a society underwrites 'normality'" (2001, 127; also see Hantke 2005, 186–187). In some respects, 1970s conservative activist Phyllis Schlafley relied on such a monster narrative in demonizing the women's liberation movement (see Solomon 1978). In essence, these "monster" discourses capitalize on the discomfort that "subversive" messages (whether from feminists in the context of the Schlafley agenda or soldiers obstructing relief workers) inflict upon an audience's self-image (Fisher 1970, 131; Solomon 1978, 56).

Beyond her concern about the inadvertent "ethical messages" workers send in relief contexts, Anderson reflects as well on a fundamental humanitarian dilemma—whether "to work, or not to work, in 'tainted' circumstances" (2007). Implying that one could be forced to compromise principles in *tainted* situations, Anderson draws on personal experience to frame the predicament:

> In 2004, as the first anniversary of the US entry into Iraq approached, I was asked by colleagues to go to Iraq to conduct some training workshops for the local staff of international non-governmental organizations. I am an American. The NGOs I would be working with receive US government funding for some programs. If I went, would I be reinforcing a military operation by advancing a "hearts and minds" campaign? Or would I be demonstrating concern and support for local people involved in efforts to alleviate suffering and contribute to redevelopment? (2007, 201)

The dilemma that she characterizes takes on particular resonance in the context of an advocacy of *coordination* prevalent among leading humanitarians such as Larry Manier, who relates that "[e]veryone associated with the humanitarian experience touts the value of coordination. . . . The public has had enough experience with multi-ring humanitarian 'circuses' to expect the worst" (2002, 19). Nonetheless Anderson passes along her own ethical reasoning that takes issue with the "coordination" narrative:

> [In view of complicated humanitarian contexts], the obvious point to make, from the experience gathered, is that there is no choice that is completely "pure." Because of the layered and complex circumstances in which humanitarians work, each choice has both positive and negative potential impacts on the lives of people to whose needs humanitarians want to respond. . . . Rather than seeking a uniform and consistent answer across all humanitarian efforts, therefore, I welcome the fact that humanitarians make differing choices. Even though I decide to shun a location, someone else will decide to go there to respond to local suffering. (2007, 221)

From a rhetorical standpoint, it is worth noting that, although the "coordination" (or convergence) agenda points to the desirability of hierarchical order (for example, an inter-governmental agency that "calls the coordinative shots"), Anderson embraces an ethic of *value pluralism* rather than *monism* associated with hierarchies (either correctly or otherwise—see TNR, 80–83). Perhaps Anderson's pluralistic approach here aligns with an *ethic of humility* (described by one ethicist) as "that meta-attitude which constitutes the moral agent's proper perspective on herself [not] as a dependent and corrupt but capable and dignified rational agent" (Grenberg 2005, 133).

Bridge Builder

The ethical thread that runs through the preponderance of Mary B. Anderson's work is that of reconciliation and unity. Further, it appears that this "preponderance" speaks more to the cardinal virtues of benevolence and justice than to explicit professional obligations *per se* (see Frankena 1973, 64).

At least on a symbolic level (and presumably, far beyond that), Anderson's advocacy for reconciliation and reunification represents *the essence of rhetoric*, persuasive appeal through *words and letters*—rather than at the point of a bayonet. The following therefore focuses upon Anderson's "bridge-building" advocacy in promoting unity between humanitarian donors and aid recipients, the humanitarian and development communities, and feuding factions within contexts of conflict or war.

Between Donors and Recipients

Mary B. Anderson endeavors to build bridges between external donor agencies that condition aid reflecting their own expectations and priorities and recipient communities with aspirations and needs irrespective of pre-conceived expectations. Anderson and her colleagues are hardly the first to address disconnects in aid systems between donors, recipients, and intermediary organizations attributed to an increasingly institutionalized aid system wherein "communication" among these amounts merely to standardized reporting procedures rather than collaborative learning (see for example Feldman 2003; Wallace 2007). Nonetheless, Anderson et al. aptly summarize the origins and implications of this industry trend to-ward standardization around two primary donor motives: (1) an intention to redirect funding priorities from response to victims and survivors of strife to preventative measures that deliver aid on the basis of longer-term sustainability and (2) greater reliance on a "business model" underwriting humanitarian effort that focuses on "the value of money," "results-based management," and "the branding of work" to make it distinguishable from other organizations (2012, 34–35).

This emergent business rhetoric in turn alienates organizations that function in local fields of operation, as evident in these reactions quoted in *Time to Listen*:

- *Many people view interventions as a money-making business, and the humanitarian as well as volunteer spirit that was the driving force has disappeared as most actors have become materialistic.* (Director of a local NGO, Kenya);
- *The NGOs become service companies that make a profit from international aid.* (An agronomist, Ecuador); and
- *They come into the camp to make profits for themselves.* (Leader in an [internal displacement] camp, Timor-Leste). (Anderson et al. 2012, 35)

Anderson and colleagues bridge the chasm between donors and recipients with a four-step strategy designed to draw donors and aid recipients into collaborative learning. First, aid agencies would commit to "early listening [wherein] all providers would engage with and listen to a variety of people in a prospective recipient country or community before developing a proposal for funding" (2012, 142). Donors would provide the resources necessary to support this discovery process. Second, donors and receivers would jointly formulate a funding proposal.

> A proposal would be expected to tell as much as needed to make the case that the plan is a good one from the points of view of the recipient groups (as well as other groups nearby who will not be included in the activity but who will be aware of it and judging it). (142)

Third, in terms of disbursement, funds would be accessible as needed rather than subject to a rigid draw-down schedule. Regarding accountability, "[a]id providers and recipients would together monitor the disbursement and use of these funds and provide transparent information to all involved to reduce opportunities for corruption or mismanagement" (142). Fourth, any reporting procedures would promote "simplicity, clarity, and honesty" that reflect a collaborative relationship among partners. In all, Anderson and her colleagues' collaborative narrative promises to bridge interests and understandings rather than drive them further asunder as alternative approaches do.

Between Communities of Professionals

Mary B. Anderson builds bridges *not only* between aid donors and recipients *but also* between communities of "humanitarian" and "development" professionals who tend to view their respective endeavors as distinct from each other. In large part, Anderson advises that "humanitarian" and "development" efforts converge when professionals from both pursuits recognize "our innate human equality and our circumstantial inequality in order to establish relationships of mutual respect and contemporaneous enjoyment of each other" (2000, 495). Her advocacy of innate human equality becomes apparent in a humorous dialogue she creates between an NGO that highly values the "coordination imperative" in disaster relief work and a wise(r) sage who is somewhat skeptical of hierarchical control and subsequent *inequalities* that coordination may entail in her book (co-authored with Peter Woodrow) *Rising from the Ashes*. Part of this conversation is as follows:

Sage: Have you ever seen a circumstance where NGO coordination bodies have taken over government functions because the NGOs thought that government was too weak or disorganized to get anything done?

NGO: Yeah. Or too corrupt.

Sage: Wouldn't it be better if the outside agencies choose to support the development of coordinating mechanisms that were in control of local people, or local government, and were effective?

NGO: If they could.

Sage: If a relief approach is anti-developmental, then coordination of it will only make its impact worse. For example, if most agencies (and government) are involved in a hand-out scheme which promotes dependency, then coordinating these efforts so everyone is fitting the handout model will do more developmental harm than good. In such circumstances, an NGO that came into this situation would want to stay free of "coordination" so that it could attempt to work with local people on a different basis. In the final analysis, anyway it is up to the local people to develop their local capacities for organizing, coordination and controlling the range of activities in which they engage with NGOs. (1989, 91–92)

From a rhetorical point of view, it is clear that the "sage" understands the "coordination narrative" and the hierarchical pecking order that evolves from it as well as in-group rhetoric that serves to reinforce the collective identities of each of these professional communities. But the "sage" proves especially adept in her (or their) selection of the *equality vs. inequality* criterion—over *humanitarian vs. development*, or *coordination vs. disorganization*—as the preeminent qualifier of competence in serving people. Once this newly selected qualifier is inserted into the discourses of *both communities*, the bridge between humanitarianism and development becomes all the more apparent (see TNR, 216–129).

Between Feuding Groups

Finally, Mary B. Anderson has devoted much effort to building bridges between feuding ethnic, religious, or political groups in the midst of war and conflict by drawing on their local capacities and interests in securing peace. Specifically she emphasizes that the purpose of the Local Capacities for Peace Project is to answer the question, "How can humanitarian and development assistance be given in conflict situations in ways that rather than feeding into and exacerbating the conflict help local people to disengage and establish alternative systems for dealing with the problems that underlie the conflict?" (1999, 1)

In *Do No Harm*, Anderson presents a framework for promoting peace between adversaries in local contexts by identifying "connectors and local capacities for peace" on the part factions on the ground" juxtaposed with "tensions, dividers, and capacity for war" (1999, 67–76). Particularly, this framework or tool accomplishes the following:

- It identifies the *categories* of information that have been found to be the most important in affecting the way aid interacts with conflict,
- It *organizes* that information, and
- It highlights *relationships* among the categories and allows one to anticipate the likely outcomes of alternative programming decisions. (1999, 75; italics in original)

Anderson nonetheless cautions that this framework cannot by itself stop war or initiate peace. But its usage encourages analysts to frame conflict in dynamic, iterative terms such that today's "tensions and dividers" leading to conflict could also be recognized as tomorrow's "capacity for peace" (69–72).

After having participated in Anderson's LCPP, a program officer with the World Vision (WV) Sudan Program reports upon how her organization benefited from Anderson's peace-building strategy:

WV Sudan entered the LCPP collaboration with the knowledge that aid does not cause wars, nor can it end them; and that we as outsiders cannot create lasting peace in Sudan. At the same time, however, we acknowledged that the work we do, not only the services we provide but how we provide them, can have negative or positive effects on existing tensions and conflicts. After 18 months, we were able to see how interventions can support or undermine Sudanese efforts to build the conditions for their own peace. (Riak 2000, 504)

Riak recalls WV's hiring dilemmas in selecting nationals to distribute food aid in civil-war-torn Sudan in the late 1990s. Specifically, Riak reports that, as the second-largest employer in the region after the army, World Vision found itself entangled in the conflict by hiring locals:

> A conflict was identified between the community and the local authorities that had developed out of a hiring procedure. The analysis showed that WV was inadvertently contributing to this conflict through a recruitment and hiring policy that depended almost entirely on the [army] and was, therefore, subject to abuse. Ways to address this included recruitment through churches, open advertising, and committee interviews. These changes provided the community with the opportunity to participate in staff selection, to seek employment, and to represent to a greater extent the diversity of [the region]. (502)

Thus it is noteworthy that Anderson's leadership in the LCPP is directed toward an "audience of speakers"—for example, World Vision in Sudan—whose subsequent discourse and action is informed by the reflective self-deliberation (or speakers speaking to themselves as well as to their other audiences) that is the cornerstone of Mary B. Anderson's bridge-building advocacy.

Waging Peace

As this sketch reveals, Mary B. Anderson has devoted a career to waging peace and mutual understanding in conflict-ridden international situations. She consistently articulates a *rhetoric of hope* and counsels her humanitarian colleagues about the arduous nature of peace-building work needed to transform hope discourse into workable realities. The next two sketches focus upon (1) Rwandan hate radio instructing Hutus to kill Tutsis in the run-up to the 1994 genocide and (2) student protests and Kent State University in 1970 and Tiananmen Square in Beijing in 1994 that led to loss of life. Readers will observe that a good deal of conversation in both of these sketches are directed toward *fear* (rather than *hope* as in the Mary B. Anderson case) that results in human deprivation and casualties. Thus, it will become evident that discourses of *hope* obligate rights advocates to significantly more effort and determination than is required of antagonists such as hate radio broadcasters in Rwanda and Governor James Rhodes in Ohio. Ironically, rhetors of *fear* encounter fewer obstacles than rights advocates speaking and toiling for *hope*.

THE RTLM, EXPONENT OF CRUELTY IN RWANDA

This sketch varies from the others in this volume that all focus on *individuals* as exemplars of rhetoric that pertains to human rights. Although it certainly relates to *individual oratory* (on the parts of radio personalities Ferdinand Nahimana, Jean-Bosco Barayagwiza, and Hassan Ngeze), the focus here is on *hate radio*—particularly as broadcast by *Radio-Télévision Libre de Mille Collines* (the RTLM) in the run-up to the 1994 Rwandan genocide—as a specific type of argumentation that mobilized committed Hutus to kill Tutsis.[2]

As discussed below, it is asserted that the broadcasted call to kill amounted to what rhetoricians classify as *epidictic genre* (as discussed below). In this respect, RTLM depictions of Tutsis as subhuman—referring to them as "cockroaches" and other animals—follow the contours of epidictic oratory intended to appeal to the audience's emotions and thus spur on action (TNR, 48–49). Nonetheless, "incitement speech" over the airwaves has spawned extended discourses concerning "who is to blame" for the influence of hate radio and what external circumstances account for its role in the genocide. Thus, the rhetoric associated with Rwandan hate radio is treated here in the following discussions: (1) conversation about the "call to violence" and its influence; (2) discussions of an accusatory (or legal) nature relating to blame and prosecution; and (3) deliberations that assess Rwandan hate radio from historical, political, and global perspectives.

THE CALL TO VIOLENCE AND SUBSEQUENT DISCOURSES

"I did not believe the Tutsis were coming to kill us, but when the government radio continued to broadcast that they were coming to take our land, were coming to kill the Hutus—when this was repeated over and over—I began to feel some kind of fear" (Berkeley 1994, 18). These were the words of a non-literate farmer from eastern Rwanda in captivity for his role as a member of the *Interahamwe*, the death squads doing the "work" of the genocide. Many of those convicted of the atrocities attribute their actions to fear instilled by broadcasts by Radio Rwanda and the RTLM:

This was the match that started the fire, they say. Their actions were motivated not by hatred, but by fear—fear of their leaders and fear of those they sought to exterminate. The stations "were always telling people that if the RPF [the rebel Rwandan Patriotic Front] comes, it will return Rwanda to feudalism, that it would bring oppression," Kiruhura says. "We didn't know the RPF. We believed what the government told us." (Berkeley, 18)

Rwandan "hate radio" emerged from the single-party government of President Juvenal Habyarimana in 1991 as part of a "self-defense" policy initiative to "protect" Hutus from the rebel (Tutsi) Rural Patriotic Front (RFP). According to a Human Rights Watch official, the role of radio was largely formulated by a high-ranking military official in the Habyarimana regime before the president's death in April of 1994:

The general outlines of the self-defence force were sketched out by Colonel Théoneste Bagosora . . . who would take the lead in national affairs after President Habyarimana was killed on 6 April 1994 [and] was known for his hostile attitude towards Tutsi. Many [of his ideas were included] in a secret national self-defence plan drawn up in early months of 1994, then implemented in the April 1994 when the civilian population was mobilized to kill Tutsi civilians. Bagasora suggested that the radio should be used in the self-defence effort. He even noted the name of Simon Bikindi, one of the most popular musicians in Rwanda, who would become famous for his songs extoling Hutu solidarity and denouncing supposed Tutsi crimes. (Des Forges 2007, 43)

Berkeley also refers to Simon Bikindi's role in the radio call to violence as follows:

"Defend your rights and rise up," the singer on the radio repeated as drums beat and guitars strummed a traditional African folk melody. . . . The singer was crooning in riddles, addressing *Mbira abumva:* "those who can understand." Beware, he told the *Bene sebahinzi*—the sons of cultivators, the Hutus—of the *Bene sebatunzi*—the sons of pastoralists, the Tutsis. "Defend your rights and rise up against those who want to oppress you." (1994, 18)

From a rhetorical standpoint, these examples of "radio speech" appear problematic in that on one hand, they qualify as epidictic oratory designed to arouse adherence though action (such as Lyndon B. Johnson's political appeals for Great Society programs and Vietnam War escalation as discussed in chapters 4 and 5). Perelman and Olbrechts-Tyteca explain:

> Epidictic oratory forms a central part of the art of persuasion. . . . The effectiveness of an exposition designed to secure a proper degree of adherence of an audience to the arguments presented to it can be assessed only in terms of the actual aim the speaker has set himself. The intensity of the adherence is not limited to obtaining purely intellectual results, to a declaration that a certain thesis seems more probable than another, but very often will be reinforced until the desired action is actually performed. (1969, 49)

But on the other hand, if there is validity to Alfred Kiruhura's claim that radio incited mobilization out of *fear*, then epidictic rhetoric turns to virulent propaganda targeting the audience's emotion rather than reason. Given the documented linkages between the Habyarimana regime and broadcasters—the RTLM was established by militant followers of the president (see Des Forges 2007)—the "call to violence" rhetoric may be best understood as institutional propaganda that falls within the definitions of epidictic genre.

The connection between the RTLM and the Habyarimana government was well documented; "the radio station received its electricity supply directly from the presidential buildings" (Misser and Jaumain 1994, 72). In referring to "argumentation and violence," Perelman and Olbrechts-Tyteca note that institutional propaganda prohibits (or closes off) subsequent debate: "From the moment the decision (to prohibit debate) is taken, the social life of the community carries with it not merely the decision itself, but also the arguments that proceeded it" (1969, 59).

Ultimately, questions about radio's "call to violence and killing" focus on whether and how this broadcast media (re)framed what might otherwise be taken as genocidal actions to appear normal and legitimate to an audience of Hutus. Generally the puzzle concerning how Rwandan radio could "transform the moral landscape" (see Fujii 2004) revolves around a pair of competing theoretical explanations. The more conventional view—that neo-patrimonial regimes in the region exert unquestioned authority over cultures that value deference to authority—may substantiate "fear" (as expressed above) as the impetus for mobilization via radio broadcasts. Such a view aligns the work of Geert Hofstede and his associates, particularly in developing indices of cultural development such as the *power distance index*—that "expresses the degree to which the less powerful members of a society accept and expect that power is distributed unequally" (Hofstede Centre website).

However, other researchers of the Rwandan genocide are skeptical of this explanation; anthropologist Darryl Li expresses his doubts as follows:

> Scholars have drawn from many of the existing theories of collective violence in order to explain the Rwandan genocide. . . . These have been widely criticized, however, to the extent that they now serve as little more than an academic piñata, though their political potency cannot be underestimated (and their potential analytical value, if properly revised, is perhaps underappreciated at this time). Primordialist approaches have been largely displaced by explanations that emphasize the historicity/contingency of ethnic identities, the role of manipulative and self-serving political elites, crushing economic and demographic pressures, the importance of racist anti-Tutsi ideologies, or often some combination thereof. (2004, 10–11)

An alternative explanation holds that the radio broadcasters (and those of the RTLM in particular) legitimized violence against Tutsis *not* by exerting unquestioned authority and instilling *fear* but instead by providing attractive, interactive programming formats that established the

> rhythms of everyday life by the proponents of the genocide was part of a dialogic process through which Rwandans actively sought to understand and confront a social world disrupted by four years of civil war, political instability, and economic crisis, now coming to a head with the assassination of Habyarimana and the eruption of widespread violence. (Li 2004, 22)

A Human Rights Watch official offers additional commentary on the RTLM's interactive format:

> Throughout the genocide, RTLM continued the interactive broadcasting that it had begun in the months before. Its journalists went out around the city of Kigali, interviewing ordinary people at the barriers, giving them an opportunity to explain on air what they were doing and why they were doing it. This confirmation by ordinary people of the

"rightness" of what they were doing contributed to the legitimacy of the genocide for radio listeners. (Des Forges 2007, 50)

Institutional theorists could simply refer to these circumstances as influential radio personalities (like counterparts in other cultural settings) who engage their audiences in ways that "make sense" of turbulent and confusing times. Such a perspective diminishes the role of the formal authority of regime leaders in power by calling attention to the "charisma and creativity" of radio personalities to interact with their audience on a seemingly personal basis (see Vokes 2007).

Subsequent discussion (below) will consider whether the emergence of "charismatic" radio in the Great Lakes region connects to pervasive institutional concerns; nonetheless, this second explanation of how radio changed the moral landscape implies that "the genocidal message" was friendly and engaging. For example, an expert in violence in the Great Lakes region quotes a program director who explains the RTLM's popularity in this way:

> These broadcasts were like a conversation among Rwandans who knew each other well and were relaxing over some banana beer or a bottle of Primus [the local beer] in a bar. It was a conversation without a moderator and without any requirements as to the truth of what was said. . . . It was all in fun. (Fujii 2004, 204, quoting Des Forges 1999, 70)

Yet Fujii also relates that RTLM programmers were strategically adept at "rehearsing the message," or constantly within the frame of "civil defense" as a unifying theme.

> Civil defense gave people the experience of conducting roadblocks, house searches, security meetings, and night patrols. It also developed the shared vocabulary, as well as the techniques, for identifying and seeking out "enemies of the people" and their "accomplices." Multiparty politics, as it took hold in Rwanda, exposed citizens to the open and aggressive promotion of an in-group, as well as to acts of intimidation and violence against those outside the group. (2004, 107, quoting Wagner 1998, 30)

Inferring a weakening of neo-patrimonial authority, reference here to the emergence of multi-party politics in place at the height of RTLM influence seems to dilute the conventional "fear of authority" explanation addressed above.

Anthropologist Darryl Li refers to on-air radio personalities as *animateurs*, referring to a person who can bring something to life, or make something happen. Although his observations largely affirm the rhetoricians' view (quoted above) that interactive programming formats can engender social roles assumed by the audience (through "lively style, good music, and off-colour jokes"; 2004, 16), Li goes further by stressing RTLM's propagandistic skill in purporting to offer "objective" reporting:

> [Rwanda radio] has often been understood simply as a means by which the station could easily "manipulate" audiences, a kind of Rwandan breads and circuses. Instead, it is also necessary to grasp how listeners interacted with RTLM's broadcasts, and how animateurs consciously or unconsciously exploited the possibilities and limits of the medium. One key performative aspect was the skill with which RTLM's animateurs played off the ideologies of the genocide, giving an impression of frankness and trustworthiness that also gave the ideology resilience in dealing with contingency. In doing so, RTLM did what any good propaganda must do: provide specific responses to opposing arguments ("balance"), even if they are based on non-falsifiable assumptions. (17)

To summarize, much of "hate radio's" call to violence can be categorized as epidictic speech with clearly emotive purposes; nonetheless, the causality here is problematic. Empirical analysis cautions against the assertion that hate radio *caused* the Rwandan genocide, since quantifiable issues of broadcast exposure, timing, and content may be found not to correlate with sequences of regional conflict (see Straus 2007). Such research disputes what some call the hypodermic needle model—"whereby media purportedly inject ideas into the body politic and thereby have a direct impact" (Straus 2007, 614)—as accurate in describing the effects of the RTLM. That said, the clear institutional nexus between the government and that broadcast medium suggests that the latter served as a *carrier* (see Scott 1995, 3) that conveyed regime propaganda instrumental in mobilizing the "work" of genocide against Tutsis. Specifically, Straus's research advises against reliance upon conventional narratives that explain genocide in static cultural terms; rather, he advances a "cumulative radicalization model pivoting around a dynamic of escalation" (Chalk

2007, 182, quoting Straus 2006, 12). Straus's more complicated narrative links political struggle whereby hardliner Hutu politicians prevail over moderates with propaganda disseminating fear of Tutsis among ordinary Hutus called to kill (Chalk 2007, 182, quoting Straus 2006, 173).

ACCUSATORY DISCOURSES

In their introductory discussion of epidictic genre, Perelman and Olbrechts-Tyteca distinguish it—eloquent prose to persuade—from two other types of oratory, deliberative and legal discourses. Here these rhetoricians briefly describe legal debate as "real contests in which two opponents [seek] to gain adherence . . . of an audience that would decide on the issues of a trial" (1969, 47). Taken simply this far, it is reasonable to classify the prosecutorial arguments in convicting RTLM officials Nahimana, Barayagwiza, and Ngeze of incitement to genocide and crimes against humanity during the (2000–2003) proceedings of The International Criminal Tribunal for Rwanda (ICTR) as *legal discourses*. Nonetheless Perelman and Olbrechts-Tyteca elaborate on the nature of strategic argumentation in legal debate that prescribes a sequential order of presentation that can effectively condition the audience: exordium (introduction), narrative, proof, refutation, conclusion, and epilogue (495).

On the basis of this "order of the [legalistic] speech and conditioning of the audience," it is useful to generalize beyond the ICTR (or other specific) trial(s) to identify continuing discourses related to Rwandan "hate radio" that parallel specific modes of presentation in legalistic argument. In these more figurative contexts of "law," it seems appropriate to substitute the adjective *accusatory*—"accusing or blaming someone: assigning blame or fault" (Merriam-Webster; m-w.com)—for *legal*. In this regard, a good deal of continuing conversation about the roles of radio leading to genocide takes the form of accusatory *narrative* that directs blame toward particular parties such as media (broadcast or print at local, national, or international levels), governments, NGOs, and international aid agencies. A related stream of continuing discourse pertains to *proof*, most often connected to problems encountered in attempting to prove or support accusatory narratives in formal proceedings.

Regarding media "blame," journalists appear particularly willing to assign themselves culpability for either ignoring or misconstruing events in the run-up to the Rwandan genocide. Allan Thompson, a former *Toronto Star* reporter who now leads a media capacity-building project in Rwanda, has compiled a wide array of reflective criticisms in his edited volume *The Media and the Rwanda Genocide* (2007), several of which deal with "hate radio." In an introductory chapter, Roméo Dallaire—the Canadian Lieutenant-General who led the United Nations Assistance Mission for Rwanda—casts a blanket indictment of Western media and their inattentive audiences:

> While the killing raged on in Rwanda, the O.J. Simpson case dominated the airwaves. Tonya Harding's kneecapping of her figure skating competitor was there as well. You had Nelson Mandela's election in South Africa. You had Yugoslavia. And, oh yes, somewhere in there, a bunch of black tribesmen in Africa were killing each other. During the 100 days of the Rwanda genocide, there was more coverage of Tonya Harding by ABC, CBS and NBC than of the genocide itself. Was that because [of various distractions]? Or was it the hand of someone above, guiding the media and getting across the subtle message, "Listen, we have absolutely no interest in going into another hellhole in Africa. We do not want to get involved in Rwanda. So don't get us involved." (2007, 14)

A British broadcast journalist based in Rwanda during the genocide argues that media reporters entered into cozy relationships with aid agencies in having framed the genocide in "humanitarian" narratives as appeals for donor funding:

> "The media presence changed the perception of the Rwandan crisis in a very damaging way," said Anne-Marie Huby, who was executive director of Médecins Sans Frontières (MSF)–UK in the mid-1990s. "In the general public's memory, the Rwanda crisis was people who die of cholera. I think people forgot the long-lens coverage of genocide. [In Goma,] I remember CNN saying "This is genocide again." . . . "We see a compelling news story, not whether it's genocide or refugees or whatever," said Larry Register, senior international editor at the time at CNN's headquarters in Atlanta. "Rwanda was such a straightforward story—a humanitarian tragedy unfolding daily." (Hilsum 2007, 169)

Hilsum adds that this "humanitarian" narrative provided governments a pretense for avoiding active involvement on the ground in Rwanda:

> Governments failed to come to the aid of the victims of genocide, but provided succour to many of the perpetrators. It was, of course, much easier to provide humanitarian aid than to try to prevent or stop the genocide, and how much outside powers could have done is still arguable. . . . One of the major outcomes of the imbalance in reporting of different aspects of the story was that governments were able to hide behind a humanitarian screen. (169)

It is the third stage of presentation—*proof*—in Perelman and Ohlbrechts-Tyteca's legal argumentation that becomes especially problematic as a forensic issue in attributing genocidal actions to broadcasted rhetoric. As a British researcher suggests, "while evidence exists to suggest there is a link between the media and real world violence there is little discussion around the direct imitation of portrayed actions in real life situations" (Morrison, 2012, 1). In particular, Sarah Morrison articulates a distinction between *incitement to attitudes* and *incitement to action*, either which can be conveyed through non-fictional or fictional media (11). She refers to Roméo Dallaire's assessment that Radio Rwanda characterized the voice of (government) authority in a culture of deference to power, suggesting that perpetrators regarded their violent actions against Tutsis as "legitimate"; such a claim follows the hypodermic needle model of media effects (discussed above). But Scott Straus's research points to the dearth of empirical evidence to support (or refute) the hypodermic needle argument that the RTLM constituted the "legitimate voice of government authority," even though the International Criminal Tribunal for Rwanda appeared to embrace it in convicting the three RTLM defendants.

One particular mode of legal conversation, that which explores the feasibility of international legal interventions to "kill the microphone" in order to pre-empt genocidal violence, presumably constitutes Perelman and Olbrechts-Tyteca's final stage of legal argumentation, the epilogue. Legal scholar Carol Pauli proposes a particular legal framework "to accomplish what the ICTR and others have not . . . to determine when a message constitutes incitement to genocide so as to justify international prior restraint through measures such as the jamming of broadcast signals" (Pauli 2010, 669). She concludes, "[o]nce identified, a broadcast incitement to genocide could be disrupted legally under several theories.

Among them is the constitution of the International Telecommunications Union gives 'absolute priority' on the broadcast airwaves to telecommunications related to saving lives" (700).

Deliberations on Political Contexts

Although Pereleman and Obrechts-Tyteca describe deliberative oratory (in distinction to the epidictic genre and legal argumentation treated above) in terms of political discourse—recommending a "course of action to be followed" (1969, 47)—it could presumably embrace argumentation about why courses of action have been taken that rely upon "analyticity" as a technique to persuade. The rhetoricians suggest that analytical arguments are directional or causal and that they incorporate *additional* evidence into explanation (rather than justifying an argument on its own terms as tautologies; 215–216). In the context of the Rwanda genocide and the role(s) of media therein, deliberative speakers look to a range of historical, cultural, and political factors that situate the relationship between hate radio and genocidal violence in broader relief.

As one example, a former director of the Office Rwandais d'Information, the governmental agency that oversees public media (forced to leave Rwanda at the onset of the genocidal violence) probes the role of the *print* media in events leading up to genocide, asking:

> Did the content of these newspapers serve as the catalyst of the genocide? The media have the potential to shape the views of their readers. [But] Rwandan newspapers reached a small proportion of the population because of their high cost and the high illiteracy rate. They certainly shaped the worldview of the political elite. . . . Having said that, the Rwanda genocide cannot be solely attributed to the Rwandan media. The media tapped into a context of social discontent, war, high population growth rate, economic crisis, regionalism, historical ethnic conflict opposing Hutus to Tutsis, bad leadership, and such external factors [of an international nature including Western structural adjustment programs]. (Higiro 2007, 86)

In large measure, Higiro's analytical discourse supports the empirical work of Scott Straus (discussed above) that disputes claims that directly attribute hate radio's messages in inciting Hutu citizens to violent actions.

Nonetheless, the former information director's assessment leads to promising conclusions:

> Rwandans who are committed to building a democratic society in Rwanda and to understanding racism and exclusionary practices . . . should be aware of the limited narratives of experts and the discourse of the [Rwanda Patriotic Front]. . . . Shifting the blame on to foreigners and ignoring deep-seated racism will only lead to cyclical violence as each ethnic group strives to achieve a zero-sum solution to oppression. (88)

Higiro's nuanced understandings of media as related to violence acquired through his official duties have been substantiated through formal research endeavors. For example, Li elaborates on the role of radio in establishing a rhythm or cadence of the everyday lives of listeners as a corrective to the disruptions attributable to Rwanda's recent history of unsettling conflict that Higiro discusses. Li relates:

> Based on available information, I would like tentatively to suggest that the appropriation of the rhythms of everyday life by the proponents of the genocide was part of a dialogic process through which Rwandans actively sought to understand and confront a social world disrupted by four years of civil war, political instability, and economic crisis, now coming to a head with the assassination of Habyarimana and the eruption of widespread violence. (2004, 22)

Fujii as well starts from Rwanda's history of conflict to accentuate radio's role as an agent of normalization that could justify genocidal violence as logical and legitimate:

> The process by which genocide became normalized as a legitimate response to fear and crisis was not inevitable. It involved multiple points of cohesion and opportunity which the *génocidaires* [those guilty of genocide] exploited to their fullest. The *génocidaires* were able to establish a genocidal rationale by framing their genocidal message in historic terms, by spreading the story through media, pop culture, and official pronouncements at every level of the administrative chain. . . . Thus were the *génocidaires* able to transform the normative landscape of Rwanda, paving the way for genocide through mass participation. (2004, 112–113)

Fujii's analysis is especially provocative in the context of human rights advocacy in asserting that radio personalities functioned as norms entrepreneurs in championing the development of a norm (in this case, the norm of *genocidal killing*) in much the same way a human rights advocate might work on behalf of gender equality or water security (see e.g., Finnemore and Sikkink 1998). From the standpoint of rhetoric, both Li's and Fujii's research efforts reflect continuing deliberative conversations that situate the speakers and audiences of "hate radio" within historical and cultural environments.

Li's analysis proceeds beyond historical explanations to support two additional narratives: "*democracy* (as a particular way of thinking about governance); and *development* (as a particular way of thinking about economy and work)" (2004, 13; italics in original). Radio advanced a democracy narrative by justifying a majoritarian will and "numerical preponderance" of Hutus over "outsider" Tutsis: "Not only did this allow the state to demonize the Tutsi as a hostile minority bent on restoring its old dominance . . . but more importantly, it squelched economic, regional, and ideological differences between Hutu in the name of ethnic solidarity" (14). The narrative of genocidal action as part and parcel of "development" stems from the Habyarimana regime's imposition of *umuganda*, a compulsory duty of collective work demanded of citizens. Li explains:

> RTLM's notorious use of "work" as a euphemism (with machetes as "tools") needs to be understood in the context of development, with participation (manning roadblocks, taking part in night patrols, conducting house searches, clearing fields) being likened to umuganda on a number of occasions. RTLM's invocation of work drew upon the existing discourses of development while simultaneously recasting communal labour as an exercise in national survival (sometimes described as "civil defence") at a moment of crisis. "Mobilize yourselves [radio personalities implored] "Work . . . everywhere in the country, come to work with your army. Come to work with your government to defend your country." (15)

In comparison to Fujii's assertion that radio normalized and legitimized violence, Li characterizes radio merely as a "medium through which Rwandans experienced and enacted the genocide" (24). The rhetorical distinctions appear significant; rather than *conditioning* its audience toward violence (see TNR, 54–55) as implied in Fujii's findings, Li implicates the listening audience as willing (rational) actors who based their decisions to involve themselves in the genocide on information transmitted over the airwaves. But again, both efforts reflect deliberative discourses that search for explanatory factors in wider contexts.

In calling attention to "hate radio's" attributions of Tutsis as "outsiders," Li's "democracy" narrative speaks to interactions within a group about *the other* group and as such takes on cross-societal significance as "us" versus "them." Presumably Li's presentation of a democratic narrative that pushes Tutsis outside of the Rwandan polity extends deliberative analysis to global considerations.

Proceeding further in situating Rwandan radio in a global context, British anthropologist Richard Vokes associates certain international development policies with the ascendance of a new variety of charismatic authority in the Great Lakes region strengthened by the technology of radio. Specifically, Vokes argues that Western structural adjustment programs supported "a proliferation of new radio stations—not to mention widely available cheap batteries" (2007, 814) to challenge the official government broadcast outlet. Vokes comments on the sociology of radio suggesting that although an individual may own one (as private property), she cannot expect to play it without drawing a crowd (that is, radio broadcasting constitutes a public good; 814).

For Vokes, the global significance of Rwandan radio goes beyond international development programs proliferating alternative broadcast entities that in turn enable charismatic radio opportunists. He argues as well that radio allowed its charismatic personalities to draw upon two alternative representations of "cosmopolitanism"—in essence, two edges of the same sword—that framed Hutu hatred for Tutsis in global perspectives. In the first frame, radio characterized Tutsis, many of whom lived outside Rwanda ("in Belgium, Canada, Kenya, Tanzania, the US, Zaïre and elsewhere"; 818), as foreigners not understanding Rwandan culture and as in alliance with many contacts in the international community. Here the "cosmopolitan" narrative reinforces the Tutsi "threat." Vokes reports that

> Based on the ICTR's archive of RTLM broadcasts, it is clear that throughout late 1993 and early 1994, RTLM listeners were constantly told that Tutsi were then in the process of mobilizing their international network in order to enslave Rwanda, and to kill all who tried to resist (the RPF invasion was represented as the vanguard of this strate-

gy). Furthermore, because of their generally "wily" nature—behaviour which, learned abroad, was further evidence of Tutsis' essentially cosmopolitan nature—the group would almost certainly be successful in duping their unsuspecting international partners to this end. (818)

But a second interpretation of cosmopolitanism takes on positive meaning as a strength of the RTLM, the "cosmopolitan" voice of Rwandan Hutus.

> RTLM presenters, as "defenders of the people," constantly played up their own cosmopolitan credentials. For example, presenters usually went to great lengths to demonstrate a good general knowledge of current international affairs. . . . [I]t was this general cosmopolitan knowledge which constructed RTLM presenters as so well placed to counter the foreign Tutsi threat to the country, because if Tutsi networks did indeed have the ear of all international radio broadcasters, it became the responsibility of RTLM presenters, with their own cosmopolitan abilities, to monitor these stations, and to uncover Tutsi mistruths wherever they were to be found. (819–820)

Vokes concludes by situating his analysis in the context of the anthropology of globalization concerning the impacts of new media in a particular time and place (821). He has also contributed (as have others noted above) to an important deliberative conversation that assesses the interaction between the RTLM as speaker of hate and its ethnic audience in historical and global perspectives.

In summary, this sketch personifies the RTLM as "a speaker" that was intent on mobilizing its Hutu audience toward violence against Tutsis in the run-up to and during the 1994 Rwanda genocide. In perverse narratives, this speaker assumed the role as *advocate* whose rhetoric significantly (but horrifically) affected the human condition. This discourse can be evaluated in reference to three oratorical types—the epidictic, legal, and deliberative—each offering different perspectives on the inhumanity of this cruel speech that may ultimately contribute to an enhanced understanding of human rights advocacy.

Clearly, Rwandan hate radio transmitted a "call to violence" leading to the genocide of Tutsis. In reference to the next sketch, it is intriguing to consider whether student casualties at the Kent State and Tiananmen Square protests were in fact precipitated by similar calls to violence or instead simply due to sequences of unfortunate circumstances.

SYLVESTER DEL CORSO, XU QINXIAN, JAMES RHODES, AND LI XIMING: RHETORS ON STUDENT PROTESTS

In response to President Richard Nixon's April 30, 1970, announcement of a decision to extend the US Vietnam war effort into Cambodia, anti-war student activists staged massive protests on many college campuses. At Kent State University several days of protests led to violence—particularly the burning of the ROTC building—that resulted in the deaths of four Kent State students shot by Ohio National Guardsmen. Two days earlier Governor James Rhodes had called out the Guard at the request of the City of Kent mayor amid significant property damage in the downtown area attributed to student demonstrations. On the next day the ROTC facility was destroyed by fire at 8:30 p.m., and Ohio National Guard troops arrived an hour later. Then on Monday, May 4, some Guardsmen opened fire on student protesters, resulting in the deaths of four students.

During a four-week period beginning in mid-April 1989, Chinese university students escalated their public demonstrations against government educational policies. Subsequently hundreds (the exact count is unknown) of student protestors were killed by military personnel in the People's Liberation Army (PLA) in its effort to "clear" Tiananmen Square in Beijing on June 4. Student activity began on April 15 as a rather non-threatening movement to mourn the death of a reformer within the Communist Party. But in a relatively short interval, student activity became more militant and increased in numbers; by May 18 nearly one million students demonstrated at the Square to support a hunger strike by some of their peers. After student efforts to prevent PLA troops from entering Tiananmen Square, the Army succeeded in gaining control of the area. Subsequently the PLA embarked on efforts to marshal tanks and armored vehicles; that action culminated in countless deaths on June 4.

This sketch focuses on the rhetoric of four principals involved in governmental responses to either the Kent State tragedy or the Tiananmen Square Massacre: Sylvester Del Corso (Adjutant General of the Ohio National Guard), Xu Qinxian (Commander of the 38th Army Unit in the PLA), James Rhodes (Governor of Ohio), and Li Ximing (Chairman of the Beijing Municipal Communist Party). The following discussion relates to (1) military voices reacting to policy actors and (2) policy voices manipulating symbols.

Military Voices Reacting to Policy Actors

At the time of the Kent State University shootings in 1970, Sylvester Del Corso served as Adjutant General (in essence, the commander) of the Ohio National Guard, having been appointed to that position by Governor James Rhodes in 1968. Del Corso had lied about his age to enlist in the military—specifically, Del Corso was all of fifteen years of age at the time. Having been raised in a poor community south of Cleveland, he attended a local college on a football scholarship. At age twenty-six, Del Corso was commissioned as a second lieutenant in the Guard. Author Joseph Kelner relates that Del Corso was one of very few officers in the Ohio Guard at the time of the Kent State tragedy with extensive combat experience. When the Guard was nationalized at the onset of World War II, he commanded an infantry company in the "Buckeye" 37th Division that fought in the South Pacific (1980, 142).

According to Kelner, Del Corso described himself "as a military man and not a politician" (143); nonetheless he was "on the record" for his contemptuous statements against the student anti–Vietnam War movement prior to the Guard's deployment to enforce martial law on campus and in the city of Kent. Kelner contends that Del Corso "regarded the SDS [Students for a Democratic Society] and the New Mobilization Committee to End the War in Vietnam as instruments of an international Communist conspiracy, that is, enemies of the United States" (143).

Adjutant General Del Corso was not present on the Kent State University campus on May 4, 1970, the day of the shootings, but had left Kent for Columbus with Governor Rhodes (and was with Rhodes when the governor called Vice President Spiro Agnew to inform him of the shootings); assistant Adjutant General Robert Canterbury was left in charge. Nonetheless, Del Corso was called as an expert witness in a federal grand jury proceeding in 1973 to testify as to whether guardsmen's fears from having been rushed by students justified the use of lethal force. Specifically, Del Corso was asked such a question sixteen times, and in each case he responded with an unequivocal "no."

That federal proceeding had been "a long time in coming" (due to political maneuvering at the onset of Watergate) despite a US Department of Justice determination of significant evidence of criminal behavior on the part of Ohio Guardsmen. Del Corso's testimony was especially critical, since most of the guardsmen called to the stand invoked their Fifth

Amendment right against self-incrimination. After the lengthy trial, the *Cleveland Plain Dealer* published excerpts of Del Corso's federal grand jury testimony, including the following:

> Based on the pictures of the shooting and the reports received, the guardsmen were not surrounded by the students at the time of of the shooting and were not threatened by the students.
>
> None of the students was close enough to the soldiers to endanger their lives. . . .
>
> There was no sniper fire before the shooting . . .
>
> "I say it was unjustifiable, because as I see it, I can't see how it was justified. And to me, overall, I would like to say, I can't see any justification in it." . . .
>
> " . . . many of these individuals that fired their weapon, there is absolutely no justification to fire, no justification. (Kelner 1980, 147)

Subsequently the grand jury indicted eight members of the Ohio National Guard for "willfully discharging loaded weapons [toward the victims] and did thereby willfully deprived said persons [of due process rights under the US Constitution]" in a Cleveland federal district court. But ultimately federal judge Frank Battisti "dismissed the charges before it went to the jury on the grounds that the government had not shown that the defendants had shot students with the intent to deprive them of specific civil rights" (Kelner 1980, 17–18).

Joseph Kelner was hired to represent shooting victims' families as plaintiffs in a civil suit against Governor Rhodes, Del Corso, Canterbury, Kent State University President Robert White, and two guardsmen. Kelner's grand strategy involved admitting Del Corso's federal grand jury testimony (discussed above) into evidence. Kelner confides to his readers that he had not revealed his strategy to other members on his legal team:

> I didn't want to let on that I had, in my apartment, a secret weapon, a blockbuster that was going to level what was left of the defense. It was nothing less than the previous sworn testimony of Adjutant General Sylvester Del Corso . . . on the justifiability of the shooting. All I had to do was qualify Del Corso as an expert. . . . If he gave different answers from those he had given the federal grand jury, I could then confront him with what he had earlier told an investigative body. He would then either have to admit his earlier testimony or find himself lying under oath. (1980, 141–142)

Unfortunately for Kelner and the plaintiffs, Judge Don Young, citing Ohio rules of evidence, refused to allow Kelner to qualify the adjutant general as an expert witness. The jury issued a verdict in favor of the defendants.

At this point, discussion turns to Xu Qinxian, a high-ranking military leader affected by the government crackdown on the massive student protests in Tiananmen Square in 1994. Thus, it is revealing to compare the pertinent discourses of Xu with those of his counterpart Sylvester Del Corso at Kent State in 1970.

"I'd rather be beheaded than be a criminal in the eyes of history." These are the words of Major General Xu Qinxian, leader of the 38th Group Army in his refusal to use military force on Chinese students during the events leading up to the Tiananmen Square Massacre in Beijing in June of 1989 (Jacobs and Buckley 2014, A1).

According to accounts in *The Tiananmen Papers,*[3] the student movement began as demonstrations mourning the death of Hu Yaobang, a Politburo member advocating educational reform, but it subsequently turned into a political confrontation against the Party occurring in both Beijing and the provinces (Zhang, Nathan, and Link 2001, 19–51). This confrontation between student masses and civilian and military authorities led up to the June 4 massacre. Zhang Liang, the pseudonym of the individual claiming to have secretly compiled documents in *The Tiananmen Papers*, speaks of the killings in the first paragraph of the document's preface:

> Twelve years is an instant in history but a long time in a person's life. For one who experienced it, June 4, 1989, weighs heavily in the memory. History seems frozen there. To write about June Fourth is to recall the blood of thousands of young people spilled on the streets around Chang'an Boulevard in Beijing. Time may wash away the bloodstains, bur not their memory. History and the people will ultimately judge June Fourth as one of the most dramatic and significant episodes in the worldwide pursuit of democracy in the twentieth century. Certainly it was the greatest event of that kind in China. (Zhiang, Nathan, and Link, 2001, xi)

Two weeks earlier, on May 19, Party officials met with high-ranking military leaders to announce martial law to begin on May 20. A member of the Politboro Standing Committee justified the imposition of martial law in his speech (excerpted here):

> The current situation in the capital is grave. Anarchy is growing. Discipline and the rule of law have been broken. After great effort we managed to get things calmed down as of late April, but in May the turbulence came back. More and more students and others got caught up in the demonstrations; universities were paralyzed. . . . It has now become clear that a tiny, tiny minority of individuals are trying to use the turmoil to reach their political goals. They want to deny the leadership of the Chinese Communist Party and the socialist system. . . . In order to stop this turmoil resolutely and restore order promptly, I stand before you [to restore order through the imposition of martial law]. (225)

Four military units, including Xu Qinxian's 38th Group Army, were dispatched to their positions in Beijing. In reports back to the headquarters of martial law troops, the various military units documented the scale of demonstrations as tens of thousands of students interfered with troop movements, thereby obstructing the implementation of martial law.

Emerging from a family of rural poverty, Xu Qinxian had enlisted in the People's Liberation Army before he was of legal age and rose within its ranks. On March 20 the Central Military Committee learned that Xu had refused to carry out martial law and took punitive action. *The Tiananmen Papers* contains the following dialogue between military leader Zhou Yibing and Yang Shangkun, chairman of the Central Military Committee:

> *Zhou Yibing*: Chairman Yang, we've just received a report from the Thirty-Eighth Army. The commander, Xu Qinxian, cannot carry out the order to enter Beijing to carry out martial law.

> *Yang Shangkun*: This is no time for jokes! This is a military order! Disobeying a military order gets you court-martialed! What do the other people in the Thirty-Eighth Army have to say?

> *Zhou Yibing*: Most are ready to carry out the order resolutely.

> *Yang Shangkun*: This is no good. It's too important. You go back and talk to Xu Qinxian right away. Work on him. Tell him that whether or

not he can see the logic of an order has nothing to do with whether he has to carry it out. (Liang, Nathan, and Link 2001, 213)

Subsequently Zhou Yibing addressed the Central Military Committee to tell of Yu's fate:

> After Thirty-Eighth Army commander Xu Qinxian disobeyed an order to carry out his martial law assignment, we obeyed Chairman Yang's order to strip Xu of his command and send him to a hospital to recover his health.
>
> All members of the Thirty-Eighth Army Party Committee were firm in their determination to carry out the orders of Party Central and the CMC and in their support of decisions regarding Xu Qinxian. The Party Committee suggested that all party committees at the army, division, and brigade levels redouble their efforts in ideological purification, sum up Xu Qinxian's mistakes as an object lesson, and take firm control of political thought. (239–240)

In sharp contrast, more recent documents (maintained by the Princeton University Library) "show soldiers troubled by misgivings, confusion, rumors and regrets about the task assigned to them." In their *New York Times* article appearing twenty years after the massacre, Andrew Jacobs and Chris Buckley report on the reactions of some who served in the military during the crackdown:

> "The situation was fluid and confusing, and we underestimated the brutality of the struggle," Capt. Yang De'an, an officer with the People's Armed Police, a paramilitary force, wrote in one assessment found among military documents acquired by the Princeton University Library. "It was hard to distinguish foes from friends, and the target to be attacked was unclear." . . .
>
> "I personally didn't do anything wrong," said Li Xiaoming, who in 1989 was among the troops who set off toward Tiananmen Square, "but I feel that as a member, a participant, this was a shame on the Chinese military." . . .
>
> In an interview, a former party researcher with military ties confirmed the existence of a petition, signed by seven senior commanders, that called on the leadership to withdraw the troops. "The people's military belongs to the people, and cannot oppose the people," stated the petition, according to the former researcher, Zhang Gang [discussed below], who was then trying to broker compromise between the

protesters and the government. "Even less can it kill the people." (Jacobs and Buckley 2014, A1)

Xu Qinxian served five years in prison, later to reside in a sanitarium for retired military officers. He offers no regrets.

Policy Voices Manipulating Symbols

For Ohio Governor James Rhodes, the first week of May 1970 proved to be eventful and tumultuous: on Sunday, May 3, he held a press conference in the City of Kent; on Monday, May 4—the day of the Kent State shootings, he had traveled back to Columbus with Adjutant General Del Corso; on Tuesday, May 5, he ran as a candidate in the Republican primary election for a US Senate seat; and in the next days after that, he focused on his public responses to the Kent State fiasco.

At his Sunday press conference—with the Guard Adjutant General and Kent Police Chief at his side, Governor Rhodes vented his interpretations of student unrest on the Kent State campus, the political motivations of student protestors, and the actions he would take, in terms of epidictic (and inflammatory) rhetoric:

> The scene here that the city of Kent is facing is probably the most vicious form of campus-oriented violence yet perpetrated by dissident groups and their allies in the State of Ohio. . . . Now it ceases to be a problem of the colleges of Ohio. This is now the problem of the State of Ohio. Now we're going to put a stop to this, for this reason. The same group that we're dealing with here today, and there's three or four of them, they only have one thing in mind. That is to destroy higher education in Ohio. . . . We have these same groups going from one campus to the other, and they use universities that are supported by the taxpayers of Ohio as a sanctuary. And in this they make definite plans of burning, destroying, and throwing rocks at police and at the National Guard and the Highway Patrol . . .
> *They're worse than the brownshirts and the Communist element and also the night riders and the vigilantes. They are the worst type of people that we harbor in America.* . . . It's over with in Ohio. . . . I think we're up against the strongest, well-trained, militant revolutionary group that has ever assembled in America. . . . *We're going to eradicate the problem. We're not going to treat the symptom.* (quoted in Kelner 1980, 165; italics added.)

As events unfolded, it turned out that Rhodes lost Tuesday's primary election to Robert A. Taft Jr., who went on to defeat his Democratic challenger in the November general election. But questions remain as to (1) whether the governor had manipulated the Kent State protests as a political ploy to capitalize on strong anti–student protest sentiment in the state and nation and (2) whether he had appropriated the Ohio National Guard as a "law-and order" symbol. Regarding the first question, it was evident that significant numbers of Ohioans (and US citizens) had been repulsed by the radical student counter-culture. At several points in his book *Kent State*, for example, prominent novelist James Michener conveys his own contempt for student demonstrators:

Why don't the universities rout out and expel their inhabitants [from the dwellings where radicals reside]? The students have done nothing wrong. There is no longer any law against young people living together; you can't expel a girl because she has set up housekeeping with a boy she likes. And as long as young radicals merely preach the overthrow of the university while refraining from taking or participating in overt action to speed their plans, they cannot be punished by either the civil authorities or the university. (1971, 80)

One question which may become increasingly significant in American life cannot be answered conclusively by reference to [particular cases at Kent State]: Does adherence to the new life style predispose a participant toward an eventual acceptance of a form of dictatorship? The answer would appear to be yes. (95)

As to whether Rhodes attempted to capitalize on this mainstream sentiment, former student-protestor Tom Hayden relates that the governor was trailing his opponent Robert Taft in days prior to the shooting and that President Richard Nixon had strongly advised Rhodes to push the Kent State issue:

Rhodes was trailing by eight percent in the final days of a Republican primary when he visited Kent State on May 3, ordered the Guard on campus and excoriated the student radicals. According to top Nixon aide H.R. Haldeman's archival notes, the President instructed his hardline political consultant, Murray Chotiner, to make sure that "Rhodes esp. rides this." (2013)

Shortly after the shootings (on May 15), Nixon referred to the Kent State protestors as "bums."

While epidictic rhetoric may bolster electoral campaigns (but perhaps *not* in regard to Rhodes's senatorial bid), it cannot provide the exacting language essential for effective policy execution. For examples, James Rhodes's April 29 proclamation to call out the National Guard to respond to Kent State protests begins: "*WHEREAS in northeastern Ohio . . . there exist unlawful assemblies and roving bodies acting with the intent to commit a felony and to do violence.*" He explicitly refers to seven Ohio counties, but not to Portage County, wherein Kent State University is located. Moreover, Rhodes based his call-out *not* on his statutory authority to have the Guard maintain martial law (as it actually *did*) but rather on the authority to have it "act in the aid of civil authorities." Recognizing the problem, the Governor and his legal adviser reverse-engineered the authorization by issuing a proclamation on the day after the shooting (May 5) on his authority to have the guard "maintain peace and order" (Kelner 1980, 160–161).

From a forensic standpoint, the question arose in state court proceedings (specifically in the civil case wherein victims' families sued Rhodes and others) as to whether the Governor's inflammatory rhetoric incited Guardsmen to discharge their loaded weapons, resulting in the deaths of the five students, each of whom was standing at least the length of a football field away from his or her shooter. When the attorney for the plaintiffs (Kelner) pressed Rhodes about the political motivation behind the rhetoric, Judge Don Young disallowed this line of questioning on the grounds that such motivations should have no bearing on the outcome of the case. Nonetheless, in his chapter "The Plaintiffs as Defendants" Kelner complains that the judge *did* allow the defense attorney to question plaintiffs about their political leanings—for example, "Have you ever made statements regarding the fact that everyone ought to be armed to defend themselves against the imperialistic government?" (1980, 117) Kelner objected, but the judge allowed the question to be answered. Ultimately, he could not .nake his case that linked Rhodes's rhetoric to inciting a few trigger-happy Guardsmen and subsequently the fatal shootings of five students.

However, the contention that Rhodes manipulated the Ohio National Guard as a "law-and-order" symbol is supported by the record. In the two years prior to the Kent State incident, Ohio ranked high among states in terms National Guard call-outs. In fact, Rhodes requested Guard assistance on 31 occasions during this time frame. Kelner reports that during this time, Del Corso had been active traveling throughout the state "giving speeches, warning of potential trouble and encouraging mayors to ask for the Guard. He also circularized Ohio's guardsmen and Guard officials in other states, at Ohio's expense, urging them to write President Nixon in support of his Vietnam policy and to condemn the peace movement" (1980, 143).

In essence, Attorney Kelner argued in the civil court proceedings that the Adjutant General had been overly deferential (if not encouraging) in allowing the governor to use the Ohio National Guard as it suited him politically. Of the thirty-one Guard call-outs in the two previous years, nearly half related to civil matters—including student protests at Cleveland State University, Ohio State University, and Ohio University. By contrast, the Ohio Highway Patrol appeared more reluctant to respond to university matters (210), although it did deploy troopers and other assets (e.g., helicopters) to Kent State just prior to the shootings. Further, Kelner contended in court that Rhodes had prematurely wrestled control over the university and city from (respectively) the university president and mayor (201–203).

Ultimately Joseph Kelner's case, which largely rested on his depiction of causal assertions, did not prevail in the state trial. In retrospect, the plaintiffs' case involved a lengthy chain of logical connections—from the governor's political whims to the availability of the Guard to be used in civil matters to Guardsmen carrying loaded weapons (even though they did not do so at a Teamster wildcat strike where they were fired upon; 143), among other factors—and appears to have been difficult to win.

Policy theorist Deborah Stone focuses upon the power of rhetoric in framing arguments within the political community (or what she calls the *polis* and presumably what Gerald Hauser calls the moral vernacular) in *Policy Paradox: The Art of Political Decision Making*. In one particular chapter "Causes," she elaborates on how effective politicians can manipulate causal phenomena to advance their interests:

"Causes" is about the language of cause, effect, and responsibility. More generally, causes theories are origin stories, stories of how a problem came into being. Every origin story implies a resolution—we learn how to get out of a mess by knowing how we got into it. Causal stories are also stories of control; they locate responsibility and blame, and assign the moral statuses of victims and perpetrators. (1997, 134)

Disputes about causation relating to the Kent State shooting still abound; in 2010 for example, a sister of one of the shouting victims founded the group Kent State Truth Tribunal[4] that appeals to the US Department of Justice to reopen the Kent State inquiry. But causal theories aside, certain hard realities were undisputable—that "Four [were] Dead in Ohio"[5] and that a Kent State student had to identify the body of his close friend with whom he had shared an apartment on March 4, 1970.

The above discussion surrounding the Kent State shootings challenges the reader to determine whether the governor intentionally constructed his Kent State rhetoric to bolster Rhodes's candidacy for a US Senate seat (even though it was unsuccessful). Readers can compare the interaction of Rhodes's student protest discourses and political agenda with similar dynamics concerning Li Ximing, a leading politician close to the center of power in the People's Republic of China at the time of the Tiananmen Square protests.

For Li Ximiang, head of the Beijing (Communist) Party Committee, student protest on Tiananmen Square posed political problems but offered significant policy opportunities. On one hand, he confronted the problem of organized dissent *within* the capital city—a locational symbol of Party legitimacy and historic struggle—and specifically *on Tiananmen Square*, proximate to many national symbols such as the National People's Congress and the Monument to the People's Heroes (Liu 1989, 48). But on the other, as a local political actor, Li was expected to report (i.e., prepare text) about the protest in a way that would allow national parties to uphold regime legitimacy. Thus his obligation to submit such a report provided the opportunity for him to frame the situation in such a way that would position Beijing's municipal role (i.e., contributing police power to a crackdown on students) in a favorable light (1989, 48–49).

Li situated himself (and the Beijing Party) advantageously relative to Zhou Ziang's (Zhou was the General Secretary of the Party—in essence, Li's national-level counterpart) sympathy for student protesters and their message. Liu presents the stark distinction between Zhou's and Deng Xiaoping's interpretations of the student demonstrations as follows:

Deng's definition of the protest as a case of "turmoil," however, was challenged by Zhao Ziyang after his return from North Korea on April

30. [B]oth Deng and Zhao were "symbolic persons"; disagreements between them would have vast consequences for the whole nation. Zhao confronted Deng with a very different interpretation of the protest. Zhao deemed the tone of the April 26 editorial "too shrill" and ventured that the nature of the protest was at best unclear. . . . He further admitted publicly that some of the protesters' grievances, such as corruption among Party and state officials, were legitimate. (52)

Liu suggests Zhou's rift with Deng and the Party had started well before the Tiananmen crisis partly because he could not tolerate the cognitive dissonance of dual loyalties to the Party and democracy movement in his advanced age. According to Liu, Zhou had addressed the Standing Committee of the Politboro in these words:

I simply can't suppress the students. I don't want to commit such a heinous crime even if it means getting the sack or death. Even if I am entirely on my own I will never change my mind on this point. As to the responsibility for economic problems, I am mentally prepared for the consequences but I never thought the students would go on hunger strike. Even though things have got out of hand I shall continue to oppose suppressing the students. (54)

Zhou left the Party soon after.

But for Deng (Liu speculates), his own prior democratic initiatives left him and others in Party leadership with a shroud of anxiety, heightened by the student demonstrations, about having diluted the revolutionary spirit within the Peoples Republic's history (56). It is within this context of "righting the ship" back toward history and memory that Li Ximing's role as a local (Beijing) Party speaker to a Central Party audience gains clarity. In essence, Li's closeness to "the action" allowed him to report to Deng and Central Party officials—remote from it —in such a way as to polarize the discourse with students (as opposed to Zhou's efforts to reconcile it) and to feature the municipality's role in aggressively quelling the turmoil (49–50).

In *The Symbolic Uses of Politics*, Murray Edelman argues that *remoteness* frees policy makers from the necessity of having to connect how they use symbols with realities "on the ground":

A traffic policeman at a busy corner may grow entranced momentarily with himself [by his power to control traffic] . . . but the lengthening line of cars in front of him and some irate honking will soon remind him that he must face reality: drivers and a prosaic chief of police. There is no such check on the fantasies and conceptualizing of those who never can test objectively their convictions. (1964, 6–7)

Yet Liu suggests that remoteness in the Tiananmen case allowed "locals," specifically Li and Beijing mayor Chen Xitong, to set the stage on which Deng could polarize discourse about student protest and in so doing, rearrange political symbolism in clearer alignment with history.

Liu explains:

Hence, in their first and most critical briefing to Deng, on April 25, Mayor Chen and Secretary Li centered their report on the protest around the key symbol of conspiracy to subvert the state. . . . Secretary Li portrayed the student movement as a gigantic worldwide conspiracy that had been planned for the past two years and that was aimed at the overthrow of the Communist Party. (1989, 48)

In rhetorical terms, Li's "up close" report on the student protest provided Deng the opportunity "break the connecting links"—in essence, Perelman and Olbrechts-Tyteca's strategy of "the dissociation of concepts" (1969, 411–414)—between his democratic reforms and the erosion of the revolutionary spirit of the past. Moreover, Liu shows the report capitalized upon the age factor so as to further enrage Party leaders:

On April 15, the date of Comrade Yaobang's death [the students' hero], a poster entitled "In Praise of Yaobang—Also To Some People" appeared on the campus of Peking University. It stated that the Party Center's criticisms of Comrade Yaobang's errors were like "those who accused others of sexual license because they were impotent themselves." . . . Some [posters] suggested inviting the Kuomintang [the political power of the Republic of China before the Cultural Revolution and currently the ruling party of Taiwan] to return to establish a two-party system on the mainland. Many "small character posters" used indescribably vulgar words vilifying Comrade Xiaoping, demanding "Down with Deng Xiaoping, End Politics of Old Men." (49)

Through the rhetoric in his report, Li Ximing convinced Central Party Leaders that "we [in Beijing] know how to solve the problem" (49).

CONCLUSION

Taken together, the three sketches in this chapter reveal a clear distinction in rhetorical reaction to circumstances of moral crisis. On one hand, Mary B. Anderson, an advocate of human rights through peace-building, appeals to her humanitarian colleagues to engage in reflective, (self-) deliberative discourses to (1) address themselves in scrutinizing their own operative assumptions and (2) understand how perpetrators of conflict frame their justificatory rationales. On the other hand, perpetrators—presumably, antagonists of human rights—pursue epidictic and forensic discourses that direct blame toward other parties. In both the Rwandan radio and Kent State/Tiananmen cases, rhetors (specifically, the RTLM radio personalities and Governor of Ohio James Rhodes) engaged in inflammatory rhetoric that cast blame outward toward Tutsis as "foreigners" and (in the Kent State context) "outside radicals" transported into Ohio. Although the direct link between inflammatory rhetoric and overt violence (e.g., killing) is difficult to substantiate, it can be reasonably asserted that the antagonistic speaker exploits "crisis" by manipulating the audience's sense of security.

NOTES

1. Although middle initials of exemplars have been otherwise excluded, an exception is made here since the initial appears central to Mary B. Anderson's identity.

2. Readers can access video clips of the RTLM on Youtube—for example, at http://www.youtube.com/watch?v=mSVKG_i_M8k. Accessed May 28, 2014.

3. The accuracy of accounts in *The Tiananmen Papers* are subject to dispute given the impossibility of verifying Zhang Liang's compiled entries. In 2004, co-editor Andrew Nathan published an article in *The China Quarterly* that largely discredits the papers.

4. See http://truthtribunal.org/about. Accessed July 15, 2014.

5. Lyrics from the song *Ohio*, written by Neil Young and performed by Crosby, Stills, and Nash—Cotillion Music and Broken Arrow Music, 1970.

4

RHETORIC IN MORAL CONFRONTATIONS

with Youssef Farhat

Bertolt Brecht's play *Galileo* portrays moral confrontation wherein a celebrated sixteenth-to-seventeenth-century Italian physicist "pushes the envelope" on behalf of scientific exploration of the physical universe against the authoritative precepts of the Church.

In confrontations moral exemplars are obliged to take risks (Hart 1992, 23). In this regard Brecht characterizes how Galileo Galilei kept the truth concealed "under his coat" (1966, 121) as ecclesiastical authorities deliberate over what to do about the scientist's public efforts promoting his improved instrument, the telescope. Scene 11 involves the pope's conversation with the grand inquisitor:

Pope: This man is the greatest physicist of our time. He is the light of Italy, and not just any muddlehead.

Inquisitor: We would have had to arrest him otherwise. This bad man knows what he is doing, not writing his books in Latin, but in the jargon of the market place.

Pope: (occupied by the shuffling of feet [heard from off-stage representing societal reaction]) That was not in the best of taste. These shuffling feet make me nervous.

Inquisitor: May this be more telling than my words, Your Holiness. Shall all these go from you with doubt in their hearts?

Pope: This man has friends. What about Versailles? What about the Viennese court? They will call the Holy Church a cesspool of defunct ideas. Keep your hands off him.

Inquisitor: In practice it will never get that far. He is a man of the flesh. He would soften at once. (1966, 109)

Brecht's inquisitor turned out to be prophetic. Since confrontations are typically episodic, an exemplar's virtue (or vice) need only be temporary, perhaps "above and beyond" his or her more enduring persona. Thus Brecht points to Galileo's shortcomings as a glutton, a braggart, and one with an affinity for comfort which compromise his moral resolve. These failings lead the physicist to capitulate when after publicizing the scientific implications of *his* improved instrument, the institutional authorities showed him *their* instruments for dealing with those who challenge legitimate dictums.

Toward the play's conclusion, Brecht imprisons Galileo *not* in physical confines but in his remorse for betraying science; the scientist verbalizes this shame in Scene 13:

As a scientist I had an almost unique opportunity. In my day astronomy emerged into the market place. At that particular time, had one man put up a fight, it could have had wide repercussions. I have come to believe I was never in real danger; for some years I was as strong as the authorities, and I surrendered my knowledge to the powers that be, to use it, no, not use it, *abuse* it as it suits their ends. I have betrayed my profession. Any man who does what I have done must not be tolerated in the ranks of science. (1966, 124)

Each of the rhetorical exemplars in this chapter assumes substantial risks in confronting either formidable realities or compelling *perceptions of reality* in ways that either address or deny human rights claims advanced by particular people. As a young boy in bonded servitude, Iqbal Masih confronts his carpet-masters and the thriving Pakistani carpet industry in his struggle against children's bonded labor, a fight that ultimately cost him his life. Pussy Riot, a group of activist Russian performers, confronts the institutions of government and established church, both intending to resurrect their respective (and symbiotic) nationalistic grandeur of the nineteenth century. US President Lyndon B. Johnson risks his own political capital accrued in reassuring the nation after the Kennedy assassination as he confronted an unpopular war that he personally loathed but nonetheless felt compelled to pursue.

IQBAL MASIH, CHILD SLAVE AS HUMAN RIGHTS REFORMER

As a young child, Iqbal Masih became a debt slave in a carpet factory in Pakistan. At the age of four, his father sold him into slavery; thus Iqbal entered into bonded servitude, a condition confronting six million children working throughout Pakistan. At ten he escaped his slavery and was set free. Iqbal appeared to be younger than his age since he suffered from malnutrition and psychosocial dwarfism (Kuklin 1998, 77). He joined the Bonded Labor Liberation Front of Pakistan, a non-governmental organization (NGO) intent on abolishing children's servitude. Iqbal managed to free over 3,000 Pakistani children and as a result achieved international notoriety. Dozens of carpet factories were closed in Pakistan as a result of Iqbal's visible crusade. When Prime Minister Bhutto visited Stockholm, Swedish schoolchildren protested against child labor in front of the Pakistani embassy; children all over the world rallied to Iqbal's cause.

On April 16, 1995, Iqbal was murdered while visiting his family's home, some six months after his tour in the United States, where he received the Reebok Human Rights Award; the ambiguous circumstances surrounding his death are discussed below. In his twelve short years of life, Iqbal Masih became a symbol of child slave labor and one of its most engaging reformers. The courage he demonstrated in breaking free from an owner who "had chained him by his ankles to a carpet loom" was applauded throughout the developed world. This sketch includes discussions related to Iqbal Masih's life and death as: (1) a voice of human collateral, (2) the "talk-back" boy as confrontational pragmatist, and (3) the target of reactionary rhetoric.

A Voice of Human Collateral

Iqbal was born in Muridke, Pakistan, in 1982 to a poor Christian family that lacked the means to send him to school to learn and read. Nonetheless he was a valuable economic asset for his parents, who used him as collateral to secure a *pesghi* (or micro-loan) in the amount of twelve US dollars from the local *thekedar*—an employer who owns a nearby carpet factory. This "transaction, no contract just a simple handshake, ended Iqbal's childhood forever" and he became a "debt-bonded laborer" (Kuklin 1998, 5). Such transactions were common among the impoverished familes in rural areas such as Muridke, "it was just the way things were done" (Crofts 2006, 19). As a child, Iqbal "gratefully" accepted his job thinking that this was his opportunity to learn a skill, earn a living, "not live their [his parents] life, and do something different" (D'Adamo 2003, 89). Author Susan Kuklin provides a detailed account of Iqbal's *pesghi* as follows:

> Under the terms of the *pesghi,* Iqbal was to weave carpets six days a week, twelve hours a day, until he worked off the 600-rupee loan. His training, the tools that he used, and the food that he ate were additional expenses. If he made mistakes while weaving the intricate designs, he would be fined. In order to learn the art of carpet weaving, Iqbal would spend a year or so as an apprentice. During this period, he would not be paid. . . . If the *thekedar* chose to pad the bill, there was no way to challenge him. There were no witnesses. No contract. Just a simple handshake and Iqbal belonged to the carpet master. (1998, 15)

Iqbal's biographer Andrew Crofts explains how Iqbal interpreted his role as a bonded slave as a matter of upholding family honor. When his older brother Aslam had reached the age of four, their father collateralized him to work as a slave in a brick kiln. Since Aslam resolved to seek out a wife, it fell upon Iqbal to work for the sum needed to pay the family of a future wife. Crofts has[1] Aslam explaining the family's economic circumstances to Iqbal and his older brother, Petras:

> "It's time for you two to work for the honour of the family." Petras now looked openly suspicious. But Iqbal was nodding in agreement. He liked the idea. . . . "Why should we do anything just because you say so?" Petras asked, knowing he was risking a slap. "Because it is our father's wish," Aslam said twisting Petra's ear. [The father had deserted the family years ago.] "I need to take a wife and that costs money. One day it will be your turn, and you will understand. "How are you going to make us?" Petras asked. "I can't make you," Aslam shrugged. "But if you refuse to do the honourable thing then Iqbal . . .

will have to take over your obligations and I would be surprised if even you could live with that shame." (Crofts 2006, 18)

Crofts goes on to add that Iqbal had heard the "family honor in bonded servitude" story many times . . . with significant variations. Sometimes it was Aslam who needed money to take a wife, other times his mother, Inyat, had to take a loan to make ends meet, and still another version had their father, a hard-core drug addict, needing a fix. In any case, Iqbal was intent on meeting his obligation.

Ambition and good nature did not stop Iqbal from walking out of the factory whenever he felt he had worked enough for the day, without waiting to be dismissed. "It didn't seem brave, it just seemed like the obvious thing to do." Crofts relates that at first Iqbal's *thekedar* responded to his indiscretions with restraint and patience. But in time after experiencing some buyer's remorse, the carpet-maker approached Aslam with his complaints about Iqbal's work habits. The brother responds, "Just punch him when he is nasty. He'll soon learn the right way to behave." "But I can't punish him. He's so small and he looks at me with those eyes . . . ," the *thekdar* replies. At that point, Aslam offers advice: "Can't you sell him to one of your friends, someone who doesn't have such a soft heart?" (2006, 24)

Acting on Aslam's recommendation, the *thekedar* sold Iqbal to a carpet-maker not nearly so indulgent; the second *thekedar* would not be swayed by Iqbal's politeness and attempts to explain "why it was a bad idea to treat people so unkindly." Under the new work regime, the child slaves were not permitted to leave the premises. Consequently Iqbal and his peers became socialized into their new realities.

Reality under this new carpet-master was one of perpetual exploitation. Specifically the "loan" was designed so that it would never be paid off as the value of the work becomes invariably greater than the original sum of the borrowed money, and the *pesghi* is often passed down to families. "These children had no idea how they would ever get back to their homes or how their families would ever be able to find them. Some of them didn't even know the names of their villages or their areas" (Crofts 2006, 35). Such a social construction involves reifying the treatment of children as objects into social reality (see Berger and Luckmann 1966).

The "Talk-Back" Boy as Confrontational Pragmatist

Although the child who "talks back" is routinely disciplined as unruly and ill-socialized, what can be said of a particular young person who demonstrates unusually seasoned wisdom at an early age? Should they not be called upon as speakers by audiences of their youthful peers, or even their "learned" elders, to impart such wisdom? Focusing upon the "wisdom-generating powers of rhetoric," communications scholar Christopher Johnstone draws upon the ethical philosophy of American pragmatist John Dewey that positions the communicative process as central to the development of the "moral self." He explains,

> The implications for rhetoric of Dewey's ethical philosophy emerge from the role of communication in the growth of personality. Growth, he tells us, is a social process; it occurs in the context of one's associations with others. "Morality is social," he writes, because "the formation of habits of belief, desire, and judgment is going on at every instant under the influence of the conditions set by men's contact, intercourse, and associations with one another." Communication is for Dewey the highest form of human activity; for it makes possible shared experience, "the greatest of human goods." (1983, 193)

But for Dewey, development of the moral self does not occur in isolation but instead within the growth and cultivation of others (Johnstone 1983, 191). The moral self emphasizes imagination and sensitivity, particularly sensitivity "of being wide-awake, alert, attentive to the significance of events. As this habit is intensified, more intelligent direction of action is made possible, and so prudence is cultivated in the person" (191).

Presuming that he was indeed blessed with Dewey's practical wisdom and sense of moral self, Iqbal needed to draw upon an awareness of the bonded-labor circumstance to awaken his peers. Amid all the harsh working conditions and the "broken spirits" of his co-workers, he realized that what matters most is to have bonded children fathom their entitled rights before anything else. Thus, he relied upon story-telling to stimulate sensory perception within the other children.

> So, I looked for the market square, It's enormous, did you know? You can't imagine how big it is. . . . Mountains of fruit, truckloads of vegetables from the country, baskets and baskets of different-colored spices. . . . They sell everything here—old things, strange things, even

rusty nails. . . . It's true, I'm telling you. And there are stalls that are like real shops and they have big radios and tapes you can put inside to hear music. There were big pots of basmati rice and chicken tandoori. It smelled so good. (D'Adamo 2003, 68–69).

Iqbal's discourses with his friends amounted to an intentional effort to lift his peers above the mental conditioning imposed upon them by the second *thekedar*. He intentionally brought up regularly those images to trigger emotions inside them, and it is then when his fellows appreciated the essential value of his message. They became bound to care for it.

Iqbal's skills raising awareness in his friends did not come easy. Early on during the first months of his slavery, He continued to do his excellent work as a skilled carpet weaver. Iqbal met every night with his friends for more stories; their conversations were nothing less than acts of higher reasoning. Iqbal attempted to push them to think critically beyond their senses by asking, "Have you ever seen anyone pay off their debt? We will never get away from here?" D'Adamo relates,

> The others did not grasp what he was saying, "You are crazy! You are wrong! You Liar!" . . . [B]ut he did not give up. [Iqbal responds,] "Since we shared the same fate and the same kind of life, you'd think we children would feel united, but instead we quarreled and separated into little groups. The big ones always bullied the little ones—as though bullying could change our destiny and make us feel better." (2003, 25)

Relating back to Dewey, Christopher Johnstone underscores the relationship between prudence and a sense of timing in moral self-development:

> [I]ntelligent or sagacious judgment requires an understanding of the relations of events to one another, a grasping of the patterns or regularities in experience. It requires, that is, that actions and events be perceived in terms of their meanings. The cultivation of practical wisdom rests in part upon the enrichment and extension of the meanings given to experience. It is in part a growth in one's recognition or awareness of the recurring events in human experience and of the implications held by these events. (1983, 192)

On a particular occasion, Iqbal resorted to theatrics when an American businessman visited the factory to purchase some carpets woven by their small hands covered with cuts and blisters where the repeated movements had worn the skin. At that time, Iqbal realized that without an act of resistance, none of the children at the factory would recognize their importance and value in their plight. After all, not only were they hopeless but they no longer remembered their significance as living human beings. For Iqbal, the visit of the client was the golden moment or a window of opportunity to restore faith in all children and to make a statement stepping up his advocacy and liberation tactics.

D'Adamo describes (through the voice of a "narrator") the day the foreign customers arrived at the factory as a "special morning" as the master had to convince the visitors that the children were treated well; "They are my apprentices. Here they learn an honest profession that will assure them a better future, one without hunger and poverty. They're like my own family." Iqbal's work was "marvelous that the foreigners would go crazy over a carpet like that" (D'Adamo 2003, 32; through a narrative voice). He was standing next to his loom and when it was his turn to show his work, "He took a knife that we all used to cut the knots, raised it above his head, and seemed to look each of us in the eye. Then he calmly turned and cut the carpet from top to bottom, right through the middle." Iqbal knew the gravity of the consequences of his act, but it was all worth it. "Courage, endurance, fearlessness and above all self-sacrifice are the qualities required for our leaders," Ghandi wrote decades earlier;[2] Iqbal was a young exemplar of Ghandi's ideals.

As could be expected, Iqbal's defiance exacted severe punitive retribution on the part of the *thekedar*, who hung him upside-down in the punishment room (known as "the tomb") for three days. Upon his release one of his peers asked, "What have you gained by destroying the carpet?" Iqbal responded,

> You took the risks, coming out at night to help me. If the master had discovered you, what would *you* have gotten out of it? I did it for you, as well as for me. This kind of life isn't right. We should return to our families; we should not be chained to our looms and forced to work like slaves. (D'Adamo 2003, 50; italics in original)

Iqbal's willingness to undergo suffering constituted moral persuasion that touched the hearts and minds of his friends and, in so doing, instilled with them a sense of "fury at injustice." While Iqbal was confined in the punishment room, his friends risked the same fate by engaging in clandestine efforts to bring him food and water each night. Iqbal then knew that he had given the other children the courage to leave their owners. When Iqbal managed to run out of the factory the master grabbed a young girl in revenge and threw her in the punishment room. The voice in his head exorted, "*Do something! For the love of heaven, somebody do something!*" Then all the other children screamed "if you send her, then send me too" (D'Adamo 2003, 50–51; italics in original).

A case can be made that Iqbal's theatrical rhetoric in seizing the moment to make his statement reflects "the argument [against] waste," or an ethic against squandering opportunities (as mentioned in reference to performers as speakers in chapter 1). Perelman and Olbrechts-Tyteca relate, "One can assimilate to this argument all those which stress an opportunity not to be missed or a means which exists and should be used. The same argument will be used to incite one with talent, skill, or an exceptional gift, to use it to the fullest extent" (1969, 279).

The Target of Reactionary Rhetoric

"It seemed as if the BLLF was on everybody's hate list" (Kuklin 1998, 57). Here author Susan Kuklin (writing for a scholastic audience) refers to the Bonded Labor Liberation Front, a Pakistani NGO organized in 1988 (having evolved from Brick Kiln Workers Front) to abolish child labor in Pakistan and throughout the world. The NGO's antagonists were quick to associate the BLLF with its counterpart in India, the Bonded Labor Front, founded earlier in 1983. Kuklin continues:

> The government called [BLLF] group members "Indian conspirators" because they participated in the Delhi-based South Asian Coalition on Child Servitude. They were accused of trying to destroy the economy of Pakistan by bringing down the carpet and brick industries. Factory owners hated the BLLF because they took away their cheap labor. Local authorities hated them because they exposed corruption. Amazingly, many of the bonded laborers hated the group [as well]. Some . . . were suspicious: "Why would an educated man like Ehsan Kahn [discussed below] take the trouble to help the poor? (57)

Kuklin's reference to corruption focuses upon the BLLF's fundamental strategy of capitalizing on the disconnect between the statutory prohibition of child labor under Pakistan's 1992 Bonded Labor [Abolition] Act and the reality of child slaves toiling in principal industries. When pressed, Pakistani authorities frequently directed blame to the West. Kuklin quotes an adviser in Pakistan's Ministry of Labor as follows: "Westerners conveniently forget their own shameful histories when they come here. . . . Europeans addressed slavery and child labor only after they became prosperous. Pakistan has only now entered an era of economic stability that will allow us to expand our horizons and address social concerns." (34)

Rhetorically speaking, the BLLF strategy to offer voice to child workers is somewhat pertinent to what Trudy Govier calls a "non-interactive audience" in her book *The Philosophy of Argument* (1999). Specifically she asks, "How much does audience matter for the understanding and evaluation of an argument? Of what significance for the theory of argument is the situation of the non-interactive audience—the audience that cannot interact with the arguer, and whose views are not known to him?" (1999, 183). It should be noted that Govier's context is that of Western mass media audiences that cannot participate in civic dialogues; nonetheless, her framework appears even more salient to invisible child laborers who are valuable in the marketplace (unlike Richard Rubenstein's "surplus populations" regarded as expendable, such as Jewish people in Nazi Germany; 1975).

Iqbal's *thekedar* explicitly warned the children not to attend public events staged by the BLLF, since the organization handed out "certificates of freedom" to children in bonded labor, thereby exposing the illegal practice to public scrutiny. Iqbal defied his *thekedar*'s orders and attended a "freedom day" rally, where he encountered the event's speaker Ehsan Kahn, a BLLF official, who would become his mentor and friend. According to Andrew Crofts, at first Iqbal had difficulty comprehending Kahn's message but finally surmised that the speaker's references to "bonded labor" related to his situation.

Crofts represents the sequence of events surrounding Kahn's acquaintance with Iqbal as follows:

"My name is Ehsan Kahn. I am the founder of the Bonded Labour Liberation Front. I am here to tell you that bonded labour is illegal in Pakistan. They have passed a law. No one can force your children to work in the factories and the brick kilns . . . "
    What is your name? [Kahn asks] . . .
    Iqbal Masih . . .

Do you work in a factory . . .
Yes . . .
How did you get here? . . .
I ran away. If they catch me, they'll punish me again. I think next time they might even kill me, they will be so angry. . . .
You'll never have to go back there, Iqbal. The government has cancelled all labour debts . . .
But the police are on the side of the carpet masters . . .
Not if you're with me. (2006, 79–83)

After the rally Kahn accompanied Iqbal, driving the boy first to visit with his mother in Muridke and then to Lahore, where Iqbal would attend the Freedom School, a learning center supported by the BLLF to educate the children it liberated. During their visit to the Freedom School, a Reebok Foundation representative met with Iqbal to learn of his story. Subsequently, the Foundation nominated him for its 1994 Human Rights Award, presented to him in the United States a few months before he was murdered. Minutes prior to the granting of the award at Northeastern University in Boston, Ehsan Kahn pleaded with Reebok Foundation officials *not* to pass on the $25,000 prize to him but instead keep it in the United States to be managed on Iqbal's behalf. Kahn anticipated that adversaries would characterize the BLLF's money-management efforts as fraudulent exploitation of a child. ABC News interviewed Iqbal the day after the award presentation and subsequently recognized him as its "Person of the Week."

Returning to Pakistan, Iqbal confronted a number of threats on his life during a period of increasing public opposition to the BLLF. Kuklin reports on a particular accusation:

The president of the Islamabad Carpet Exporters Union told his colleagues, "Our industry is the victim of enemy agents who spread lies and fiction around the world that bonded labor and child labor is utilized in the production of hand-knotted carpets. They are not and have never been." He condemned the BLLF and its allies as "Jewish and Indian enemies who want to damage the reputation of Pakistan's carpet industry." (1998, 87)

The circumstances surrounding Iqbal's murder and the assassin's motives are anything but clear. He was shot during the evening of April 16, 1995, when he and a few friends were walking along a dirt road near his home. The confessed assassin, a man by the name of Ashraf, was known in the area as a confused individual. After his apprehension he claimed that he was in some manner provoked and shot aimlessly toward the youths. In his confession (that he later retracted), Ashraf related the following:

> I had never met Iqbal before. I fired in utter confusion. I am an absolutely impoverished man. I am not familiar with rich persons. I have no acquaintance with any carpet manufacturer. I am supported by my parents through hard labor. [My bosses] are simple people and have no business except tilling the land. They have nothing to do with the carpet business. (Kuklin 1998, 93)

The ambiguity surrounding the tragedy led the various interests to frame Iqbal's death in ways that suited their respective agendas. BLLF officials discounted Ashraf's statements as absurd (if he in fact *was* the actual killer) alleging the murder was directed by the carpet industry. The police accepted the confession at face value in their attempt to thwart the BLLF from exploiting the murder. Kuklin reports, "The police raided BLLF offices. Their files and equipment were confiscated. Two people were arrested, a volunteer and an accountant" (95). Carpet makers as well claimed that the BLLF was exploiting the tragedy and that in fact Ehsan Kahn (who was in Europe at a conference at the time of Iqbal's death) had stolen the boy's prize money. Andrew Crofts reports that even Prime Minister Benazir Bhutto shared her own narrative concerning Iqbal's death:

> The prime minister, when questioned about the murder on television, suggested that Iqbal had been shot by a farmer when he, Iqbal, was caught copulating with the farmer's donkey. The image [corresponded] with another myth that was being circulated that Iqbal had not been a boy at all but a midget, who Ehsan had been passing off as a child for publicity purposes. The prime minister only knew what she had been told and it was impossible to know at which stage of the journey the story took this final grotesque turn. (2006, 240)

The Reebok Foundation bestowed its human rights award (posthumously) again on Iqbal in 2000.

During his short life, Iqbal Masih drew upon inner courage and a strong sense of moral pragmatism to advocate on behalf of other children in bonded labor. In addition, he was willing to take calculated risks and to accept responsibility for the consequences of his actions. Readers can assess whether, and to what extent, the Russian punk rock group Pussy Riot demonstrates similar attributes in their campaigns against the policies and actions of Vladimir Putin and the Patriarch of the Russian Orthodox Church.

PUSSY RIOT: ADVOCATES THROUGH DISOBEDIENT ART

Pussy Riot is a group of feminist artists who perform provocative punk rock in unusual public places, usually in and around Moscow, to voice protest against entrenched power in Russian society. Consisting of about 11 members at any given time, the group typically performs in flamboyant pink costumes with balaclavas (masks) on their heads. Pussy Riot often directs its protests directly at President Vladimir Putin, whom they regard as a dictator, but also toward the Russian Orthodox Church, which they allege is complicit in supporting Putin's new nationalism that would restore the Church's cultural authority to that in imperial times prior to the Bolshevik Revolution. Although the group pursues an active protest agenda, this sketch primarily focuses upon its confrontation with religious authorities at the Church of Christ the Saviour, an expansive cathedral in Moscow that is a visible symbol of the Orthodox Church in contemporary Russia. In February of 2012, Pussy Riot intruded on sacred space in Christ the Saviour to perform an offensive song to express its grievances with President Putin and the Orthodox Church hierarchy.

Fools?

Does the "carnivalesque" (Seal 2013, 295) specter of five women protesting in gaudy punk apparel, at the altar of a nationally historic cathedral no less, qualify as obscene foolishness? If these women are not *five individuals* but instead *one idea*, who assesses whether that idea is foolish or sound? The answers to these two questions lie in a third: Who controls the "frame," or the authority to cast judgment on the (il)legitimacy of this collective discourse?

In this case, the idea was conveyed through the two-minute performance of a song by the punk-rock group Pussy Riot at the Cathedral of Christ the Saviour in Moscow on February 21, 2012. The lyrics of that song, entitled "Virgin Mary, Put Putin Away," appeal to Mary to recognize how Putin and the Patriarch of the Russian Orthodox Church manipulate ecclesiastical symbols to expand their respective power bases. Denysenko explains that Pussy Riot put these verses to the melody of a segment of Rachmaninov's *Vigil* that is often performed by choirs in the Orthodox liturgy. But he also asserts that the group's demonstration lends itself to various interpretations:

> One could suggest that the women were mocking the Church and its ancient liturgy, but this section of the performance expresses such authenticity that I believe it was not intended to mock but to illustrate the women's desire to belong to the Church. Pussy Riot was attempting to capture the attention of the most general portion of its intended audience: the pedestrian Orthodox Christian in Russia. (2013, 1070)

So who can authoritatively frame the discourse of the lyrics in this song, performed in the midst of a prayer service, . . . the mass public in a society that traditionally relegates its "foolish" dissidents to insane asylums and prisons: media (both in the West and East) known to unduly satirize *women* protestors (Seal 2013, 294)? A trial judge? The Russian President identified in lyrics? The Cathedral's Patriarch? Or the five women as *one speaker* addressing a global audience?

Some Pussy Riot supporters understandably gravitate toward the societal legacy of institutionalizing or incarcerating dissidents to establish the group's "foolishness" in a lineage with revered intellectual critics whom group members admire. For example, digital journalist Stephen Morgan alludes to such a connection in his book *Pussy Riot vs Putin: Revolutionary Russia*:

> Referring to dissident artists [of the KGB era], Nadia quotes one of the most famous dissidents, Alecksander Solzhenitsyn, in order to express her belief that they would succeed. Despite the persecution and imprisonment by Putin. "Just like Solzhenitsyn," she says, "I will break cement." . . . Maria Alyokhina also compared their trial to the Soviet Union's persecution of Jospeh Brodsky in the 1960s. His poems were defined as "so-called" poems; the witnesses for the prosecution hadn't actually read them—just as a number of witnesses in our case didn't

see (our) performance itself and only watched the clip online." (2013, 95)

Nonetheless, this "persecuted dissident" narrative misses the potent religious significance packed into the song's lyrics and played out in one of the most sacred spaces in Orthodox Russia. As a scholar of Byzantine liturgy, Nicholas Denysenko offers a wide-ranging interpretation of Pussy Riot's "appeal to Mary" in song that connects the depth of the Byzantine tradition with contemporary events at the Cathedral and that illustrates the converging agendas of elites both in the faith and in government. For Denysenko, it is important to understand *context*, in terms of (1) the physical architecture of sacred space in the Cathedral (perhaps to determine if there was space for the group's foolishness in its confines) and (2) a particular occasion in the corporate life of the Cathedral's faithful that offered an opportunity to reframe the Byzantine tradition in ways that serve present-day purposes.

In terms of its physical presence, the *current* Christ the Saviour is a new structure—unlike many other older cathedrals having undergone renovations over the year—presumably symbolizing the renewal of the Orthodox institutional mission after the fall of the Soviet Union. Denysenko relates to the Church's reinvention in this way: "The emerging Russian church would have a new symbol in Christ the Saviour cathedral, and the process of rebuilding the destroyed cathedral would likewise close the painful chapter of the Soviet era and its persecution of the Orthodox Church" (2013, 64).

But the decision to invest over $340 million in this rebuilding effort took on controversy at a time of pronounced poverty and unemployment after the collapse of the Soviet Union. Some related the ostentatiousness of the new cathedral to the personal wealth of the Orthodox Church's Patriarch Kyrill, known to wear a watch valued at thirty thousand dollars (Denysenko 2013, 1067). However, the Orthodox Church defended the rebuilding of Christ the Saviour to serve as a "national ecclesial symbol where Church and state pray together," much like Westminster Abbey in Great Britain or the Washington National Cathedral in the United States (2013, 1066). Thus the Cathedral's edifice speaks to a contemporary convergence of religious and political interests in a new Russia.

The ecclesial architecture of Christ the Saviour is like that of most Orthodox churches: The sacred space includes the sanctuary, the location of the Eucharistic table with its multivalent symbolism of dining table, tomb, and resting place of the martyrs; the verticality of the Church, conveying the awesome power of God in the divine presence of the Church, overseeing the almighty creation and heightened by some arrangement of domes and/or cupolas; the iconostasis and accompanying iconographic program, conveying the participation of God, Jesus, Mary, and the saints; . . . and the assigned seating, where the laity occupy the area of the nave with the clergy in the sanctuary, performing their holy duties by leading the people in worship. (Denysenko, 1065)

It is not surprising that Pussy Riot's occupation of the area near the Eucharistic table in itself signified the subversion of the Church's authority over sacred space. Beyond this, the song, according to Denysenko, self-identifies them as *illegitimate* in the new Russian convergence of Church-government interests and thus they "align themselves with the people who mindlessly obey the Church; with supporters of gay pride who are sent away to Siberia; and with feminists. The perpetrators of mindless obedience and persecution of marginalized groups are Church leaders, symbolized by their black robes and limousines" (1069–1070). Thus, when this illegitimate punk group seized sacred space for its obscene performance, it weighed in as a contender to reframe the traditional Orthodox narrative in a radically different discourse from that of the Church and its Patriarch.

The seventh verse of the "Appeal"—referring to the belt of the Virgin Mary—connects Pussy Riot's demonstration to a momentous occasion that had transpired one year earlier at the Cathedral, the public veneration of the belt of Mary. On loan from a particular monastery, this sacred artifact drew over 3,000 citizens to Christ the Saviour. From an institutional perspective, the event served to link the "new" church-state nexus with the Marian-Byzantine tradition that has appealed to Mary as protector of Russia against its threats. Understandably, this symbolism of divine protection has been appropriated by imperial regimes of the past (prior to the Bolshevik Revolution), and presumably it will be used to support political agendas in the future. Beyond this, Denysenko draws on the work of Vera Shevzov, who traces the role of Mary in the Byzantine interpretation that essentially associates the Mother of God with Russia as a chosen nation. Specifically, he relates—

Shevzov shows how Mary "stood at the interface between religious and national identity" in numerous Russian historical contexts, appearing already in the medieval Primary Chronicle, protecting Russia during the Time of Troubles, and even delivering Tsar Alexander III from harm at a train derailment in 1888. Mary's military intervention on behalf of Russia serves as another demonstration of the Russian continuation of Mary's Byzantine heritage. (1074–1075, quoting Shevzov 2004, 244–257)

If the Patriarch Kyrill had intended to capitalize on the belt's visit to the Cathedral, Pussy Riot's subsequent "Appeal to Mary" appears to have been a calculated effort to reframe the Marian-Byzantine narrative so as to subvert the Patriarch's new church-state project. Denysenko argues that

[t]he core of their message seems to be directed to Mary herself, an appeal to Mary to unseat Putin and assume the kind of intervening control attributed to Mary in Russian and Byzantine history, with the assumption that the people will restore a correct sense of order once the problematic figures are removed. If Pussy Riot attempts to find a place in the traditional Russian narrative of Marian [theology of salvation], their journey will at best be rocky, because Pussy Riot targets perhaps the two most powerful Russian figures: President Putin and Patriarch Kyrill. (1075–1076)

As could be expected, the Patriarch railed against the Pussy Riot demonstration as blasphemous but perhaps helpful in testing the "faithful's" resolve to uphold sacred values when they are under attack by blasphemers:

I cannot shake the thought that this is an exploratory attack . . . to test the depth of faith and commitment to Orthodoxy in Russia. . . . And today, I think those who launched this provocation have seen that standing before them is not a faceless, quiet mass but a people that is capable of protecting what it holds sacred. Those who would invite us all to mock our shrines, reject our faith and, if possible, destroy our churches are testing the people's ability to protect their holy places. (Astrasheuskaya and Gutterman 2012)

However, a prominent writer on church issues, Andrei Kuraev, appeared more circumspect regarding the group's demonstration. As a reporter of a US-based arts blog writes,

> A missionary in the Russian Orthodox Church, who has said that the feminist punk band Pussy Riot should have been shown mercy instead of jailed for their 2012 performance in Moscow's Christ the Saviour Cathedral, . . . Deacon Andrei Kuraev said that Pussy Riot had a dramatic impact on the church. Although he continues to condemn the form of their protest, in which they sang a prayer to the Virgin Mary to save Russia from Putin and Patriarch Kirill I, Kuraev said they should have been treated with mercy, adding that he would have served them blini and talked to them. (Kishkovsky 2014)

But does the "form of protest" that Pussy Riot pursued constitute *foolishness* and, if so, in what sense of that term? Members of the group take pride in affirming their identities of "non-legitimacy" at least in the context of the contemporary presentation as a spectacle of "unity" among the Russian Orthodox. For example at her trial, Nadya Tolokonnikova argued that many in the Orthodox faith had become disillusioned with the church:

> I know that a huge number of Orthodox believers also defend us, and some are even praying for us outside the court. . . . And this alone shows that there is no single social group of Orthodox believers, as the prosecuting counsel would have us believe. . . . Every day it dawns more and more on people that if this political system has armed itself to the teeth against three girls who performed in Christ the Saviour Cathedral, then that only means that the system is scared of the truth, afraid of the sincerity and directness we represent. (Dugdale 2013)

In many ways the group's discourses appear as ethical critiques that are grounded within the Marian-Byzntine liturgy and tradition. The "Appeal to Mary" demonstration in essence "breaks in" to the Church's presentation of "unity," disrupting its grandiosity to show its contradiction with the humility of Mary. If Pussy Riot members can be dismissed as fools, they are calculating fools intending to annoy and provoke—to speak what they believe needs to be said (Cox 2012[3]; Denysenko 2013, 1082). And as Timothy Beal asserts, these "fools" are far from blasphemers but are instead those who understand religious truths as "in process" rather than as static "finished products" (2012).

Prosecutors, the Law, and So-Called Justice

Ideally, the adjudicative process incorporates two legitimacy discourses—the first speaks for the legitimate task of validating charges against one who violates a duly adopted law and the second of defending the "upright," legitimate citizen against those charges. As the trial began, the women were charged with "hooliganism" and "religious hatred," but at the conclusion they were convicted of "cruelly undermining the social order" and sentenced to two years of confinement at a labor camp (Morgan 2013, 41). Framing the Pussy Riot (July 30–August 17, 2012) trial within such a (Western) legitimacy narrative, as a number of celebrities and news outlets did, served both to distort the group's identity and to compress explanations of state motivations into a stereotypical category of "arbitrary law." According to a British criminologist, performers such as Sir Paul McCartney and Madonna, as well as newspapers like the *Guardian*, framed the trial in terms of East/West and democracy/authoritarianism binaries reminiscent of the Cold War era. In particular, Lizzie Seal asserts:

> News stories did create a discourse of deviance, but of Russia as a deviant state and Putin as its deviant leader—Russia remained the "terrifying Other" and was the Western news media's object of censure. In further support of the West/East and democracy/authoritarianism binaries, Russian public opinion on Pussy Riot was reported as being negative. . . . Representation of the verdict in the Western news media was therefore shaped by geopolitical concerns, and by established discourses of Russia as unlike Europe and the USA. (2013, 297)

That binary narrative erroneously casts Pussy Riot members on trial as "legitimate," defenseless young women and that "Putin had brought the full force of the state down upon them—three giggling, embarrassed and helpless young women. This portrayal of Pussy Riot as silly naïve girls, seemingly unaware of the full meaning of their actions, patronized and trivialized them" (Seal 2013, 298). To the contrary, through their "Appeal to Mary" performance at Christ the Saviour group members projected personas of illegitimate deviance that would precipitate state retribution . . . as well as global attention through the Internet and related visual technologies. Indeed, their gaudy apparel, complete with balaclavas, promoted identities of deviance, worthy of digital dissemination. They appeared anything but legitimate.

Second, the binary frame masks nuances of state (in)tolerance of freedom which, according to Seal, has expanded significantly since the Soviet collapse—freedom of expression through the media is tolerated but political activism involving public protest is not. In fact, freedom of expression through the media allowed for scathing accounts of state injustice in the conduct of the Pussy Riot trial on a par with the *Guardian* and *New York Times* so as to invalidate the binary narrative. For example, the editor of *GQ Russia* wrote that "The Russian authorities took a marginal act of arty protest and, through sheer cruelty, made it into an international cause . . .[suggesting that] coverage of the trial amounted to long infomercials against investing in, visiting and generally dealing with Russia" (quoted in Lynskey 2012).

But the Russian daily newspaper *Vedomosti* was even more critical in its article entitled "This Is Not Blasphemy" in the run-up to the trial. Reporter Ella Paneyakh begins her article

> Three members of the punk band Pussy Riot charged with hooliganism will start having their case heard in the Khamovniki Court today. The trial will begin, of course, but there is no law that would justify the scale of the process—i.e., a law against sacrilege and blasphemy. . . . There is no such law. . . . For a long time, the church was above criticism. But today, when all of a sudden it has come under criticism, both the authorities and a part of society would like to see the old desecration laws that existed in imperial Russia reinstated. Blasphemy, sacrilege and offensive behavior in church were punishable because the Orthodox faith was in effect Russia's official religion. (2012)

Further, Paneyakh reports how opinions of those attentive to the case changed between the time of arrest and the announcement of the indictment. Although these citizens regarded the stunt as "disgusting and offensive," it did not appear to justify court action beyond imposing penalties for a minor administrative offense. She goes on to say that even those who believe Pussy Riot members are "guilty as charged" are nonetheless "outraged by the fact that decisions of medieval church councils are being used as a basis for secular charges, by ridiculous 'expert analysis' brought forth by the prosecution, and by the court ignoring the defense."

Some of the group's sympathizers from the West followed the binary narrative in describing the legal proceedings as a "show trial" as "a combination of the methods of Stalin's show trials mixed with the logic of Alice in Wonderland" (Morgan 2013, 28) and "an amazing piece of political theater" (Miller 2012). A loose rhetorical interpretation of motives for this spectacle could follow Putin's advantage in serving as a protector or a conservator of the Orthodox Church and its liturgical tradition against "blasphemers" such as the accused. In such a narrative it might then follow that Putin encouraged court prosecutors to (ab)use the law in a manner appropriate to conserve these traditions.

But other observers publicly debated *who* in fact was running this "show trial," *who* the prosecutors actually were, and *who* or *what* was really under indictment. This alternative frame casts the accused as the prosecutors: "Once they were granted a platform [for their trial testimonies] that they had never sought, the three women, with admirable clarity and dignity, used it to put their accusers on trial" (Lynskey 2012). Or as the political writer for *Vedomosti* put it in his article "Modern Art: Confession of the Regime":

> The perpetrators of the punk prayer service struck at the sorest spot in the system, and in the most radical way possible. . . . Pussy Riot has revealed the formula behind today's Russian state system. They demonstrated that what we consider to be traditional Christian virtues— loving thy neighbor, tolerance, compassion, forgiveness and other humane ideas—are not the qualities that the church leadership wants to cultivate. They showed that the principle of the separation of church and state is a dead letter in the nonfunctioning Basic Law, and that not only are those two institutions not separate, but they are in fact inseparable, like the two heads of the eagle on the state coat of arms. (Glikin 2012)

Indeed the assertive tone of (both the opening and closing) testimonies of the accused were predictably taken as insolence by the judge, a regrettable misinterpretation from the group's perspective. But even in Western adjudication, trials as advocacy platforms—at least up until the post-9/11 court cases of jihadists accused of terrorism—have been somewhat rare. Regarding analogies to notable US cases, perhaps the so-called Chicago

Seven trial of alleged conspirators charged with instigating riots at the 1968 Democratic National Convention comes close. During those proceedings, defendant Abbie Hoffman offered Judge Julius Hoffman (no relation) a copy of co-defendant Jerry Rubin's book *DO IT! Scenarios of the Revolution* (1970) with the inscription "Julius, you radicalized more people that we ever could. You're the country's top Yippie" (Lynskey 2012).

Transnational Communicators

Just as Abbie Hoffman and the other Chicago Seven defendants did in their 1969–1970 trials, the three Pussy Riot perpetrators turned the proceedings against them into court theater to speak out so as to ridicule Russia's political, social, and cultural institutions. But unlike some of the Chicago Seven, whose convictions were eventually overturned on appeal, the Pussy Riot defendants lost in their appeals processes and served time in prison—beyond their lengthy pre-trial detention—until their sentences were commuted in the run-up to the 2014 Winter Olympic Games in Sochi. Either in part or in full, the rhetorical arguments of each of the three, in the form of their opening and closing court testimonies, have been published on Internet websites (e.g., "Pussy Riot Testimonies"; Dugdale 2013) and in books such as *Pussy Riot! A Punk Prayer for Freedom* (Alyokhina, Tolokonnikova, and Samutsevich 2013) and *Words Will Break Cement: The Passion of Pussy Riot* (Gessen 2014).

Clearly the defendants expected a guilty verdict, as Ekaterina makes evident in her closing testimony: "I have mixed feelings right now about this trial. On one hand, we are expecting a guilty verdict now. Compared to the judicial machine, we are nobodies and we have lost. One the other hand, we have won. The entire world can see that the case against us is trumped up" (Gessen 2014, 220). Thus, a strong case can be made that Nadya, Maria, and Ekaterina envisioned (or mentally constructed) an audience of attentive citizens of a *global community* that might interpret their testimonies as indictments of Russian institutions designed to stifle individual thought and social critique. Even had these women not advertently pitched their rhetoric to extend far beyond the courtroom, the fact remains that they have indeed done so through the assistance of supportive journalists and writers such as Steven Morgan of Belgium and Masha

Gessen (now) of the United States and publishers, for example The Feminist Press.

Given their current status as published texts accessible to an international readership, there is reason to treat Pussy Riot's trial testimonies as textual messages to a global community rather than as pleas to persuade their adversaries within what a Russian Amnesty International official calls "a parody of the administration of justice" (Roth 2014, A4, reporting on a similar case). Denysenko speaks to the global message as follows:

> Pussy Riot's appeal to Mary essentially stole Patriarch Kyrill's thunder and diminished the exuberance of initial success enjoyed by the Russian Church in the period immediately following the visit of Mary's Belt. Pussy Riot literally seized Patriarch Kyrill's stage through a performance that lasted less than two minutes, but in the information and social media age, it was disseminated virally and introduced to a global audience. In fact, Pussy Riot is no longer on merely the patriarch's stage, but now has a global audience. (2013, 1077)

Two excerpts from Nadya Tolokonnikova's closing testimony focus not only on state injustice but also on the complicity of the Orthodox hierarchy in blessing this so-called justice. She begins:

> In the scheme of things it is not really three Pussy Riot vocalists who are on trial here. If that were the case, then what happened here would have no significance. On trial here is the state system of the Russian Federation. This imitation of the judicial process is reaching its predetermined end, such were the prosecutor, judge and investigator we had. And those who stand behind them as well, those who gave the political order to repress. Where should the blame lie for the performance in the Christ the Saviour Cathedral and the subsequent trial? It lies with the authoritarian nature of the political system. (Gessen 2014, 195)

With the re-emergence of civil religion in contemporary Russia, Tolokonnikova could not find solace in the church but instead had to submit to both institutions working in tandem. Such a complaint appears to clarify the symbolism in the band's intrusion into sacred space at Christ the Saviour as a claim on space inside the church but outside of subservience to the state. As Denysenko affirms, "the time was ripe" for unconventional advocacy for personal freedom against the reinforcing controls of both institutions:

> In the era of Putin's leadership, legitimately free vehicles for a public critique of the political and ecclesial processes and their leaders were largely absent. And it was during this ripe time of the apparent hoarding of power on the part of Russian leaders that the Pussy Riot punk prayer performance occurred —in the sacred space of Christ the Savior cathedral—bringing under question the symbol of a post-Soviet institution. Pussy Riot's performance sent an important message to the people that creatively drew from a repository of Russian liturgical and spiritual tradition while appealing to a nontraditional demographic. (2013, 1068)

Nadya concludes her closing testimony by referring to the song at the heart of the criminal case:

> And in conclusion, I would like to quote a Pussy Riot Song. Strange as it may seem, all of their songs turned out to be prophetic. Among other things, we prophesied that "the head of the KGB [Putin] and the chief saint [Patriarch Kyrill] march the protesters to pretrial detention under guard." But what I want to quote now is, "Open the doors, rip off your epaulettes, taste the smell of freedom with us!" That's all. (Gessen 2014, 208)

She apparently found personal freedom within herself.

Maria's closing statement as well reflected a personal sense of liberation in the presence of a contrived legal system that justified a pre-ordained verdict in spite of the evidence.

> I am sad that we have said so many words and you have not understood any of them. Or are you lying when you talk of our apologies as though they were insincere. I don't understand. What more do you need to hear? For me, only this trial can rightly be referred to as "so-called." And I am not afraid of you. I am not afraid of the lies and fictions and of poorly coded description in the verdict of this so-called court, because all you can do is take away my so-called freedom, the only sort that exists in the Russian Federation. (Gessen 2014, 216)

But Nadya's and Maria's searches for individual freedom and truth through critical inquiry appear inimical to the collective mindset of the obedient, particularly those in the Orthodox Church, the *direct* audience of Pussy Riot's "Appeal to Mary."

Not only does the rigidity of the law serve to accuse the non-obedient (as it often does), but in this case it insulates the "creation of a Russian world which would preserve Orthodox culture in the context of imminent globalization" (1070). In an excerpt in her final statement, Ekaterina asks a question about Putin's "new Russia" as related to the church:

> Why did Putin need to use the Orthodox religion and its aesthetic? Putin could have used his own secular instruments of power: national corporations, for example, or his own terrifying policing systems. Or his obedient judicial system. Perhaps it's because of the harsh and unsuccessful policies of Putin's government: [she mentions several embarrassing incidents]—all these and other unhappy moments in his political career might have made him stop and wonder whether the citizens of Russia might just give him a helping hand with his resignation. And that must have been the point when he needed to find a unique, cast-iron guarantee of a long life at the summit of power. (Gessen 2014, 217)

In large part, Denysenko responds to this question in his analysis of Byzantine rites and liturgy that draws upon mystical philosophy within Marian iconography that supports pietism in the church and national exceptionalism in the political sphere (2013, 1075–1079). The American columnist David Brooks traces the connection between the Church's mysticism and Putin's nationalism to the rhetoric of his favorite philosophers:

> To enter into the world of Putin's favorite philosophers is to enter a world full of melodrama, mysticism and grandiose eschatological visions. . . . Three great ideas run through this work. The first is Russian exceptionalism: the idea that Russia has its own unique spiritual status and purpose. The second is devotion to the Orthodox faith. The third is belief in autocracy. Mashed together, these philosophers point to a Russia that is a quasi-theocratic nationalist autocracy destined to play a culminating role on the world stage. (Brooks, 2014, A19)

Further along in her statement, Ekaterina reaches a similar conclusion to those of Denysenko and Brooks:

Logically enough, the Russian Orthodox Church, which has a long-standing mystical connection to the state, became the main agent of this project in the media. It was also decided that the Russian Orthodox Church should counteract all the detrimental influences of contemporary mass culture, with its concepts of diversity and tolerance, as opposed to the Soviet period, when the Church mainly opposed the violence done by the authorities against history itself (Gessen 2014, 219).

From the standpoint of piety derived from mysticism, Pussy Riot's performance at Christ the Saviour constitutes blasphemy. But Ekaterina maintains that these charges of blasphemy emerge from a rigid, legalistic (mis)understanding of the Gospel:

> Many of them have said, "He is possessed by a demon and insane. Why do you listen to him?" . . . It's remarkable that it is this verse that the Russian Orthodox Church uses to express its own view of blasphemy. . . . In expressing this view the Russian Orthodox Church cites the Gospels as static religious truths. The Gospels are no longer seen as the revelations they were from the beginning. They are seen as a monolith that can be broken up into quotes that can be stuffed anywhere, into any document, used for any purpose whatsoever. (Gessen 2014, 214–215)

Although Ekaterina and her co-defendants refused to allow the rigidity of mysticism to disqualify them from their searches for freedom, they were nonetheless convicted of undermining the social order and sentenced to two years imprisonment in a labor camp.

As a postscript, it is worth noting that some observers place the Pussy Riot trial in a context of a Russian "culture war" that pits national pride and religious faith against a well-off urban elite with the former engaged in a continuing crackdown on dissent (e.g., vanden Heuvel 2012, 5; Paneyakh 2012). For the most part, band members appreciate their support from the West but, as a correspondent for the *Guardian* reports,

> The circus of western celebrity sits uneasily with Pussy Riot's stern rejection of fame and capitalism. "We're flattered, of course, that Madonna and Björk have offered to perform with us," a member using the pseudonym Orange told Radio Free Europe. "But the only performances we'll participate in are illegal ones. We refuse to perform as

part of the capitalist system, at concerts where they sell tickets."
(Lynskey 2012)

Since the three band members were released from incarceration in
December of 2013, various individuals associated with Pussy Riot have
been actively engaged in demonstrations against authorities. Six group
members protested at a Sochi Olympics site in February of 2014 and were
subsequently horsewhipped and pepper-sprayed by Cossack auxiliary police offering security at the games (Wolken 2014). Less than one week
later, Pussy Riot members protested in Moscow in sympathy for other
dissidents who were handed down sentences by a court (Myers and Reevell 2014, A11); on that occasion, band members were detained twice
during the same day.

As did Iqbal Masih, members of Pussy Riot project strong convictions
in their advocacy supported by an integrity, or wholeness of resolve and
spirit. Attention now shifts back into history to focus on US President
Lyndon Johnson and his advocacy to escalate the Vietnam Conflict in the
1960s. Among other issues, comparisons between Pussy Riot (and for
that matter, Iqbal) and Johnson in the context of Vietnam raise questions
about psychological fitness and pressures encountered in advocacy work,
whether directed toward human rights causes or other agendas. Further,
this comparison lends perspective on whether gifted oratory (and "word
magic") can compensate for a rhetor's agonizing self-deliberations.

LYNDON B. JOHNSON, MAN OF PEACE
AND ESCALATOR OF A WAR

In a tragic and chaotic moment in US history—immediately following the
assassination of John F. Kennedy in Dallas, Texas on November 22,
1963, Lyndon Johnson became the thirty-sixth president of the United
States. This sketch deals primarily with Johnson's discourses surrounding
his eventual decision in 1965 to escalate the US military campaign
against the North Vietnamese, *even though* he believed the conflict to be
unwinnable. A second commentary on President Johnson's rhetoric associated with his efforts to enact civil rights legislation appears in the next
chapter. Both sketches center upon Johnson's words and actions during
the first three months of 1965, a turbulent year following his election.

This sketch comprises the following discussions: "Prophet of Self-Prophecy," "Author of Convenient Fiction," and "Patient on the Couch, or Astute Atrategist?"

Prophet of Self-Prophecy

At this writing, four US presidents are assembled with prominent historians and other notables at the *Civil Rights Summit* at the LBJ Library to commemorate the 50th anniversary of President Lyndon Baines Johnson's signing of the Civil Rights Act of 1964. For biographer Doris Kearns Goodwin, Johnson's place in history is, and will be, most often prefaced by the phrase "if it hadn't been for Vietnam," insinuating that this external quagmire will forever overshadow LBJ's good works at home (1991, 251). Yet his first press secretary (and long-time staffer) George Reedy calls attention to the irony that early on Johnson predicted that the Vietnam fiasco would cause his political demise: "There was nothing he wanted less than to be a 'war president.' This was readily apparent in the epitaphs he constantly composed for himself. He hoped by suitable public relations, he could persuade posterity to attach to his name what he regarded as 'good' adjectives" (1982, 159). But instead he saw the White House surrounded "by half-naked hippies chanting '*Hey! Hey! LBJ! How many kids have you killed today?*'" Johnson in fact verbalized this self-prophecy as he confided with his biographer:

> I knew from the start that I was bound to be crucified either way I moved. If I left the woman I really loved—the *Great Society*—in order to get involved with that bitch of a war on the other side of the world, then I would lose everything at home. All my programs. All my hopes to feed the hungry and shelter the homeless. All my dreams to provide education and medical care to the browns and the blacks and the lame and the poor. (Goodwin 1991, 251–252)

From a rhetorical standpoint there could be relevance in the assertion that, as shown (above) in casual conversation with Goodwin, a crude Texan could naturally speak in such literary prose. Although it is unlikely that rhetorical analysis can unravel the paradoxes of history, it can offer insights about the (in)capabilities of principal actors who steer policy in addressing complex international conflicts. In the memoir of his time in the Johnson Administration, George Reedy asserts that Johnson functioned magnificently in filling out the remainder of the term after John Kennedy's assassination but proved ill-suited to address the challenges of his own after his 1964 election—particularly the trials of Vietnam. Reedy's argument focuses primarily on Johnson's oratorical skill that succeeded in reassuring citizens and government officials to remain confident and steadfast in their national allegiances. Put another way (as discussed below), Johnson was a gifted wordsmith proficient in reinforcing existing viewpoints—but not so able at changing opinion. Regarding the latter, Reedy suggests that strategic argumentation was not among LBJ's strengths.

In terms of rhetoric, the key to Johnson's effectiveness as a speaker was not so much in his choice of argumentative strategies but rather in how he arranged the "contact of minds" between his understanding of audiences and himself. Rhetoricians Perelman and Olbrechts-Tyteca explain how an *epidictic genre* (or oratorical skill) resides "alongside the deliberative and legal types of oratory" (1969, 47) often to impart aspirational reassurance. These rhetoricians differentiate themselves from colleagues who discount the epidictic as argumentative (49).

In regard to presidential politics, it appears that the epidictic genre is at the heart of Theodore Roosevelt's claim that the successful politician is "he who says what everybody is thinking most often and in the loudest voice." Related to LBJ's statements on Vietnam, there is empirical (content analysis) evidence that "the message was the audience" (Miller and Seligman 1978, 71). Analyst Roderick Hart asserts that Johnson was at "home on the range," having made far more speeches in the friendly atmosphere of his native state than other modern presidents (except for Ronald Reagan); in addition, he selected Republican states three times more often than Democratic areas as sites for addressing international conflict (1978, 92).

Although Johnson's discourses on Vietnam may well have been effective in intensifying adherence to his intractable position among sympathetic audiences, the question here focuses on whether his epidictic prose, laced with metaphors and anecdotes, preempted outcomes other than those predicted. To be sure the causal ordering here is murky. On one hand, it hardly appears reasonable that one's manner of oratory in itself can initiate a chain of circumstances (or "dominos") that predestines history. More fathomable is the contention that LBJ used epidictic rhetoric to compensate for his inexperience in the area of foreign affairs and the personal insecurity that inexperience engendered (Goodwin 1991, 256).

The rhetoricians suggest that from a conceptual standpoint epidictic speech "is more reminiscent of a procession than of a struggle" (TNR, 51). In terms of processions, Senator Eugene McCarthy, a critic of the president's Vietnam stances, claimed that Johnson escalated the conflict as if he were driving cattle: "You start them very slowly. The thing to tell them is they are not going anyplace. Then progressively you increase the pace, and at the end you stampede them, if you have to, to get where you want them" (Yuravlivker 2006, 461). With Johnson this "processional" oratory appears interwoven with self-justification aimed at increasing *his own adherence*. In essence he followed the behavior of war presidents who frame reality to preclude rational deliberations with their critics (Hart 1987, 921; Yuravlivker 2006, 461) Goodwin explains how LBJ transferred his sense of confidence from his areas of competence to foreign affairs issues beyond his grasp:

> When Johnson chose to pursue a legislative goal, having determined it to be realistic, he did so with a conviction that was often genuine. "Whatever conviction I had with people resulted from a deep, intense feeling I was right . . . intensity of conviction is the number one priority." He brought the same kind of conviction to the goals and principles of foreign policy, its intensity increased by the fact that he was not sure how to achieve them. (1991, 257)

Nonetheless, self-assuredness appears to have abounded, for example: "Yet everything I knew about history told me that if I got out of Vietnam and let Ho Chi Minh run through the streets of Saigon, then I'd be doing exactly what Chamberlain did in World War II. I'd be giving a big fat reward to aggression" (Johnson, quoted in Goodwin 1991, 252).

On the other hand, it is quite reasonable to assert that Lyndon Johnson's choice of epidictic "invocation" over deliberative dialogue brought early closure to debate—or in the vernacular, nipping it in the bud—and thus it helped actualize the self-prophecy. In large part, Johnson rejected challenges to speak deliberatively by discrediting potential audiences of adversaries, whether of North Vietnamese officials, ranking members of Congress, or even key people within his own administration. Negotiations toward a settlement with the North Vietnamese were unspeakable because the enemy would interpret such an initiative as weakness to be exploited.

In his (February 17, 1965) conversation with Senate Minority Leader Everett Dirksen, LBJ characterized the folly of such negotiation: "They do not keep their word, so whatever you agree on is of no value. That we know, from Munich on, that when you give, the dictators feed on raw meat. If they take South Vietnam, they take Thailand, they take Indonesia, they take Burma, [and then] they come back to the Philippines" (Beschloss 2001, 181–182). He then goes on to implicate prominent liberals in the Senate who expressed different sentiments: "The Communists take our speeches and they quote what Mansfield says or what Church says or what de Gaulle says, what McGovern says, and they think that's the government of the United States" (182).

In regard to his own administration, Johnson was typically impatient with cabinet members and advisers who broached alternative opinions. In some cases he would undercut dissenting speakers in his inner circle by stigmatizing them as "house moralists"; in particular, LBJ marginalized them—for example, he discredited then–Press Secretary Bill Moyers by greeting him as "Here comes Mr. Stop-the-Bombing" (Dobel 1999, 103).

Lacking a credible audience (or alternative speaker) left for debate, the premonition stood as a fait accompli.

Author of Convenient Fiction

For the speaker epidictic rhetoric can soothe the anxieties of the faithful in real time only to postpone coping with difficult realities. In his generalization that "Vietnam is not the first example in history of a hell whose access roads were paved with good intentions," George Reedy grapples with the incompatibilities of LBJ's words and actions that appear(ed) then and now as willful intents to deceive the public (1982, 19). Others in immediate contact with Johnson as well had problems working through these contradictions. For example, Josef Berger, one of Johnson's speechwriters, "said that [Johnson] seemed to have been involved in a 'spiral' of policy and politics that he could not break. 'I am certain,' he said, 'that Johnson didn't know where he was going,' with the Vietnam situation" (Benson 1974, 14). Speech professor Thomas Benson conducted this interview with Berger in December of 1965, "at the end of a year when the United States had increased its troop commitment in Vietnam from

23,000 to 180,000 men, when the administration hinted at further escalation to half a million men, when the White House referred to its Christmas bombing pause as a 'peace offensive'" (1974, 13–14).

In reference to Reedy's struggles to reconcile Johnson's myriad contradictions, the former press secretary (and speech professor as well) tells of listening to his priest's homily about a fictional book entitled *Humility and How I Achieved It*. In his mind Reedy concluded that if there *were* such a book, LBJ surely would have written it—and then have circulated it to his friends with the inscription "I thought you would like to know about my most lovable characteristic, which is humility." Further, Reedy relates that "[LBJ] would never have grasped the irony in either the title or the note. . . . In his mind, the printed word conferred qualities of grace upon those to whom it referred. . . . He subscribed to what was essentially a primitive form of word magic and he cared very much about the words of characterization" (1982, 12). For Reedy "word magic" engendered *moods* within audiences such that "Johnson's inability to connect words with reality [amounted to] 'come to Jesus' proposals that would be accepted by hearers," even if they lacked factual validity (13–14).

In rhetorical terms, Johnson's "word magic" and fictional proposals can be understood as the speaker's "knowledge of an audience [that] cannot be conceived independently of the knowledge of how to influence it . . . [or] how to bring about its conditioning." Perelman and Olbrechts-Tyteca liken this oratorical tactic to the work of a theatrical stagehand: "Various conditioning agents are available to increase one's influence on the audience: music, lighting, crowd effects, scenery, and various devices of stage management" (1969, 23). However, stagehands may be less likely to mesmerize themselves by their own efforts. Presumably LBJ's characterizations of his distinction from Barry Goldwater in his 1964 campaign and of events leading up to the infamous Tonkin Gulf Resolutions stand out as prime examples of convenient fictions, perhaps inadvertently co-authored by conditioned audiences buying in to them.

During his 1964 campaign, Johnson authorized a provocative campaign ad that distanced himself from his characterization of Goldwater as a reckless warmonger, which in retrospect appears as both a fictional proposal and an anything but subtle attempt to condition his audience. Still accessible through the Internet,[4] the ad shows a small girl counting the petals she picks from a daisy blossom. When she reaches "nine," her voice gives way to that of a man eerily counting down to the explosion of a nuclear bomb. Specifically, the script proceeds as follows:

Girl: [picking petals] One, two, three, four, five, seven, six, six, eight, nine;

Male voice: [echoing] Ten . . . nine . . . eight . . . seven . . . six . . . five . . . four . . . three . . . two . . . one . . . zero!

[close-up visual of the girl's face]

[video and audio of fiery detonation and then "mushroom cloud"]

LBJ: [emphatically] These are the stakes! To make a world in which all of God's children can live, or to go into the dark. We must either love each other, or we must die!

Announcer [a recognizable sportscaster's voice]: "Vote for President Johnson on November 3. The stakes are too high for you to stay home."

Ironically, the detonation of that blast constituted political overkill, since the election's outcome appeared certain to political insiders (such as Reedy) given Goldwater's fundamental campaign gaffes along the way. Perhaps this epidictic fiction is aptly assessed by Johnson's own communications expert:

Johnson's failure to understand the role of the communications process in a democratic society contributed more than anything else to his undoing. He could not understand the distinction between a speech and a soliloquy in a play. To him, both were intended to move the audience—but only to wild applause. He did not even understand the question of using words that were appropriate. He once demanded from his staff several paragraphs of humor to go into a Rose Garden statement on behalf of efforts to improve the lot of [mentally challenged] children. (Reedy 1982, 18)

Although perhaps not a prudent presidential candidate (see Miller and Seligman 1978, 72), Barry Goldwater did manage to goad LBJ or at least push the president to face his own personal insecurities. Specifically,

Goldwater's strident national defense rhetoric moved Johnson to worry that his own advocacy of peace and restraint toward the North Vietnamese—pledging that he would "never send American boys to do the fighting that Asian boys should do for themselves" (Goodwin 1991, 198)—could be construed as weakness. Goodwin argues that, regardless of the specifics concerning the alleged North Vietnamese torpedo attack on an American vessel in the Gulf of Tonkin, the incident afforded LBJ justifications both for ordering a military reprisal and to recast his rhetoric to exude strength (198). In other words, the circumstance provided the occasion to construct a narrative to bridge incompatibilities of people's perceptions (at least in LBJ's mind) regarding his strength in dealing with the Vietnam conundrum. In Goodwin's words:

> In one stroke, Johnson had been able both to flex his muscles and show restraint, to act abroad as he had done at home . . . [to] pursue contradictory policies and apparently make them work. . . . He was able to demonstrate that the "man of peace" was not a man of weakness or timidity. And on the verge of the campaign, the Tonkin affair allowed this consensus President to speak by his actions to each of his constituencies, satisfying them all in one stroke. (1991, 198–199)

Such contradictions can be found in his "Peace without Conquest" address at Johns Hopkins University on April 7, 1965; an analysis of that speech finds that "[LBJ] sought to answer Vietnam critics with 'unconditional discussions' and a billion-dollar electrification project for Southeast Asia, but he also reaffirmed his determination not to withdraw" (Yuravlivker 2006, 457).

In his memoir of his service in the Johnson administration, George Reedy concludes his discussion of the Vietnam experience with the statement, "I will never share the conviction of the left wing that [LBJ] deliberately precipitated the war" (1991, 163). Reedy then proceeds to explain how subsequent information (beyond the grasp of Johnson and other officials at the time) offered little evidence to corroborate the earlier claim that the North Vietnamese had actually fired upon the US ship. That information, he argues, casts the "retaliatory" strike as a monumental blunder.

Yet beyond the mistaken understandings that led up to creating the Tonkin narrative, Reedy is unmistakably harsh in criticizing how Johnson *used* this fiction:

The use that Lyndon Johnson made of the Gulf of Tonkin resolution was another matter altogether. When he presented the text to congressional leaders the night of the retaliation, there was no doubt that he left in their minds the unmistakable impression that it would only be used in connection with the specific incident. . . . To use it later as a blanket justification for prosecuting the war was disingenuous, to say the least. . . . I suspect he may have meant what he said the night that he met the congressional leaders and later rearranged the facts in his own mind to the later interpretation. He was capable of such self-deception. (164–165)

Sometimes fiction in response to contradictory claims "sticks" and is freely and willfully accepted by audiences as a means of reconciling incompatibilities. But in the case of the Tonkin narrative, it appears that fiction led to self-deception and dissonance for the President and many in his national audience.

Patient on the Couch or Astute Strategist?

Available evidence suggests that the dissonance associated with decisions concerning the Vietnam conflict inflicted a psychological toll on the President that was observable to those around him, In particular, historian Michael Beschloss adds his commentary to published entries in Lady Bird Johnson's personal diary that speak to her concerns of her husband's state of mind—including two made during the same week in February of 1965:

While Lyndon and Hubert [Humphrey] were talking, I was rather startled to hear [Lyndon] say something I had heard so often, but did not really expect to come out of his mouth in front of anyone else. "I'm not temperamentally equipped to be Commander-in-Chief," he said. They were talking about the crisis in Vietnam, the long nights with phone calls about planes going out . . . the necessity of giving orders that would produce God knows what cataclysmic results. He said, "I'm too sentimental to give the orders." Somehow I could not wish him *not* to hurt when he gives the orders. (February 11, 1965; Beschloss 2001, 177)

and

Lyndon's liking for [McNamara] is so evident that I almost fear that it might make other people gang up on him out of jealousy. He said, "[I]f I got word that Bob had died or quit, I don't believe I could go on with this job." (February 14, 1965, 178)

The timing of these diary entries coincided with a stressful period of indecision following a January 27 report from McGeorge Bundy and Robert McNamara concluding that the US war effort was failing and recommending a significant step-up in the military offensive against the North Vietnamese. On February 6, Johnson received word of a guerilla raid on a US Army barracks that killed nine soldiers. Other advisers and members of Congress critiqued the escalation option claiming that if the United States "did nothing, [South Vietnam's] collapse would not be serious. However, if escalation was tried and failed . . . then the consequences would be profoundly serious" (Goodwin 1991, 262). Later reflecting on the dilemma Johnson relates, "Suddenly I realized that doing nothing was more dangerous than doing," to which Goodwin summarizes, "In the end, coolness with which Johnson agreed to the bombing betrayed the pressures he had endured. Action, after so much discussion, was always a relief for Johnson" (263).

Pointing out that prior to the Kennedy assassination LBJ was skeptical of waging a war in Asia, George Reedy wonders why he did not disengage soon after his assumption of the presidency.[5] Reedy speculates:

One possible answer may lie in a simple misunderstanding. . . . [After the assassination] the Kennedy people knew the realities of power and they were looking to [LBJ] for a cue to their future conduct. *He, on the other hand, was looking to them for a cue as to what Kennedy would have done.* His lifetime in politics had taught him that what counted was the opinion *of the man who had been elected.* He did not want to take off on his own until he had been elected. (1982, 160; italics in original)

However, during these first weeks after his inauguration in 1965, Johnson sought validation from two former presidents. Michael Beschloss's *Reaching for Glory* includes transcripts of telephone conversations with both Dwight Eisenhower and Harry Truman initiated by Johnson on the same day—February 15, 1965—pleading with each to visit him at the White House as a token of their support for his Vietnam policies.

Each of these conversations seem to reveal a sitting president in need:

LBJ: General, I want to visit with you in the next day or so on our problems out in Southeast Asia, and I just wondered what your schedule was . . .

Eisenhower: Well, of course, I could do anything.

LBJ: I don't want to put it up like we are in deep trouble. Because I don't think it's reached that point . . . I don't know whether you have anything you need to do back this way or not. But if you did . . . I could have a Jetstar pick you up. . . . I'm a little concerned about leaving the appearance that we've got an emergency or something . . .

Eisenhower: I've always got a publisher in [New York], Mr. President.

LBJ: Why don't you come down here and spend a day with me at the White House and let me say, for the public, that I understand you were going to be in New York and I wanted to advise you on general problems . . . so it doesn't look too dramatic, that we've got a real emergency . . . I'll put you in Lincoln's bed.

Eisenhower: [chuckles] Lincoln's bed?

LBJ: Well . . . I would love for you—I wish you would stay at the White House. I need you a little bit. I need a little Billy Graham these days. You come prepared to stay with me for a day or two. Don't be in a hurry because I need you. (Beschloss 2001, 178–179)

and

Truman: What's the trouble?

LBJ: Well, I got a little bit . . . with Indochina. The Vietnamese . . . I just thought I'd call you and try to get a little advice and a little inspiration. I've been reading history and saw how much hell you had, and you handled it pretty good, and I just thought maybe I could learn something from you.

Truman: I think you're handling it pretty good, too. . . . You know how to do it. And I know you can do it. . . .

LBJ: All I know to do out there is what I am doing. I think when they go in and kill your boys, you've got to hit back. And I'm not trying to spread the war and I'm not trying to—

Truman: You be [as] you have [been]! You bust them in the nose every time you get a chance. And they understand that language better than any other kind. (Beschloss 2001, 180)

Eisenhower accepted the invitation, but Truman at that point was too ill to travel.

From a rhetorical standpoint, the question arises as to whether Johnson's appeal to his predecessors for counsel is indicative of insecurity and self-doubt or of a strategy to attain buy-ins from two former presidents noted for military success. Regarding the former, the term *aporia* refers to a rhetorical device whereby a speaker doubts his own position (however disingenuously) in a manner to ask those in the audience how *they* would proceed; in other words, to present the paradox to the audience (see Nordquist n.d.). Perelman and Olbrechts-Tyteca remind their readers that "all argumentation is indicative of a doubt, for it assumes the advisability of strengthening, or of making more explicit, agreement on a given opinion, which would not be sufficiently clear or compelling" (1969, 479–480). So to the question of whether Johnson's interactions with Presidents Eisenhower and Truman reflect authentic self-doubt or a bid for endorsements, the best response is likely *both of the above*.

CONCLUSION

As characterized in this chapter, none of the human rights advocates capitulated in confronting injustice, as did Bertolt Brecht's Galileo. Rather, young Iqbal Masih confronted his circumstance as a child in bonded labor head-on, defying his carpet-masters and the Pakistani carpet industry; subsequently, his courage cost him his life. Pussy Riot used disobedient art to reframe the Russian Orthodox Church's liturgical narratives intended to restore that institution to its exalted status in Vladimir Putin's new nationalism. Ironically, Pussy Riot's (pre-ordained) conviction after its sham-trial offered the group a visible "podium" for speaking truth through its letters from prison. It is significant that both Iqbal and Pussy Riot directed their respective confrontational messages to global audiences, so as to cause a "boomerang effect" (see Keck and Sikkink 1998) in bringing international pressure to bear upon their adversaries.

By contrast, US President Lyndon B. Johnson intended for his epidictic rhetoric to reassure the anxieties of his national constituency concerned about the legitimacy of US hostile actions in Vietnam in the early 1960s. Unfortunately for Johnson (and perhaps the nation), those discourses appeared *not* to convince Johnson himself of the war's virtues nor spare him from psychological dissonance in prosecuting a war that he had predicted to cause his political downfall.

NOTES

1. The quotes appearing in Andrew Crofts's book *The Little Hero* are representations of his conversations with Ehsan Kahn and others while he was in Pakistan in preparation for the book. In my personal (e-mail) conversation, I asked Crofts about the authenticity of his quotes. He responded, "It is rather a long time since I wrote the book but I seem to remember that I received a lot of contradictory stories from the people that I met who were involved and I ended up dramatizing what I thought was probably a close representation of the true story" (July 2, 2014). Nonetheless I use Crofts's representations—as well as D'Adamo's (2003)—of conversations as depictions of particular moral vernaculars (Gerald Hauser 2008) surrounding the life and death of Iqbal.

2. See "Full Text of 'Mahatma Gandhi & Karl Marx; A Study of Selected Social Thinkers,'" 21. http://archive.org/stream/mahatmagandhikar00sinhrich/mahatmagandhikar00sinhrich_djvu.txt. Accessed July 23, 2014.

3. In my personal communication with Harvey Cox, the noted Harvard Divinity School professor commented, "I am even more of a fan of P[ussy] Riot now [than when he wrote his op ed. piece in 2012]."

4. Several postings of the "Johnson Daisy Ad" are available on youtube.com; for example, see https://www.youtube.com/watch?v=dDTBnsqxZ3k. Accessed April 29, 2014.

5. However, there is evidence that Johnson *did* attempt to convince congressional leaders and others to disengage from Vietnam. Legal Counsel Lee White relates, "Some of the harshest critics of the Johnson Administration's Vietnam policies . . . remarked that upon hearing the tapes of LBJ's conversations, espe-

cially with Georgia Senator Richard Russell [his close friend and chair of the Senate Armed Services Committee], they realized how hard LBJ tried to disengage from Vietnam" (2008, 134–135).

5

RHETORIC IN MORAL PROJECTS

If moral projects "create more principled ways of doing things" (Hart 1992, 24), there is ample reason to question whether Starbuck's initiative to divine rain for a draught-stricken Texan community in N. Richard Nash's play *The Rainmaker* qualifies as "principled." It is after all common to react skeptically to someone's *project* as a political agenda, ideological mission, or self-aggrandizing scheme.

In Nash's play, Starbuck's more immediate *project* is to seduce Lizzie Curry, a lonely spinster trapped in her self-perception of unattractiveness. After Lizzie's father H. C. takes on Starbuck as a hired hand at the Curry Ranch, Starbuck proceeds to charm her by extolling her beauty. Both Noah (Lizzie's elder brother) and H. C. (Noah's as well as Lizzie's loving father) see through Starbuck's ruses to divine rain for the community and make a lifetime commitment to Lizzie. Outraged by his sister's impending victimization, Noah takes up a pistol to do Starbuck in.

H. C., however, remains more circumspect in valuing his daughter's (however fleeting) happiness with Starbuck's affections and seizes on the occasion to dress down his self-righteous son. Provocative ethicist Joseph Fletcher celebrates H. C.'s response to Noah in this especially memorable scene in *The Rainmaker*:

> On the stage and as a movie [*The Rainmaker*] was a great success. But the key to it, ethically, lies in a scene where the morally outraged brother . . . threatens to shoot the sympathetic but not "serious" Rainmaker because he makes love to [Lizzie] in the barn at midnight. The Rainmaker's intention is to restore her sense of womanliness and her

hopes for marriage and children. Her father, a wise old rancher, grabs the pistol away from his son, saying, *"Noah, you're so full of what's right you can't see what's good."* I nominate the Texas rancher as co-hero [along with Starbuck]. (1966, 13; italics added)

Presumably H. C.'s (as well as Nash's and Fletcher's) distinction between *the right* and *the good* can be instructive in examining moral projects in general and human-*rights* related efforts in particular. The three sketches included in this chapter each depict a rhetorical exemplar's *project*, either to promote either the *rights* or well-being (i.e., the *good*) of some segment of society over others—at least as understood within the status quo. US President Lyndon B. Johnson champions a *good* (that is, better or "great") society that threatens to undermine Southern white perceptions of the *right* way to live as separate and distinct from people of color. Julian Assange's project to have government secrets published in order to force transparency as the *right* way to operate a government allegedly obstructs security as a public *good* in an age of global terrorism. By contrast, Geert Wilders's project to protect the well-being (or common *good*) of native Dutch citizens from the recent influx of immigrants jeopardizes the cultural and political *rights* of Muslims in the Netherlands, a nation with a strong human rights identity.

LYNDON B. JOHNSON, CHAMPION OF A *GREAT* SOCIETY

In assuming the presidency under tragic circumstance in November of 1963, Lyndon Johnson inherited President Kennedy's resolve to eliminate discriminatory policies and public attitudes directed toward racial minorities. The year following the Kennedy assassination stoked racial tensions, particularly in the South with intensified Ku Klux Klan activity, and generally as the Director of the Federal Bureau of Investigation waged a campaign to discredit civil rights leader Martin Luther King. Although President Johnson retained key Kennedy staffers connected with civil rights initiatives, he aspired to establish his own legacy in using the nation's robust economy to improve the lives and livelihoods of all citizens, including those that had been marginalized by discriminatory policies, actions, and behaviors. At a 2014 ceremony commemorating the fiftieth anniversary of the signing of the Civil Rights Act, President Barack Obama praised LBJ's efforts to open the doors of racial equality, saying: "The doors swung open for you and they swung open for me. That's why I'm standing here" (Lederman 2014, A5). This sketch comprises the following discussions: "Proponent of Abundance" and "Master of Dialogue . . . and Pragmatic Hardball."

Proponent of Abundance

Antagonistic rhetoric leaves virtually no middle ground for compromise. As US Senate Majority Leader, Lyndon Johnson witnessed the antagonistic stalemate between the Southern segregationists and Northern liberals that blocked passage of civil rights legislation. Johnson's Press Secretary George Reedy describes the situation:

> By the mid-fifties, the issue had produced total exhaustion on both sides. Everything had been said that could possibly be said with the only result a hardening of positions and increasing polarization of attitudes. Movement in any direction was impossible because the question was not being treated as a legislative matter. Instead, it [the impasse over civil rights legislation] was a clash between the mores of two cultures—deep-seated moral beliefs that could not be compromised. (1982, 121)

In this context of stalemate, Reedy calls attention to Johnson *not* merely as a deal broker and overseer tallying political IOUs but also as a leader who could envision space for movement where none seemed to exist. In short Johnson sensed that Southerners might soften their stance toward a specific focus on *voting rights* in deference to their fierce devotion to the Constitution. Success in securing voting rights, Johnson reasoned, would be instrumental in supporting subsequent legislation for gaining economic and social rights in the long game. In human rights parlance, it could be said that LBJ understood CP (civil and political) rights not merely as ends unto themselves but also as means to ESC (economic, social, and cultural) rights. Reedy proceeds in detail to recount how Johnson managed to broker a deal on the Civil Rights Act of 1957 that facilitated President Eisenhower's voting rights proposals, the first piece of rights legislation passed since 1875. Referring to the passage of this bill as a "legislative miracle," Reedy relates how Johnson ushered in a compromise between Northerners who demanded federal enforcement powers and Southerners who wanted violators protected from criminal prosecution (1982, 127–131).

Johnson's eye for "space" gazed upon significantly broader horizons with respect to civil rights after he was duly elected president in 1964. His State of the Union address on January 4, 1965, set forth an expansive vision of abundant living not only for blacks deprived of rights but for all citizens:

> Yet the Presidency brings no special gifts of prophecy or foresight. You take an oath, you step into an office and you must guide a great democracy. The answer was waiting for me in the land where I was born. It was once barren land. . . . But men came and they worked and they endured and they built. And tonight that land is abundant, abundant in fruit and cattle and goats and sheep and there are pleasant homes and lakes and the floods are gone. Why did men come to that once-forbidding land? There was a dream—a dream of a place where a free man could build for himself and raise children to a better life. (Goodwin 1991, 215)

Johnson's use of epidictic discourse evident in this passage is reflective of "enchantment" as described by political philosopher Jane Bennett:

> The overall effect of enchantment is a mood of fullness, plenitude, or liveliness, a sense of having had one's nerves or circulation or concentration powers tuned up or recharged—a shot in the arm, a fleeting return to childlike excitement about life . . . in early modern Europe, the terms for wonder and wonders—*admiratio, mirabilia, miracula*—"seem to have their roots in an Indo-European word for "smile." (Bennett 2001, 5; quoted in Howe 2006, 440)

According to Doris Kearns Goodwin, Johnson wanted not only equality for all but also, beyond that, a decent life *not* in some distant future but all at once. She comments, "There was no justification for delay in providing what had already been denied. . . . So the agenda was established; the Great Society would offer something to almost everyone [Medicare, tax rebates, farm subsidies, food, etc.]" (1991, 216). Discourse in this speech is presumably indicative of Roderick Hart's comment, "[Johnson's] first presidency—a domestic one—was a roaring, brawling drunk" in distinction to the second (an international one involving Vietnam; see the previous chapter) as a "painfully slow process of detoxification" (1987, 90).

A case can be made that Johnson's emphases on abundant lives ties into an "enchantment" narrative that restores intrinsic meaning in a view of modern life that has been conditioned by rationalistic assumptions of value-neutrality and competition for scarce resources. Administrative theorist Louis Howe understands the ethical power embedded within the enchantment narrative as a means by which people in difficult situations find strength, perseverance, and self-actualization. Howe refers to a passage of theologian Katie Cannon that speaks to how confidence in the abundant life has served to empower within the American context of rights-deprivation:

> [The] New Testament helps Black women be aware of the bad housing, overworked mothers, underworked fathers, functional illiteracy, and malnutrition. . . . However, as God-fearing women they maintain that Black life is more than defensive reactions to oppressive circumstances of anguish and desperation. Black life is the rich, colorful creativity that emerged and reemerges in the Black quest for human dignity. (Cannon 1995, 56; Howe 2006, 425)

At this writing, racial tensions flare from the police killing of an unarmed eighteen-year-old male of color in Ferguson, Missouri. Tensions escalated after the city police used "hardware" such as riot helmets and armored vehicles (acquired through a US Department of Defense program to offer war paraphernalia to civilian law enforcement agencies) to confront citizen protesters. In response, Governor Jay Nixon placed state trooper Ronald Johnson, an African American raised in Ferguson, to oversee the turbulent situation. Describing how Johnson approaches an angry and frightened crowd, a journalist writes:

> And so the residents came, held back at first behind yellow police tape until Captain Johnson urged them to join the crowd near the podium. He began answering questions and recounting conversations, including one with his daughter after he returned home early Friday. They talked about the story of Jesus Christ and an apostle, Peter, walking on water. She said, "When Peter got scared, Jesus picked him up and said, have faith," Captain Johnson said. "And I'm telling you today, we need to be just like Peter because I know we're scared." The crowd cheered. (Blinder 2014, A13)

Trooper Johnson's epidictic rhetoric of hope and enchantment appears to work for him as it did for others facing trying circumstances in the past. It is coincidentally fitting (probably more in regard to his views on race than gender) that Lyndon Johnson's orientation toward *abundance* (rather than scarcity) mirrored the historical strengths of those he intended to find particular prosperity in the Great Society. Howe's abundance narrative is evident in LBJ's Oval Office speech in March of 1965 after he deployed federal troops to quash civil unrest in Alabama. In that speech, the President related his teaching experience in rural Texas to the unforgettable faces of poverty he saw in his students (Goodwin 1991, 230). As Goodwin relates, this presidential oratory amounted to both a "summons and a sermon" (280) reflecting the abundance narrative expressed through the epidictic genre—Johnson in his element.

The significance of this abundance or enchantment narrative becomes apparent as Howe contrasts it with the presumptuous, rationalist assumptions of academic liberals in their "understanding" of the public arena: "[a]cademic liberals and secularists . . . advocate a neutral framework within which a deontological [obligatory] notion of public reason can flourish. To oversimplify, public reason is conceived as a form of 'metaphysical abstinence' that understands society to be made up of prudential individuals unconnected to one another except by rational consent" (2006, 426). Put another way, Howe complains that rationalists squeeze all of the fervor (idealistic, religious, and so forth) out of a "reasoned" view of public affairs—leading to what Paul du Gay calls "soulless instrumentalism" (2000, 56).

But Lyndon Johnson thrived on "irrational" fervor, and his frequent use of epidictic rhetoric (described in the previous chapter as aspirational reassurance) reflected it. Presumably epidictic conversation expands, rather than reduces as rationalist discourse does, social life to new possibilities. Goodwin relates to Johnson's expansive discourse in this way: "There was almost nothing beyond the practical capacity of a united and determined America. . . . What was unique about Johnson was the confidence he possessed, powers of will and persuasion which could convince an entire nation that his policies represented the necessary and wisest course toward the kind of America that all should desire" (1991, 220).

Master of Dialogue . . . and Pragmatic Hardball

From a policy perspective, it can be said that the broad strokes of epidictic "boosterism" neglect the details of program implementation that call for the rhetoric of deliberation to determine, for example, what "educational opportunity" actually means. For the rationalistic bureaucrat, Johnson's Great Society discourse could have been interpreted as a harbinger of implementation complexities to follow. Goodwin emphasizes that Johnson typically framed programs in terms of vague generalities: "so it went message after message. The subjects might change, but the essentials remained the same: in the opening, an expression of dire need; in the middle, a vague proposal; in the end, a buoyant description of anticipated results" (1991, 219). But at the formulation stage, Johnson worked his rhetoric well in Congress, where he could deliberate one-on-one with members he knew so very well.

Unconstrained by the formal divisions between executive and legislative roles, President Johnson appeared to relish his interactions with his former colleagues in gaining support for various Great Society programs. Specifically, Goodwin suggests that LBJ felt comfortable engaging in deliberative discourse with a familiar audience and that he could effectively persuade legislators if they were provided information protecting them from a media ambush (1991, 224). But at a more fundamental level, the above quote speaks to Johnson's ability to adapt to his audience, in this case his former colleagues in Congress. Perelman and Olbrechts-Tyteca suggest, "In argumentation, the important thing is not knowing what the speaker regards as true or important, but knowing the views of those he's addressing. To borrow Gracian's [a seventeenth-century Jesuit philosopher's] simile, speech is "like a feast, at which the dishes are made to please the guests, and not the cooks"" (1710, 23–24). There is evidence that Johnson devoted considerable effort to assessing the mood of his congressional audience in a given circumstance, as in a comment offered to his biographer in reference to his strategy to address conflicts between advocates of parochial and public schooling in formulating an education bill:

"In some ways Congress is a dangerous animal that you're trying to make work for you. You push him a little bit and he may go just as you want but you push him too much and he may balk and turn on you. You've got to sense just how much he'll take and what kind of mood he's in every day. For if you don't have a feel for him, he's liable to turn around and go wild. And it all depends on your sense of timing." (Goodwin 1991, 227)

Johnson differentiated those in his congressional audience both in terms of "talkers" rather than "doers" and "show-horses" as opposed to "work-horses," and became particularly irate when a "work-horse" he felt could be counted on would drop the ball. With regard to the education bill, Johnson had been depending upon Adam Clayton Powell, an Afro-American who served as Chairman of the House Labor and Education Committee, to report the education bill out expeditiously. However, Powell had stalled progress on that bill in reaction to another of LBJ's Great Society initiatives for (white) Appalachia—thus incurring the President's wrath in a March 1, 1965 meeting:

LBJ: Adam, what the hell has been happening to your committee? I thought you told me two months ago you were going to have a bill for me.

Powell: All hell broke loose because—

LBJ: What the hell are you blackmailing me on a—

Powell: Let me—

LBJ: The hell you didn't. . . . You damn near defeated the best education bill I've got. I hope you're going to be proud of it! . . .

LBJ: For Christ's sake. . . . If there's anything going to happen on Appalachia that's anti-Negro, I won't let that happen. Period.

Powell: I'm not talking Negro. I am talking about . . . the education bill.

LBJ: For *God's* sake, don't get sucked into it. They [opponents] *used* you for three weeks and murdered me! . . . I want that bill reported out tomorrow morning. (Beschloss 2001, 197–199)

On that same day, Lady Bird Johnson recorded the following in her diary: "It was really a virtuoso performance. He gave [Powell] all the reasons why he ought to get that bill out of his committee in words that were dazzling, homey, and unanswerable. If I had been on the other side of the line, I would have ended by saying yes without waiting to quite decide why" (199).

By knowing and adapting to his audience (and its individual members such as Adam Clayton Powell), Johnson at times became a harsh and punitive task-master. But similar tactics appeared to work as well on LBJ's clienteles outside of the government. Johnson's White House Counsel Lee White talks about his participation in a March 1965 meeting with black clergy pressing a particular complaint (that White does not recall). But before the pastors could air their grievance, Johnson took control of the conversation:

> "I don't know what y'all want to talk to me about, but let me tell you whatever it is, it isn't as important to [your] people as the Education Bill that's up for a vote tomorrow. The count looks mighty close and we need all the help we can get. Lee, tell Larry O'Brien to come down and bring his tally sheet with him so we can get working on it . . . [after O'Brien appears, the President continues] Now which one of you has some way of getting to that one?" [and so on down the tally sheet] (White 2008, 126–127)

This classic example of co-optation depended upon a speaker's knowledge of his audience.

Lyndon Johnson's admiration for "doers" (and contempt for "talkers"—for example, his Vice-President Hubert Humphrey; Reedy 1982, 88) relates to a rather esoteric topic in the study of rhetoric, the difference between *persuading* and *convincing*. Although Perelman and Olbrechts-Tyteca are dubious of this hypothetical distinction as clearly delineating actual discourse (1969, 29), they nonetheless acknowledge other rhetoricians who emphasize it. In essence, *convincing* needs to address universal "convictions" pertaining to "absolute truths" to be determined through "pure reason" whereas *persuading* relates to particular contexts (or audiences) in which "a person is satisfied by affective and personal reasons" (27). Presumably, persuasion's attention to affect in particular contexts aligns closely to pragmatic argumentation that aims toward an ethic of utility in contrast with a conviction in deontological (or principles-based) ethics.

As indicated above, Lyndon Johnson admired "doers"—even those whose political views differed from his—because they were approachable and therefore could be persuaded. He particularly respected the "silent senator," Carl Hayden from Arizona, who was willing to be persuaded and ready to make a deal. Johnson would ask, "Why can't there be more like Carl Hayden? Can't those damn fools understand that he passed a forty-million-dollar bill through the Senate the other day just by nodding his head?" (Reedy 1982, 88) Reedy adds, "What [LBJ] disliked were men who searched their conscience Hamlet-like for hours on the floor to no purpose he could see" (88). If *persuading* (rather than *convincing*) lends itself to pragmatic argumentation in politics as the art of the possible, it also allows for "enchantment," particularly as reflected through *abundance narratives* (discussed above). Put another way, insistence on *convictions* as matters of absolute truth leads to antagonistic discourses that preempt political action through compromise. By extension, it could be argued that human rights advocacy that depends on firm *convictions* in universal truths may fuel antagonisms that preclude pragmatic accommodation in particular contexts of human deprivation.

On occasion short words, such as two- and three-letter prepositions, can mean a great deal. George Reedy suggests that this was the case with Lyndon Johnson's pragmatic philosophy of American Government as "government *for* the people" (coincidentally, the title of legal counsel Lee White's 2008 book) rather than "government *by* the people" (1982, 86–95). Reedy explains:

> This attitude left no room in the LBJ philosophy for the Senate as a *deliberative* body in which speeches could change the outcome of legislation or as an *educational* body in which speeches were intended to inform the public on the issues of the day. He did not believe that any amount of words could have either effect. In his view, bills were changed by carefully brokered applications of political power and the public was "educated" by the lobbying groups that represented the special interests involved in the issues. (88; italics in original)

Reedy subsequently argues that Johnson's pragmatic brokerage politics offered him a centrist position from which to play both ideological extremes against the middle. Referencing Scottish "ploughman" poet Bobby Burns, Reedy suggests, "Under any circumstances the right and the left will always see and hear hobgoblins and things that go bump in the night. Paranoia is an essential ingredient of ideologies that anchor the two ends of the political spectrum. The extent to which it should be encouraged is a question of conscience" (90).

But in the end, Lyndon Johnson's hardball pragmatism on behalf of the Great Society in general, and civil rights in particular, exacted a heavy political cost for Democrats, especially in the South. Nonetheless, LBJ prophesied this outcome, as his legal counsel Lee White recollects:

> The Voting Rights Act has had the revolutionary effect on national politics that all predicted it would have. That includes the shellacking the Democratic Party suffered in the southern and border states. At the time, LBJ predicted that the Voting Rights Act would spawn at least a generation of bad news and his forecast proved to be right on the nose. (2008, 132)

In rhetorical terms, it appears that Lyndon Baines Johnson—in stark contrast to his image as a pragmatic politician who mastered the art of persuasion—was indeed capable of self-deliberation. Thus, it appears then that Lyndon B. Johnson relied on persuasion in public life but acted on personal conviction of the truths embodied in civil rights.

In the following sketch, Julian Assange and his "cypherpunk" associates engage in an advocacy campaign for "truth" in the name of government transparency with respect to secret documents. Yet it will become apparent that, in contrast to Lyndon Johnson who framed his advocacy for the Great Society in a *rhetoric of hope*, Assange and his colleagues resorted to narratives of *fear* to win the hearts and minds of the public. Readers can compare Johnson and Assange in terms of the (in)effectiveness of their respective discourses.

JULIAN ASSANGE, CYPHERPUNK ADVOCATE AND WIKILEAKS FOUNDER

Julian Assange, the founder of WikiLeaks, stands out as a provocative public figure who, by advocating for individual privacy and governmental transparency, has taken on the wrath of government officials and corporate executives. On one hand, he is honored as a humanitarian in having accepted Transparency International's 2009 media award. And on the other, Assange eludes the questions of Swedish prosecutors about sexual misconduct during his 2010 visit in Sweden. The following sketch highlights not only Assange's rhetoric but also that of his WikiLeaks cohorts (and disciples such as Edward Snowden) as well as institutional adversaries. Assange in fact serves as a trustee of the Journalistic Source Protection Defence Fund "dedicated to building support for Edward Snowden, his human rights, his long-term liberty and his right to asylum" (JSPDF "Free Snowden" website). Specifically, attention here is directed to (1) identity rhetoric that clarifies how the WikiLeaks protagonists understand themselves and their advocacy, (2) rhetoric associated with how WikiLeaks has *institutionalized itself*, (3) the rhetoric of interaction between WikiLeaks and non-governmental institutions, and (4) that with governmental institutions.

Hackers in Search of an Advocacy Identity

Breaking with its tradition, Britain's Television Channel Four called upon a controversial figure—former US security contractor Edward Snowden living in Russian exile to avoid prosecution under the US Espionage Act—to deliver its 2013 Christmas Day message. For this occasion Channel Four usually features non-political speakers for this occasion, such as Queen Elizabeth II, who commented in 2012 that the birth of her great-grandson Prince George symbolizes hope for the future. But in 2013 this media outlet offered Snowden, an international fugitive, a national if not global audience to identify himself *not* as someone who "wants to change society" but as "want[ing] to give society a chance to determine if it wants to change itself" (Castle 2013). Further, Channel Four provided Snowden the opportunity to identify himself and his cypher-privacy colleagues by projecting the natures and motives of the institutional adversary as "an all-knowing Orwellian state."

Clearly, Edward Snowden is a traitor to some—such as John Bolton, former US Ambassador to the United Nations who opined that Snowden "ought to swing from a tall oak tree" (Reilly 2013)—but a hero to civil liberties groups such as the Partnership for Civic Justice Fund that purchased a "Thank You, Edward Snowden" advertisement painted on the side of a Washington DC public transit bus (Savage 2013). Nonetheless, Snowden's global notoriety stems from his actions leaking volumes of classified secrets to WikiLeaks and his public statements *as an exponent of a cyber-privacy (and government transparency) community*—of which

WikiLeaks founder Julian Assange is a central figure—rather than as an advocacy leader in his own right. Indeed, questions of identity concerning "who members of this cyber-privacy advocacy community *really are*" (criminals? patriots? sociopaths?) and "from whence they came" appear elusive even to Assange and his cohorts.

In fact, Assange's book *Cypherpunks: Freedom and the Future of the Internet* (2012) consists of conversations wherein he and three of his associates retrospectively reflect upon the collective identity of their advocacy movement, the evolution of their privacy and transparency concerns since the 1990s, and the rationales of their government and private sector adversaries. Similarly, Assange's principal collaborator and WikiLeaks spokesperson Daniel Domscheit-Berg accounts for his "time with Julian Assange at the world's most dangerous website" (until his break with Assange) in his book *Inside WikiLeaks* (2011). As an outsider, Australian journalist Suelette Dreyfus focuses on the infancy of the current movement in the 1990s by describing the youthful experiences of particular hackers that would later become influential in the WikiLeaks community in the book *Underground* (2012) that she co-authored with Assange. Referring to him in particular, Dreyfus attributes a combination of identities—as talented youths, biblical heroes, and budding anarchists—to those in the cypher-underground of the 1990s:

> You think that a boy up the road leads a perfect middle-class Australian life, trotting off to secondary school every day, sitting quietly at the back of the class, and playing harmless computer games in his boyish room at home. In reality, he is knee-deep in NASA networks. . . . There is the David and Goliath theme, as the little guy pits himself against the giants. Julian, WikiLeaks, and the young hackers in this book all find themselves battling the likes of the US military, NASA, and the Australian Federal Police. There is irreverent humor and a clear willingness to flip the finger at those who huff and puff, angrily demanding that the little guy gets back in the box. (2012, xiv)

Each of these books focuses on identity rhetoric, discourses, and narratives that project the "realities" of government and corporate intentions regarding cyber-technology.

As especially apparent in *Cypherpunks*, the interaction between Assange and his colleagues reflects a rhetoric of self-deliberation (see TNR, 40–41) whereby the deliberator (or in this case, co-deliberators) assume(s) the roles of both *speaker and audience* while also relating to their readers as a universal audience. What becomes evident to both the discussion participants and to readers is how various concepts of identity interact in ways that coalesce an increasingly significant meaning within their advocacy. For example, one of the *Cypherpunks* participants (Jeremie) relates back to their common background of teenage hacking to infuse meaning and moral purpose into what otherwise could be taken as mischief:

> It is interesting to see the power of the hackers—"hackers" in the primary sense of the term, not a criminal. A hacker is a technology enthusiast, somebody who likes to understand how technology works, not to be trapped into technology but to make it work better. . . . I suppose that when you were five or seven you had a screwdriver and tried to open devices to understand what it was like inside. This is what being a hacker is, and hackers built the internet for many reasons, including because it was fun, and they have developed it and have given the internet to everybody else. (Assange 2012, 67)

Through their retrospective discourse these cyherpunks impose identities upon their adversaries—mainly, governmental bureaucracies (and to a lesser extent, private sector entities) that "abuse" cyber-technology—in ways that affirm their own altruism. Addressed to their audience of readers, they identify governmental institutions that demand cyber-security as manifestations of "the secret state." Suelette Dreyfus presents the advocates' account of how "the secret state" emerged after the Cold War and how the young "underground" hackers encountered it:

> Although the Cold War had recently ended, the Secret State was still on the rise. The world's most powerful Western spy agencies were reinventing themselves to spy on their own citizens instead of KGB agents. The cryptography that we now take for granted in our web browsers was still classified as a weapon by governments, many of whom banned it from export. It was the era when *War Games* met *Sneakers*. (Dreyfus 2012, xvi; italics, upper-case in original)

Moreover, Domscheit-Berg (Assange's WikiLeaks spokesperson) relates how a terse and testy e-mail message from a German intelligence officer reacting to a webpage publication reinforced the group's identity of recognition from an institutional adversary; that e-mail begins:

Dear Sir or Madam:

On your homepage you enable the download of a classified report of the Bundesnachrichtendienst. I hereby demand that you immediately block this ability. I have already ordered a review of possible criminal consequences.

Sincerely,

Ernst Uhrlau
President, Bundesnachrichtendienst

In response, one of the cypherpunks impertinently responded, "Dear Mr. Uhrlau, We have several BND-related reports. Could you be more precise?" (2011, 57–59)

Having established the Orwellian "all-knowing" and secretive natures of cyber-intensive bureaucracies, these privacy/transparency advocates cast themselves as "restorers of faith" in governmental institutions (notwithstanding Dreyfus's remarks about their anarchistic tendencies discussed above). Edward Snowden alluded to this restorative mission in his 2013 Channel Four Christmas address:

> The conversation occurring today will determine the amount of trust we can place both in the technology that surrounds us and the government that regulates it. Together, we can find a better balance, end mass surveillance and remind the government that if it really wants to know how we feel, asking is always cheaper than spying. (Castle 2013)

To a lesser extent, this altruistic "restoration project" motivates them to reveal the "reality" of the institutional imperative to expand coercive power through the clandestine use of information technology. Stated another way, these advocates portray their institutional adversaries as power-aggrandizing (a common accusation directed toward bureaucracies) but argue further that "official" institutional justifications for secretive, classified policies simply serve as *pretenses* for their power-seeking behaviors.

Assange et al.'s underlying assertion that the (supposed) "need to classify sensitive intelligence" merely serves as a ruse becomes evident in their rhetoric in a broader claim that government endeavors to "militarize cyberspace." At one point in the *Cypherpunks* discussion, Assange relies upon analogy to support this assertion:

> I see that there is now a militarization of cyberspace, in the sense of a military occupation. When you communicate over the internet, when you communicate using mobile phones, which are now meshed to the internet, your communications are being intercepted by military intelligence organizations. It's like having a tank in your bedroom. It's a soldier between you and your wife as you're SMSing. We are all living under martial law as far as our communications are concerned, we just can't see the tanks—but they are there. (2012, 33)

From there, he expounds on the *pretense of secrecy* as a ruse for institutional power, and in response his cohort (Jacob) refers to this pretense in terms of rhetoric that plays upon powerful biblical imagery: "The Four Horsemen of the Info-pocalypse: child pornography, terrorism, money laundering, and the war on some drugs." In that rhetoricians concern themselves with the "effects of analogy" (see TNR, 381–385), there is reason to speculate as to exactly how this analogy works, particularly as to how meaning transfers from imagery from the book of Revelation to these advocates' insistence that the need for secrecy around government's use of the Internet is simply a fabricated justification for a power-grab. Given the numerous (and sometimes contradictory) interpretations of the Revelation passage, the exact structure and logic (or transfer) of this analogy appears anything but clear; but perhaps they needn't be—Assange et al.'s audiences can be left to figure that out for themselves. The implication that the state exploits public abhorrence of child pornography, terrorism, and so forth for its own institutional purposes likely provokes strong emotional reactions from many in those audiences.

In summary, a large measure of Julian Assange's advocacy rhetoric (among other purposes) appears intent upon affirming high-minded identities of those connected with the WikiLeaks and the embryonic hacker-underground movements. As evident in the above discussions, various strains of identity rhetoric appear to evolve over time and sometimes in a contradictory manner—for example, association with the "weak" (like David vs. Goliath) but also "strong" and effectual as in the case of incurring the wrath of a German intelligence official. In the early years, this group found identity as "anti-institutional" outsiders; such an identity called for some revision as WikiLeaks itself became institutionalized as a business and media source with a global constituency.

Rebels as Keepers of an Institution

The self-identities of the "cypherpunk" cohorts became subject to re-examination and interpersonal conflict as WikiLeaks matured from random hacking forays into a working enterprise unto itself. Reality at this point dictated that young people committed to "taking on" institutional systems would now need to institutionalize WikiLeaks. This in turn led to quandaries about how committed *they themselves* would be to transparency (that they so shrilly demand of others) and to whether one of these young radicals could step forward as a competent institutional leader. Again, the rhetoric here is primarily of a self-deliberating nature whereby members of the cohort debate issues that pit the empirical facts of institutional life (such as how to sustain funding streams) with the importance of staying true to values and advocating "new" norms different from those of conventional media organizations.

Rhetoricians point to a distinction between a speaker's efforts to *convince* and *persuade* (TNR, 2–3; 26–31); in attempting to convince, the speaker argues the need to come to grips with, or conform to, indisputable facts, but in persuading refers to only a first stage in the progression toward desired action. In *Inside WikiLeaks* (2011), Domscheit-Berg speaks to his own frustrations in convincing Julian Assange to deal with the pressing business aspects of WikiLeaks—given Assange's preoccupation with visionary idealism. Thus it became unclear where co-deliberative argumentation should start (with the necessities of institution-building or with advocacy?) and whether long-term goals make much sense to advocates with anarchistic tendencies. Indeed, Domscheit-Berg (although in a somewhat different context) refers to German anarchist Rudolf Rocker, whom he quotes as saying, "I am an anarchist not because I believe that anarchism is a final goal, but because there is no such thing as a final goal" (2011, 113).

Arguments about the *reality* and *direction* of institutional development focused as well upon the appropriate design, or architecture, of the WikiLeaks system. Referring to the term "philosophy of technique," Assange approached the architectural design issue as a sociologist theorizing upon the correlation between organization design and patterns of political power during particular historical eras. Starting with the early twentieth century's need to centralize control in the mill era, Assange ultimately arrived at the current semi-conductor manufacturing setting as analogous to the organizational logic of WikiLeaks: "thousands of people in it who have to wear hairnets to keep every little skin flake, every bit of hair away from the semi-conductor manufacturing process, which is a multi-step process that is extremely complicated" (Assange 2012, 26–27).

As the "culture" (presumably meaning environmental condition) of air purity is to making computer semi-conductors, so is that of "Internet liberation" essential to WikiLeaks' organizational processes. Thus, in the desired WikiLeaks culture, system architecture needs to control the external political (that is, governmental and corporate) environment to exact concessions on behalf of the individual user. More specifically, appropriate design for Assange should serve individuals (characterized elsewhere as the little guy that powerful institutions shove "back in the box"— Dreyfus 2012, xvii) not only to share sensitive data files with them but also to extend their unfettered voice. Regarding the latter, in *Cypherpunks,* Jeremie responds to Assange, "The printing press taught the people how to read; the internet taught the people how to write. This is something very new, this is a new ability for everyone to be able to write and express themselves" (Assange 2012, 82).

Furthermore, this cohort understood that decentralized architecture could serve as an antidote against censorship. Assange argued that the structured nature of WikiLeaks' counterparts accounted for their vulnerability to government censorship: "We have Facebook completely centralized. Twitter completely centralized. Google completely centralized. All in the United States; all controllable by whoever controls coercive force. Just like the censorship that started after WikiLeaks released Cablegate [WikiLeaks' release of diplomatic cables in 2010], when Amazon dropped our site from its servers" (Assange 2012, 76). As in the case of rhetoric asserting that "security concerns" serve merely as pretexts for expanding bureaucratic power, the debate surrounding appropriate WikiLeaks architecture depends upon analogy as an argumentative strategy

Finally, the rhetoric associated with institution-building (or lack thereof) needs to question whether Julian Assange, the founder of WikiLeaks, can serve as a competent institutional leader. At several junctures in his account of working with Assange, Daniel Domscheit-Berg casts doubt on Assange's organization leadership skills, particularly in his aversion to deal with pragmatic issues such as budgeting and defining clear strategic goals. One could infer that Julian Assange fits squarely into the category of "founder celebrities" with little if any aptitude for guiding organizations through successive stages of development. In fact, the Italian *Rolling Stone Magazine* named Assange its 2010 "rock star of the year" and showed him on its December 2010 cover as the star of a (fictitious) film entitled *The Man Who Fell [from the Web] to the Earth*. The magazine's editors said that they "decided to feature the Australian whistle-blower on its front cover because although he is not a musician, he best embodied a rock-and-roll behaviour during 2010" (Karotki 2010).

But could it be the case that emerging forms of organizations, such as WikiLeaks with its decentralized architecture and mission to liberate the Internet, call for a radically different institutional logic and sense of direction, perhaps compatible to Assange's philosophy of technique? Journalist Suelette Dreyfus, clearly Assange's defender, emphasizes his sense of vision:

> Julian sees solutions others can't see. His lens is not focused on the foreground. His thinking reflects the cypher punk community of the 1990's where he cut his teeth. . . . They believed in the right of the individual to personal privacy—and the responsibility of government to be open, transparent, and completely accountable to the public. (2012, xii)

Such a strategy of argumentation, in addition to calling direction (that is, appropriate stages and processes) into question, appears to enlist the rhetoricians' technique of contradiction and incompatibility (TNR, 195). Thus, it would appear that only those in the audience inclined to entertain non-conventional ideas, or at least those with a capacity for nuance, would be receptive to Assange's approaches to organization.

Transparency Advocates and Non-Governmental Institutions

For Julian Assange the transparency advocate, principle and nuance seldom if ever coexist, ostensibly because the ambiguities of life and institutional circumstances lack relevance. Domscheit-Berg presents the unvarnished WikiLeaks "principle" in succinct terms: "Publishing everything we received was part of our concept of transparency. What else could we do if we didn't want to open ourselves up to accusations of playing favorites? Whether the material affected the political right or the left, the good guys or the idiots, we published it" (2012, 27). As discussed below, Domscheit-Berg muses as to whether WikiLeaks operated as a cult with Assange as cult leader who prohibited others from using discretion in determining what should be published.

Legal recriminations from the principled actions of "publishing everything" included a law suit filed by a Swiss Bank in 2008 as well as legislative inquiries and grand jury investigations on the part of government. Yet in a paradoxical twist, public attention to early WikiLeaks legal tribulations afforded it visibility through coverage extended by the mainstream media organizations such as the *New York Times* and *Der Spiegel* as well as broadcast organizations. WikiLeaks's early Internet disclosures (posted at numerous websites) relied upon anonymous sources—it is unclear how carefully these accounts were screened. In 2008 for example, Assange and Domscheit-Berg received anonymous e-mail messages alleging the culpability of the Swiss bank in providing wealthy investors a means of tax evasion involving "sums between $5 million and $100 million per client" (Domscheit-Berg 2011, 17). Claiming that a former employee legally bound by a confidentiality agreement had leaked records of individual investments, the bank sought injunctive relief ordering WikiLeaks to take down a particular website disclosing those records (but was apparently unaware of others that showed this information as well).

But the payoff for WikiLeaks was its formation of a symbiotic relationship of sorts with the established news institutions and itself. Specifically, the *New York Times* devoted several articles to the case, and a CBS News headline stated that "Freedom of Speech Has a Number"; the body of that account included WikiLeaks's IP number for both donors and adversaries to contact. According to Domscheit-Berg, this notoriety placed WikiLeaks on the global map. In this relationship WikiLeaks "published everything" on principle so the established media institutions could then analyze the subtle and nuanced implications of these disclosures.

Shortly after the bank disclosures, Assange and Domscheit-Berg were in receipt of secret documents—the handbooks of the Church of Scientology—sent by a group calling itself "Anonymous," an international alliance of Net activists who had declared war on Scientology and whose members concealed their faces with masks of Guy Fawkes, the late-sixteenth-century British revolutionary associated with Gunpowder Treason, during their public protests and in YouTube videos (34). Anonymous's website stated the following:

> Scientology has no qualms about persecuting ordinary citizens who protest against their machinations. What we mean by persecute is shadowing and harassing individuals just because they do not share Scientology's view of the world. We are only protecting ourselves against intimidation and harassment. The Scientology organization is incredibly wealthy. It has an unbelievable team of lawyers at its disposal and is known for its nuisance lawsuits. That's the reason for the masks. (Domscheit-Berg 2011, 35)

Although not providing the scale of visibility that the bank disclosures had, the publication of the Scientology handbooks created the opportunity for WikiLeaks to protect the privacy of anonymous sources by "running interference" against the legal liability of Anonymous and other parties thereafter. In this regard, Domscheit-Berg maintains that "the leaders of the sect were either cleverer than our adversaries at the bank or lucky enough to come after them. The case of [the Swiss bank] had shown the whole world that one could only lose by suing us." He also relates that Anonymous defiantly challenged Scientologists in demonstrations by holding up placards that read "Sue WL, you f*****s!" (41)

It was through this experience that, in becoming familiar with the writings of Scientology founder L. Ron Hubbard, Domscheit-Berg began to associate Assange's rigid insistence on "principles" with cult behavior that may have seeped into the WikiLeaks operating culture. In particular, he self-deliberates:

> Looking back, I ask myself whether WikiLeaks itself has developed into a kind of religious cult. It's become a system that admits little internal criticism. Anything that went wrong had to be the fault of something on the outside. The guru was beyond question. The danger had to be external. This mind-set encouraged internal cohesion. Anyone who offered too much criticism was punished by having his rights suspended or by being threatened with possible consequences. Moreover, WL participants were only allowed to know as much as was absolutely necessary for them to carry out their appointed tasks. (2011, 42–43)

If Domscheit-Berg's reflection is accurate, it reveals a culture far removed from Assange's espoused institutional architecture of decentralization described above.

In 2011 the *New York Times* released *Open Secrets*, an extensive compilation of its coverage of its WikiLeaks articles and editorials, which described the symbiotic but contentious relationship between WikiLeaks and both the *Times* and UK's *Guardian*. In his reflective introduction (titled "The Boy Who Kicked the Hornet's Nest"), *Times* editor Bill Keller speaks to the ethical dilemmas of reporting on WikiLeaks disclosures by acknowledging the delicate nature of the media's social responsibility:

> A free press in a democracy can be messy. But the alternative is to give the government a veto over what its citizens are allowed to know. Anyone who has worked in a country where the news diet is controlled by the government can sympathize with Thomas Jefferson's oft-quoted remark that he would rather have newspapers without government than government without newspapers. (2011, 17)

But in comparison to the *Guardian*, which serves readers who sometimes savor criticism of the United States, the *Times* has an obligation to an audience that has been directly affected by the 2001 terrorist attacks and that continues to cope with the policy conundrum of pitting security against free expression (Keller 2015, 15). Nested within this policy dilemma are other related paradoxes—or at least contradictions with conventional logic—that affected how established media organizations dealt with WikiLeaks. From one perspective (that of journalist Suelette Dreyfus), the advent of WikiLeaks is characterized as a reaction to a weakened media. Dreyfus quotes an Australian federal official who argued, "The establishment media does not necessarily report what society should know—that is why WikiLeaks is succeeding. It is fulfilling a role that has been ignored for too long" (2011, 447).

Yet Dreyfus presents an additional logical challenge that calls attention to the supposed contradiction between irresponsible radicalism of youth (as personified by Assange) and legitimate public stewardship:

> Here comes the interesting paradox. The anarchist-inspired ethos of the early computer underground has contributed to a new creation— WikiLeaks. Yet the existence of this publisher with its single-minded

intent to publish or perish *may be the very thing that ultimately prevents the spread of anarchy.* It may be the front line to put an end to the Secret State and its oppressive security. For just that reason, this new media creation is embraced by those who have fought on both sides of the computer underground—the orderly and the anarchists. Neither side wants to see rights and protections quietly stolen away. (2011, 450)

Apart from their substantive merits, the thrust of these rhetorical arguments aligns with what rhetoricians recognize as statements prompting dissociation that incline audiences to reconsider ideas (TNR 1969, 442). Thus the symbiotic relationship that has existed between WikiLeaks and established media institutions, as strained and turbulent as it has been, has instructive value for effective advocacy. Speakers may do well to attend to the paradoxes involved in how their audiences respond to themselves as messengers, particularly those who appear disheveled and subject to unfortunate fates.

WikiLeaks Advocates and Governmental Institutions

By late 2010 WikiLeaks faced prosecution under the US Espionage Act and the wrath of many in the Obama administration over three particular WikiLeaks actions during the year. In April it released a video entitled "Collateral Murder," which showed American Rangers firing from two Apache helicopters fatally shooting over 20 Iraqi civilians in a suburb of Baghdad. The video had been provided by Army Private Bradley (or Chelsea) Manning, who was arrested some seven weeks after WikiLeaks published "Collateral Murder." The audio presented a cavalier, business-as-usual tenor of these military personnel as they proceeded. In July WikiLeaks published the Afghan War logs, over 91,000 reports covering the war in Afghanistan from 2004 to 2010; in October it put out the Iraq war logs, by its own description the largest military leak in history. Assange relates the following in a Web interview on British television the day of the release:

Well, these documents cover the periods of 2004 to the beginning of 2010. It is the most accurate description of a war to have ever been released. Within them, we can see 285,000 casualties. That's added up, report by report. . . . Now, looking at particular groups of casualties,

we can see, for example, over 600 civilians killed at checkpoint killings, including thirty children, previously—mostly previously unre-
ported, that three-quarters of those killed at checkpoint killings, according to the United States military itself, were civilians, and only
one-quarter, according to the US military internal reporting, were in-
surgents. (Goodman 2010)

To questions about the claims of General Stanley McChrystal and
others that these leaks put the lives of US soldiers at risk, Assange responded:

> Well, this is the same old argument that the Pentagon has been trotting
> out every time there is media exposure of their abuses for the past fifty
> years. They tried it with the Afghan war logs. . . . So, on the one hand,
> we see no credible evidence of harm being committed. . . . So then we
> look at the other side of the equation. What is the possible benefit? Can
> this material save lives? Can it improve the quality of life in Iraq? Can
> it tend to shape our perceptions of how war should and should not be
> conducted? Can it shape our perceptions of who should be conducting
> war and in what manner? And the answer to that is a clear yes. (Good-
> man 2010)

If Assange had (rhetorically) asked *"Who are the beneficiaries..?"* of
censoring leaks rather than "What are the possible benefits?" responses
could point to security and intelligence elites in government who enjoy
unusually wide discretion (if not autonomy) within their purviews. In
their *New York Times* account of NSA Director James Capper's testimony before the Senate Armed Services Committee in February 2014, Sanger and Schmitt suggest that continuing Congressional investigations of
security place considerably greater scrutiny on the Director than is typically the case:

> The continuing revelations have posed a particular challenge to Mr.
> Clapper, a retired Air Force general and longtime intelligence expert,
> who has made no secret of his dislike for testifying in public. Critics
> have charged that he deliberately misled Congress and the public last
> year when asked if the intelligence agencies collected information on
> domestic communications. He was forced by the Snowden revelations
> to correct his statements, and he has been somewhat more careful in
> his testimony. (2014, A8)

WikiLeaks's release of nearly 250,000 diplomatic cables in 2010—revealing US officials' distress over Iran's nuclear agenda (Sanger, Glanzer, and Becker 2011), al-Maliki's fears of nations on Iraq's borders (Gordon 2011), and Yemen's engagements with Al Qaeda (Shane 2011), among many other issues—shed light on the work and correspondence of diplomats that typically passes under the radar of public scrutiny. Clearly, many of these cables confirmed skepticism of US motives on the part of adversaries, such as Iran's supreme leader Ayatollah Ali Khamenei, who now had evidence to validate their distrust in the Obama administration (Peterson 2010). Deftly, then–US Secretary of State Hillary Clinton attempted to salvage a measure of prestige for her agency by suggesting that the leaked cables offered glimpses of the essential work diplomats perform on a daily basis. Columnist Mark Landler writes:

> Mrs. Clinton's reaction to shouldering the burden has been every bit as artful as the cables that landed her in so much trouble. "It was a DoD system, and a DoD obviously military intel guy," she said. "But we're part of one government, and we're part of one country, and we have to work together, and that's what we're doing." (Landler 2011, 218)

But there is little doubt that the cable leaks, in exposing the substance of backchannel (unofficial and off-the-record) communications, have had a chilling effect on international diplomacy. Diplomatic pressure brought to bear by US officials to derail Spanish court investigations linked to the Iraq war and military prison at Guantanamo Bay found their way into *El Pais*, a leading Spanish newspaper, by way of WikiLeaks cable disclosures in 2010 (Yardley 2014, A7).

For US Representative Ron Paul, Julian Assange stood as a champion of public accountability since the released cables raise fundamental questions like—

- Do the American people deserve to know the truth regarding the ongoing war in Iraq, Afghanistan, Pakistan, and Yemen?
- Why is hostility mostly directed toward Julian Assange, the publisher, and not our government's failure to protect classified information?
- Are we getting our money's worth from the $80 billion dollars per year we spend on intelligence gathering? and

- Was it not once considered patriotic to stand up to our government when it was wrong? (Mackey 2011, 228–229)

Some (probably most) members of the US Congress assailed Assange as a traitor in its grand jury proceedings under the Espionage Act. In *Cypherpunks*, Assange explains the situation as follows:

> The Grand Jury investigation is not the only avenue of attack on Wiki-Leaks. In December 2010, in the wake of Cablegate, various active US politicians called for the extrajudicial assassination of Julian Assange, including by drone strike. US senators labeled WikiLeaks a "terrorist organization" and named Assange a "high-tech terrorist" and an "enemy combatant" engaged in "cyber warfare." (2012, 14)

But reactions to the Edward Snowden leaks appear to divide Republican members of the US Congress, whereby libertarians such Robert Good-latte of Virginia, Chair of the House Judiciary Committee, appear more critical of the NSA than of Snowden—while Chair of House Intelligence Mike Rogers of Michigan views Snowden as a common criminal. Questioning FBI Director James Comey in an Intelligence Committee hearing, Rogers asks, "So if I'm a newspaper reporter for—fill in the blank—and I sell stolen material, is that legal because I'm a newspaper reporter? If I'm hawking stolen, classified material that I'm not legally in possession of for personal gain and profit, is that not a crime?" Comey responded that although "hawking stolen jewelry" may be a crime, "I think [reporting leaks is] a harder question because it involves a newsgathering function and could have First Amendment implications" (Savage 2014b, A13). Nonetheless, pressure from the government, according to Assange, has led to Internet service providers discontinuing service to WikiLeaks, amounting to censoring it.

But as becomes apparent in President Obama's comments about the need to overhaul NSA protocols in accessing private telephone conversations, the WikiLeaks project in general and Snowden's leaks in particular force institutional responses intended to restore legitimacy. In the President's words,

> I recognize that because of these revelations that there's a process that's taking place where we have to win back the trust, not just of governments but, more importantly, of ordinary citizens. And that's

not going to happen overnight, because I think that there's a tendency to be skeptical of government and to be skeptical in particular of US intelligence services. (Savage 2014a, A16)

Despite myriad efforts to demonize Assange, Snowden, and other Wiki-Leakers from within government institutions, the thrust of their actions appear parallel with reform traditions aimed at curbing intrusive government.

In the sketch to follow, Geert Wilders serves from within government as a Dutch parliamentarian, in contrast to Julian Assange who attempts to reform public agency practices in handling secret documents from outside of government. Nonetheless, both Assange and Wilders engage in rhetoric that is highly critical of government. Readers may find it instructive to trace the similarities in their respective discourse strategies.

GEERT WILDERS, ADVOCATE OF INTOLERANCE

Geert Wilders, a current member of the Dutch Parliament, is the founder and leader of the Party for Freedom, the third largest party in the Netherlands. Wilders unleashes shrill populist messages against the "elite establishment" policies of the Dutch national government and the European Union—most notably, those encouraging multiculturalism and immigration. His alienating rhetoric against both the influx of Muslim immigrants into Holland and (what he considers) the "anti-Western" ideology of Islam have led to threats made on his life; thus he is frequently surrounded by security personnel in public appearances.

Wilders's antagonistic statements against that faith have elicited harsh reactions from many national leaders in Europe and elsewhere. In 2009 Dutch prosecutors charged Wilders with violating the Dutch anti-hate speech law, but he ultimately won an acquittal in a two-year trial that bolstered his celebrity among followers. Wilders's political influence reaches beyond the Netherlands as he assumes prominence among other populist party leaders in Europe such as Marine Le Pen of France and Nigel Farage of Great Britain. This sketch of Geert Wilders as an advocate of intolerance includes the following discussions: "The Proprietor of a One-Stop Populist Shop," "The Antagonist in Visual Space," and "The Unwitting Dialectician."

The Proprietor of a One-Stop Populist Shop

Geert Wilders's rise to power as a rights-antagonist and populist must be understood, oddly enough, within the contexts of the Dutch institutional commitment to international humanitarian concerns and a policy environment that values the consensual over the adversarial (Oomen 2013, 63). From an institutional perspective, the Dutch constitution explicitly embraces human rights as an overriding international norm and recognizes the outcomes of international justice mechanisms as binding upon the Netherlands as well as other nations. Furthermore, it leaves its "bill of rights" open-ended (rather than stipulated), perhaps under the rationale that such a proactive nation in the realm of international justice need not limit rights only to those specified (56).

Yet as Barbara Oomen explains, the Netherland's outward orientation toward international justice, dating back to the Hague Conferences of 1899 and 1907—intent on establishing "world government" and a "world court," actually serve in the national interest. In particular Oomen refers to an influential international law professor who then maintained that the nation should assume the mantle of moral leadership in the international realm:

> [van Vollenhoven] argued that the Dutch history and position as a small country put it in a unique position to advocate an international court that would adjudicate both written and unwritten law, as well as an international police force. . . . Advocating this, he argued, was the Dutch vocation: 'If, in our days, the circle of the influential and powerful other nations—its diplomats, lawyers, military—smile apathetically and in disbelief at this noble aim of world justice strengthened by a world military force, then let the Netherlands dare be the Joan of Arc.' (2013, 46)

But over the years, the domestic policy outcomes on the nation's institutional commitment to human rights have taken some intriguing twists, leading up to current political realities that animate Geert Wilders's anti-Islamic discourse. Specifically, Oomen relates that

> Many historians have pointed out how developing the international legal order was very much in line with Dutch self-interest, as "*ploutos sits on pax' lap*" (wealth is a child of peace). A small player like the Netherlands, that earned much of its income on the world seas and in

trade, only stood to benefit from international rules and institutions to enforce them vis-a-vis the larger countries. (2013, 49)

Thus, she asserts that "human rights" should be understood as a Dutch "export product" for a "niche market" wherein the Netherlands assumes the role of a "guiding nation . . . to elevate backward countries" (44–49). Oomen's inference here is that the social construction of what human rights *actually mean* and how they are to be implemented play out on a "two-level playing field" (2013, 53). On the domestic (or local) level, human rights acquire meaning within the context of a local community that places a premium on the individual's freedom of expression and (to a lesser extent) values freedom of religion. Given this populist construction of rights, Oomen maintains that it becomes incumbent upon ministry heads and civil servants to take leadership roles in formulating and implementing rights particularly as they relate to the international realms. In other words, these officials are so consumed in the details of that craft as to relegate parliamentarians such as Wilders to the sidelines of rights policy-making. As a result, members of Parliament enjoy wide latitude in either pushing or obstructing human rights causes.

Thus, in the institutional and political contexts in which parliamentarians such as Wilders operate, opportunities emerge by which legislators can capitalize on the "fall-out" from Dutch rights-talk. Such opportunities become especially attractive since the national interest in human rights in the international sphere has not permeated the social consciousness of the Dutch public (which has relatively little awareness on their own rights, much less of international human rights). This enables legislators to frame these issues (most notably, those related to immigration) to serve their purposes. Regarding the latter, Oomen comments:

Even if civil servants leave The Hague with formal instructions, they have a great deal of negotiating freedom. . . . If ministers still have entire departments to work on their policy preferences, parliamentarians in the Netherlands are typically one-stop-shops, with at best one personal assistant, who are overloaded with information and are under a strong pressure to score in the media. In the "drama-democracy" parliamentary priorities are generally determined more by the newspaper headlines than by the ability to persistently and over a long time period engage with tenacious policy issues, thus making it important for advocacy groups to first solicit media attention for a particular topic, and subsequently engage parliamentarians. . . . In his PhD, *So, how do we tell parliament*, Enthoven quotes a parliamentarian who states: "There is no parliament, there are 150 one-person-shops." (2013, 70)

"Scoring in the media," according to Dutch political scientist Maartin Hajer and Wytske Versteeg, depends largely upon the politician's capability to accommodate media preferences for expression *in narrative form*, especially those with storylines of crisis and instability. Specifically the researchers assert,

[S]weeping statements are exactly what the media are interested in; news is not *news* without a narrative. Drama, clashes, and conflicts sell—as does strong, symbolic language. This means that there is a built-in logic of escalation in the interactions among politicians, publics, and the media, which becomes particularly acute in times of heightened conflict or dislocation. (2009, 5)

Further, Hajer and Versteeg argue that political narratives that translate *concrete* situations into *abstract values* can be especially effective in resonating with audiences and in fending off reactions from adversarial voices. Regarding the former, *Islamization*—Geert Wilders's abstraction of choice—leads to a variety of subsequent opportunities to frame situations that occur (in his rhetoric) as outcomes of *Islamization* in ways that validate uneasiness with the presence of Muslims in Dutch society. Excerpts of Wilders's speech to an anti-Islamic organization in Beverly Hills, California, document the emotive quality of Wilders's Islamization narrative:

As you know, the current Islamization of Europe is not an invasion like those we have seen in the past. This time it is not a military invasion with swords, this time we have to deal with a stealthy invasion. Nowadays, the armies are replaced by cultural relativism and mass immigration. It is this dangerous cocktail that is the main cause of the Islamization and is responsible for the introduction of Sharia law in Europe.
    As you know, Sharia is Islamic law, effective in barbaric countries such as Saudi Arabia and Iran. Beheadings, hangings, chopping off hands and feet, stoning to death, lashings, it all happens because Sharia

law prescribes it. Now, radical Muslims want to implement Sharia law into our Western societies. (quoted in Hajer and Versteeg 2009, 4)

Among other assertions, Wilders's narrative blames "elites" (presumably those public officials who do *not* engage in his rhetoric) for allowing "Islamization" to take root. Hajer and Versteeg maintain that right-wing populist voices project an authentic sense of honesty: "A common reaction to both politicians was that they finally dared to say what so many people had thought; the suggestion was that the tolerance and calm of the previous years had been nothing but a conspiracy of silence by the leftist media and political elite" (2009, 3).

In terms of trumping critics, moderate politicians find it difficult to respond to rhetoric such as Wilders's that is packaged in an abstract, value-laden narrative. Most often, responses of logic and fact do not resonate with target audiences but are instead taken as an ad hominem attack on the protagonist. As a case in point, Hajer and Versteeg call attention to a 2009 response to Wilders on the part of the Dutch Minister of Foreign Affairs, Maxime Verhagen: "*Wilders sows the seeds of conflict with his generalizations. The statements of Wilders make Holland a country of 'us against them.' That is not the Netherlands where I want to live. I want to live in a Holland with shared values*"—to which the researchers comment, "[I]t is doubtful whether his words had any positive effect beyond that specific audience; indeed, a quick glance at a news site's online forum reveals a flurry of criticism for Verhagen, who came across as having attacked Wilders" (2009, 6). Moreover, speakers intending to rebut extremist rhetoric should anticipate the effects of their discourses on what Hajer and Versteeg call the "politics of multiplicities" or in rhetorical terms, multiple audiences:

In this sense, politics in the mediated age seems like playing a pinball machine set at a steep angle and with only short flippers at your disposal; politicians can hit the pinball all over the playing field but even if they hit their targets, the ball is likely to come back at them from unexpected angles, requiring them to rebut or respond on little notice and with sometimes unanticipated consequences. (2009, 7)

Nonetheless, Verhagen's reference to Wilders's "us versus them" rhetoric—in essence, the discourse of *antagonism* (as discussed below) is significant in its inference that there is virtually no place for dialogue here; rather, it begins with "the absolute truth" and ends there as well. To paraphrase another Dutch political scientist, "If you step into someone else's [value abstraction], you will almost always lose" (de Bruijn 2011, 12–13).

Although the power of Wilders's Islamization abstraction clearly defames Muslims, it is not surprising that populist extremists wield their rhetoric so as to stigmatize other adversaries whom they label as "elites." Obviously the established politicians (having "lost their way") are targeted, but so too are civil servants branded (along with NGO officials and other advocates) as "useful idiots" who unknowingly aid the Islamic "conspiracy," including—

> Smooth-talking public administration graduates in designer glasses; the department of muddling through; the government of delay and cancellation; the palace on the Amsterdam canal ring; . . . the Dutch branch of Friends of the Earth; the arts crowd; mandarins; professional lobbyists; those with a spine full of whipped cream; those who would rather have a fat bank account than principles; grant guzzlers; and the fat and lazy left-wing canal ring elite. (quoted in de Bruijn 2011, 39)

Human rights advocates and organizations fare no better, as described in Wilders's book *Marked for Death: Islam's War against the West and Me* (2012) as naïve functionaries of the "Islamic conspiracy":

> The West must also stand up to intolerant Islamic regimes. They should recognize that human rights exist to protect individuals, not religions and ideologies. Member states of the Organization of Islamic Cooperation [OIC] that do not renounce the Cairo Declaration, which elevates Sharia law over human rights, should be expelled from the United Nations. (215)

> One of the most dangerous vehicles of Islam today is [the OIC]. . . . Its efforts have met with some success, such as the approval in March 2012 by the United Nations Human Rights Council of a resolution criminalizing "defamations of religions." The resolution, authored by Pakistan on behalf of the OIC, explicitly mentions only one faith: Islam. For the OIC, Islam is the only religion worthy of protection. (116–117)

No organization, local or international, official or unofficial, has bothered to expose what is happening to [subjugated Islamic women]. . . . Why do the human rights activists ignore their suffering as though they do not exist? Why isn't the cry of these millions of women heard, and why isn't it answered by anyone, anywhere? Why? Why? Why? (210)

Wilders's Islamization narrative has spawned a derivative, perhaps even more powerful, "anti-EU" storyline that blames that confederation's open borders policy for the unwieldy movement of Muslims among European nations. As an indication of a changing political narrative, a *New York Times* reporter relates, "Mr. Wilders has turned his party's emphasis from opposition to Islam to opposition to the European Union, and his Party for Freedom is likely to elect the largest number of European legislators from the Netherlands" (Erlanger 2014, A4). If there is indeed a change in Wilders's narrative of choice, it may coincide with opportunities to leverage his political leadership among his populist counterparts in France (Marine Le Pen), Great Britain (Nigel Farage), and in other nationalist parties in Europe.

To summarize, Dutch parliamentarians function within an unstructured legislative environment as independent, one-stop-shops—free to politick on issues concerning Muslim immigration in the virtual absence of institutional accountability. Geert Wilders has found success advancing an antagonistic narrative of Islamization that capitalizes on the public's fear of large numbers of Muslims in Dutch society. That narrative affords Wilders the opportunity to exploit concrete issues and situations that arise in contemporary society by superimposing a variety of frames that attach emotive meanings to particular issues. In his insightful analysis, Hans de Bruijn (2011) identifies a number of frames commonly used by Wilders and offers examples of Wilders's rhetoric associated with each, for example:

- The "problem and ideology" frame: "*I prefer to call them 'colonizers'—Islamic colonizers—because they come here not to assimilate but to take over the country and subjugate us*" (26);
- The "risk of major disaster" frame: "*The time will come when our daughters and granddaughters will have to wear headscarves*" (29); and
- The "totem pro parte" [whole referring to part of the whole] frame: "*A bus driver from the city of Gouda sent me an email last week:*

'Mr. Wilders, We are being terrorized by Moroccans. Yesterday, one of my colleagues was robbed at knife-point on his first run of the day by a Moroccan. His friends were waiting for him in a car, and they all drove away happily as if they just stopped at a cash machine to draw money'" (33).

The Antagonist in Visual Space

Roughly analogous to "Harry and Louise"—the fictional couple portrayed in the Health Insurance Association of America's 1994 televised ad campaign against Clinton healthcare initiatives, "Henk en Ingrid" surface in Geert Wilders's political videos as "common Dutch citizens" whose financial well-being suffers from the "drain" on the nation's welfare system that "accommodates" Muslim immigrants. Politicians apparently reap benefits when bad things happen to imaginary people. In that regard, a television news reporter who followed Wilders on a March 2013 campaign trip in the northern region entitled "Looking Out for Henk and Ingrid" captures his conversation as follows:

> We are campaigning for the common people . . . who have lost their trust in the Dutch political elite, because they do everything that is not in the interest of what we call the Dutch common people like Henk and Ingrid when it comes to mass integration, when it comes to the raising of taxes, when it comes to the very best healthcare system for the elderly we have in Holland today, when it comes to the unsafety of the Dutch's streets, . . . we fight for *them*.[1]

Subsequently the reporter focuses on a woman protester along the route of Wilders's campaign voicing opposition to the candidate's anti-Islamic narrative: "He says that Henk and Ingrid should not be paying for Ali and Fatima, and I'm against that. We've got a social welfare system that's for *everybody*" [Italics indicate inflection].

Thus, through the television media, Wilders uses visual space to conjoin the narrative of Islamization with the concepts of citizen identity and relative deprivation (see van Velzen 2012, 29–30). Wilders's campaign rhetoric appears to capitalize in particular upon the ambiguity of what Dutch citizenship requires of minorities, and the associated implications for religious practices, which have been in flux since the 1990s. In his analysis of "Dutch governmental rhetoric on good citizenship," Wagenvoorde reports that the liberal integrative policy of the 1990s has given way to a more strident demand that minorities become aware of the defining features of Dutch society:

> Since the 1990s, citizenship has become an important topic in Dutch integration policy. In hardly twenty years, the government's rhetoric has changed from a liberal approach, in which citizens are considered free to express their own value system in the public sphere, to a more communitarian approach that gestures towards a clear-cut picture of how citizens should behave. (2011, 2)

Comparing respective government documents, she finds that the earlier conception of citizenship called for an integration wherein minorities can "decide for themselves to what extent they will keep and possibly further develop their cultural identity" (3). By contrast, largely due to a changing political environment that veered toward Wilders's brand of populism, a new policy thrust focused on "socio-cultural adaptation." In this regard, Wagenvoorde discloses that the latter document titled *Make Sure You Belong to It!* replaces the permissive integration stance of the earlier policy. Yet in addition, the government now reaches out into visual space with its ten-minute film *Coming to the Netherlands* to address foreign audiences who anticipate emigration *prior to their arrival*. Specifically, this video alerts viewers that they must pass the Civic Integration Examination Abroad that tests (1) knowledge of Dutch society, (2) ability to speak and comprehend the Dutch language, and (3) reading and comprehension in the Dutch language to be granted immigrant status.

Yet beyond priming immigrants about the stiff linguistic challenges awaiting them, the film informs its audience about what life will be like in Dutch society. But the message is ambiguous—one hand, the moderator welcomes people from different cultures, but on the other she confronts viewers with difficulties that immigrants encounter in everyday life. The film begins with the narrator's assertion that, unless people are financially solvent, they will probably be housed in low-income public housing in crowded conditions with other immigrants (and features a middle-aged, Turkish man who cautions viewers to "think hard" about their decision—had he to "do it all over again," he would have likely remained in Turkey). Subsequently, the moderator stresses the benefits of settling in small villages, wherein it is easier to connect with Dutch citizens (and adapt to the culture) than in large cities, where ethnic ghettos are common. Eventually, the topic turns to religion. Here viewers learn that, in addition to having a traditional Christian cultural identity, the Netherlands had endured eighty years of religious strife in the sixteenth century between Catholic rulers and Protestant rebels, the latter eventually prevailing through William of Orange's rise to power; the presumed inference here is that anything close to a repeat performance will not be tolerated.

Although *Coming to the Netherlands* implies that immigrant Muslims might incite religious strife, one particular conflagration that *did* emerge can be attributed to the visual rhetoric of a native Hollander and political figure, Geert Wilders—rather than to a Muslim. As Wilders tells it,

> In late 2007, I decided to make *Fitna*, a 15-minute documentary film about the Islamic threat. The most common translation of the Arabic word *fitna* is "ordeal" or "trial." The title of the film symbolizes my view that Islam is an ordeal currently confronting the West. I was assisted in making the film by Koran experts who, to protect their personal safety, remain anonymous. Featuring an exquisite copy of a Koran I bought in East Jerusalem, *Fitna* juxtaposes Koranic verse calling for violence, particularly against non-Muslims, with footage of terrorist attacks and other violent deeds these verses inspire, along with clips of Islamic leaders inciting violence for the sake of Allah. (187)

Table 5.1 shows selected scenes in the film depicting particular combinations of verse and depictions of contemporary violence Wilders's attributes to actions precipitated by faith in the Koran. In *Marked for Death*, Wilders relates that, after having released the film, he was besieged by myriad hostile responses from those *within* the Netherlands, and that the nature of those responses essentially proved the point of the film; "outraged at my film's suggestion that the Koran advocates violence, furious Islamic activists unleashed wild threats of violence" (2012, 188).

Fitna was first released on the UK video website *Liveleaks.com* and eventually run by *Youtube.com* and elicited nearly 250,000 comments between February and May of 2008. As could be expected, particularly emotional comments came from the immigrant community: [message begins] "Wilders must die" [and ends] "F*** all those who support Wilders because you had better realize: one will reap the consequences of one's actions!!!!" Wilders also reports that "people with the last name Wilders, though unrelated to me, received letters threatening that if they failed to prevent me from releasing *Fitna*, 'The first deadly victim will be you, one of your children or grandchildren'." (188). Nonetheless, he reports as well of heated reactions from non-Islamic citizens, particularly business and labor leaders who feared international boycotts of Dutch products in reaction to the film. Wilders also alleges that police "provided pre-printed forms that people could use to press criminal charges against me" (189).

Almost simultaneous to *Fitna*'s release, the Dutch prime minister issued a scathing rebuke of Wilders, saying that the film "equates Islam with committing atrocities. We reject this interpretation. . . . In fact, the victims are often also Muslims. Hence, we deplore that Mr. Wilders has released this movie. We do not see what purpose this movie serves both to offend the feelings of others" (Wilders 2012, 190). Similar statements were issued by UN General Secretary Ban Ki-Moon and European Union officials; Indonesian President Susilo Bambang Yudhoyono banned him from that country for life, and the king of Jordan threatened to issue him

Table 5.1. Wilders's Association of Visual Depictions with Koranic Verses in the *Fitna* Film (Selected Examples)

Verse in Koran	*Visual Depiction*
Surah 8, Verse 60 "Prepare for them whatever force and cavalry ye able of gathering to strike terror in the hearts of enemies, of Allah."	Airliners crashing into the World Trade Center twin towers on September 11, 2001, and other terrorist sites.
Surah 4, Verse 56 "Those who have disbelieved our signs, we shall roast them in fire. Whenever their skins are cooked to a turn, we shall substitute new skins for them that they may feel the punishment: Verily Allah is sublime and wise."	An Islamic cleric brandishing a sword threatening beheading; a Muslim toddler referring to Jews as "apes and pigs" in the eyes of Allah.
Surah 47, Verse 4 "Therefore, when ye meet the unbelievers, smite at their necks and when ye have caused a bloodbath among them, bind a bond firmly on them."	The murder of Dutch politician Theo Van Gogh.
Surah 8, Verse 39 "Fight them until there is no dissension and the religion is entirely Allah's."	Various predictions that Islam will dominate the world; Muslims holding a sign: *Freedom Go to Hell*.

an international arrest warrant"—to which Wilders reacts, "Nothing happens in the Hashemite Kingdom without the acquiescence of the King. King Abdullah II is a direct descendant of the barbaric prophet Muhammad. That explains a lot" (192). In each of these cases, from a rhetorical point of view, it appears that the speakers (or "judges") mentioned above have rendered critical judgments on Wilders and in turn Wilders attempts to disqualify these judgments by his own that rely on ad hominem argumentation, as in his reference to King Abdullah II (TNR, 298; 111).

Wilders's production and release of *Fitna* represents an advocate's (or a politician's) use of visual spaces that differs significantly from traditional campaigns through the video media—even efforts to create fictional figures such as "Henk en Ingrid," "Harry and Louise," and the "Swift Boat Veterans for Truth" (who emerged to disqualify John Kerry in the 2004 presidential election in the United States). As co-authors who have published several analyses of *Fitna* as rhetoric explain, the film creates a contentious debate "that is strongly articulated with Web 2.0 practices (van Zoonan, et al. 2011, 1284); Web 2.0 refers to a second generation of services through the Internet. In the case of *Fitna*, this interaction involves *visual* debate on a global scale in that expression not only includes written comments but hundreds of posted videos—posted by Wilders's detractors and supporters—as well. Moreover, these researchers suggest that the Web 2.0 technology elicits the participation of "ordinary people" who would typically not register their views in traditional media fora, particularly those dealing with religion and politics.

For scholars of mass media (such as van Zoonan and her colleagues), Web 2.0 video interaction piques research interest in the emerging methodology of "cybermetric network analysis" that discerns how communities of comments, subscriptions, and "friends" on the Web cluster in reference to a particular topic, such as *Fitna* (van Zoonan 2011, 1290–1296). From these spatial relations of networks, it becomes possible to study substantive questions connected to the *nature* of the discourse, particularly as compared with standards of democratic dialogue, by analyzing common rhetorical qualities of messages within various networks.

Against the researchers' three-fold criteria of *antagonism* (narcissistic self-expression that stifles civic engagement), *agonism* (pluralistic acknowledgment that adversaries are not enemies), and *dialogue* (speech supporting civic discourse); van Zoonan et al. find that Wilders's *Fitna* has, perhaps not surprisingly, polarized global audiences so as to attract antagonistic responses that preclude engagement, such as these:

- Wilders is saving our country, can't you see you cancer morons; most of you are paedophiles [sic] still living with your parents; f*** the haters, nothing is gonna stop Islam; (van Zoonan et al. 2011, 1291); and
- I laugh that you claim a book of myths/deceit which is fixated/ obsessed with hate, sex, punishments, genitalia, barbarity has quality. First prove an allah before you dribble such IMMATURE junk. (1291)

By comparison, a distinct minority of posts and/or comments qualify as agonistic, such as this:

I was provoked by the apologetic attitudes by a certain segment of EU citizens, who chose to apologise to all Muslims everywhere for Fitna on behalf of the entire EU. We should never apologise for practising our free speech. Especially not in the face of massive anti-democratic Islamist activity within Europe. . . . My video was a message to European apologists. It's not anti-Islam, but anti-Islamic extremism. However my video is not aimed at Muslims, but at the people who will bend over backwards not to step on Muslim toes. They are doing a disservice to free speech and democracy in Europe. (1291)

Fitna appears to elicit antagonistic responses that stoke hostility in visual space beyond the initial reactions that Wilders provoked.

The Unwitting Dialectician

In some respects, Geert Wilders's rhetoric through Fitna garnered predictable and (most likely) intended results in (1) having been renounced by his "elite" establishment adversaries and (2) bolstering support for populist politics in the Netherlands and other nations—particularly in the United States. After Fitna's release, Wilders embarked on an international tour that consisted of speeches to officials in some European capitals as well as in Australia and the Unites States. Telling of his visit to Capitol Hill, Wilders relates: "America behaved as befits a free country. On

February 26, 2009, I showed *Fitna* at the US Capitol at the invitation of Arizona Senator Jon Kyl" (2011, 96).

But as van Zoonan et al. relate in their article on women's responses to *Fitna*, Wilders's antagonistic discourse in visual space set dialectical forces in motion that led to deliberative dialogue and civic engagement among Muslim women. First, van Zoonan et al. associate *Fitna*'s depictions of Muslim women with an Orientalist discourse "in which women are presented as the current and future victims of the oppression of Muslim men and Islam" (2011, 97). Specifically they argue that the film presents Muslim women as victims of extreme violence, as complicit in promoting hatred toward the West, and as part of "allegedly changing the Dutch landscape" (98). Muslim men, they contend, are cast either as vitriolic preachers or as parts of large, threatening crowds. By contrast, non-Muslims are shown as victims or (in the case of women) aid workers. These depicted roles converge into a gendered narrative wherein Wilders and others—such as Theo Van Gogh, his political mentor who was assassinated by a Muslim—emerge as heroes:

> The narrative that articulates these roles into a coherent traditional gender discourse of male activity versus female passivity is that of men fighting over the control of women and femininity: Muslim men as individuals or as collective are shown as perpetrators who preach and enact violence, oppress and abuse Muslim women; non-Muslim women and some men, especially homosexuals, are cast as real or future victims of this aggression, specifically within the Dutch national context. White Dutch male heroes, embodied in the figures of Theo van Gogh and Geert Wilders himself, are seen to come to the rescue of non-Muslim women. (van Zoonan et al. 2011, 113)

These authors then conclude that the "protection scenario, in which the well-being of Oriental (and non-Oriental) women depends on the benevolent intervention of non-Muslim Western men from the patriarchal order . . . [in which] women are denied agency, and appear as victims whose safety lies in the hands of male protectors" (114).

Second, this critique contends that Web 2.0 technology provides a platform for Muslim women, as well as others around the world, to assert their authentic voices in expressing reactions to *Fitna* and postings related to it. From their data base of sixty-three YouTube video postings by (generally young) Muslim women between February and May of 2008, the researchers maintain that "YouTube clearly offers an alternative space to express one's opinions in different formats than those of mainstream media coverage; cut-and-paste and testimonials are the typical YouTube genres that young women from Muslim and non-Muslim backgrounds (otherwise marginalized actors) used to criticize Geert Wilders and his film" (2011, 125). Thus they reason further that the technology provides a space for Muslim women to refute the gender stereotypes of the Orientalist discourse. As an example, they call attention to a particular YouTube posting by a British woman who was especially receptive to Jordan's Queen Raina who posted a call for Muslim women to send her examples of stereotypes of females in Islam that she could publically address. A Moroccan woman and Dutch citizen wearing a bright pink hijab spoke on her own posting, asserting that "if Wilders's goal was for Dutch non-Muslims to turn against their fellow Muslims citizens she thought he had failed" (2011, 123).

Third, the YouTube platform affords Muslim women agency in claiming the right to speak within Islam. Van Zoonan et al. conclude that "the YouTube videos uploaded by women showed that YouTube clearly offers an alternative and an important space to discuss *Fitna* and Islam" (2011, 125). Their comments about two particular postings by Egyptian women are especially poignant in documenting how the technology aids women in expressing their own claims within the faith:

> Of all the uploaded videos the concerted effort of a group of young Egyptian women is the most elaborate and consequential example of Muslim women speaking for themselves. . . . A female voice-over reads the verse, which is followed by written texts of different colours on black background explaining their meaning and putting them in the context of the complete verse they were taken from. First, the pure act of women reading [contests the stereotype of women's subservience in the practice of Islam]. Second, the additional act of women interpreting the true meaning of the Quranic verses is also rather uncommon and puts these videos right at the heart of liberal modern Islam. (2011, 123)

Finally, through their efforts to respond to various gendered stereotypes in the Orientalist discourse, Muslim women have utilized new media technology to claim civic identity in the global sphere. In their acts of either listening to (merely by uploading posts) or speaking about (actually posting videos) that contribute to global conversations about Wilders's *Fitna*, these women speak out about their actual experiences within their faith. In essence, they claim roles as citizens who are willing to engage in discourses of deliberation, both within local and global communities.

Paradoxically, Geert Wilders's antagonistic rhetoric may in fact offer an exemplary contribution to global human rights, through the assistance of women who utilized available Web 2.0 technology to extend their voice in global dialogue.

CONCLUSION

In this chapter Lyndon B. Johnson re-emerges *not* as a rights antagonist as in chapter 4 but as an advocate of (the) human "good" (if not *rights*) in his discourses on behalf of a "Great Society" project. It is significant that the *ir*rationality (if not *supra*-rationality) of his epidictic rhetoric follows an enchantment narrative that affirms *abundance*—in stark contrast to the resource *scarcity* theme in the conventional conversations of "rational" policy-making. In justifying their WikiLeaks project intended to facilitate absolute transparency in the operations of business and government, Julian Assange and his cypher-punk associates base their advocacy *not* on enchantment but on a deep suspicion of institutional motives. Their rhetorical arguments principally rely upon the strategy of using vivid, provocative analogies that call attention to stark contradictions and incompatibilities between societal rights "talk" and the actual usurpation of those rights.

In the current context of far-right European politics, Dutch legislator Geert Wilders is proficient in building narratives that support his media-related projects intended to denounce the religious practice of Islam and stop its adherents from immigrating to the Netherlands. Wilders recognizes that "news" means nothing if not packaged within a provocative narrative. Further, he knows that by speaking in shrill ideological abstractions, he can trap moderates whose dialogue is destined to fail in treading this rhetorical quicksand. However, new social media offer Wilder's victims—particularly, Islamic women—a platform for presenting concrete realities (for instance, YouTube depictions of themselves as Dutch citizens who happen to practice Islam) that discredit Wilders's antagonistic abstractions.

NOTE

1. See https://www.youtube.com/watch?v=G15Z0mItK_g. Accessed March 12, 2015.

6

RHETORIC IN MORAL WORK

Moral work focuses on one's vocational calling (beyond income and other extrinsic payoffs) that stands out as significant because "it is the key to a worthy life for the vast majority of us. It refers to the intentional decision of an individual always to think and act in virtuous ways" (Hart 1992, 24–25).

Commenting on the nature of moral virtues, ethicist William Frankena understands virtues as dispositions or traits governing actions, most of which derive from the two moral principles of beneficence (a will to do good) and justice (1973, 64). Among other virtues derived from these principles (such as optimism, courage, and wisdom), *perseverance* and *mental toughness* surface as especially critical in human development work.

In William Gibson's play *The Miracle Worker*, novice teacher Annie Sullivan demonstrates mental toughness in dealing not only with her deaf-blind student Helen but with the entire Keller family, particularly with Helen's outspoken father. Early in the play Annie holds the Kellers accountable, chiding them for *pitying* their disadvantaged daughter rather than challenging her to develop her mental capacities. In the midst of one of Helen's tantrums, Annie becomes assertive in grabbing Helen's hands; the Kellers react with anger to Annie's "callousness" in this exchange:

> *Keller [the father]:* Miss Sullivan! You would have more understanding of your people if you had some pity in you. Now kindly do as I—

Annie: Pity? For this tyrant. The whole house turns on her whims, is there anything she wants she doesn't get? I'll tell you what I pity, that the sun won't rise and set for her all her life, and every day you're telling her it will . . .

Keller [addressing his wife]: Kate, for the love of heaven, will you—

Kate: Miss Annie, Please. I don't think it serves to lose our—

Annie: It does you good, that's all. It's less trouble to feel sorry for her than to teach her anything better, isn't it?

For Annie *pity* has no place in teaching Helen, and for development scholar Peter Uvin *charity* has no place in human rights work. In his book *Human Rights and Development*, Uvin states his case for demanding accountability (from aid donors as well as from rights-abusers) as follows:

At the heart of any rights-based approach to development are concerns with mechanisms of accountability, for this is precisely what distinguishes charity from claims. As the Human Rights Council of Australia states, "Accountability is the key to protection and promotion of human rights." Indeed, the very move from charity to claims brings about a focus on the mechanisms of accountability. If claims exist, methods for holding those who violate claims accountable must exist as well. If not, the claims lose meaning. (Uvin 2004, 331; his references omitted)

Since the rhetoric of "human rights" and "human development" can be easily appropriated, it is important to distinguish those who routinely direct their work toward empowering people to claim their rights from others who engage in rights discourse in their own self-interest. Two of the sketches in this chapter focus on performers who draw upon their careers in music to promote inter-cultural understandings that heal the wounds of historical tragedies. Daniel Barenboim conducts symphonic music and directs performances in ways that introduce Jewish audiences to his symphonic interpretations of Richard Wagner's compositions; thus, Barenboim's work offers insight into German cultural vernaculars that led to the rise of the Third Reich. Lucius Banda uses his vocal talents to call attention to human rights abuses in the Sub-Saharan African nation of

Malawi; these injustices are to a considerable extent perpetuated by political regimes in power since the nation's independence from colonial rule
in 1963. On the other hand, another sketch (positioned between those on
Barenboim and Banda) focuses on a US law enforcement official—Sheriff Joe Arpaio of Maricopa County, Arizona—who professes to teach his
(largely Hispanic immigrant) prisoner population the virtues of self-re-
spect and hard work while he incarcerates them. Nonetheless as a "law
and order" sheriff, Arpaio appears more committed to rooting out those
found on the wrong side of "the law" than to human development endeavors.

DANIEL BARENBOIM, HUMANIZER OF SOUND

Daniel Barenboim is a pianist and internationally renowned conductor
who currently serves as the General Music Director of the Staatsoper
(State Opera) in Berlin and of the La Scala Opera House in Milan. Born
in Buenos Aires, he gave his first public concert in that city at the age of
seven and then performed internationally in Vienna and Rome at the age
of ten. One year later, he moved with his family to Israel. As a person of
Jewish faith, Barenboim was criticized for conducting (1981–1999) at
Bayreuth, in the enclosed pit that composer Richard Wagner, a known
anti-Semite (even though he himself may have been of Jewish ancestry),
had built in his home town in Germany; the conductor is particularly
drawn to the techniques that Wagner used in his compositions. Barenboim served as Music Director of the Chicago Symphony Orchestra from
1991 until 2006.

For Barenboim, music is an art form that transcends national interests
and cultural barriers. Both within the concert hall and beyond it, the
conductor has endeavored to channel his artistic interests in ways that
nurture intercultural dialogue and understanding. Barenboim articulates
his ideas about music and its social implications in *Parallels and Paradoxes* (2002), which he co-authored with his close friend Edward Said, a
professor of English at Columbia University (until his death in 2003). The
conductor and English professor (from respectively Jewish and Palestinian backgrounds) partnered to shepherd significant initiatives to promote
intercultural dialogue through the arts, as described in this sketch. This

sketch includes the following discussions: "Teaching Maestro," "The Agonist and the Taboo," and "Steward of Inter-Cultural Performance."

Teaching Maestro

As evident in *Parallels and Paradoxes* (2002), Daniel Barenboim the orchestra conductor assigns himself the role of teacher in helping his audiences discover truth through a musical performance. Yet from a rhetorical standpoint, one could ask whether the conductor who leads the performance of a piece is any *more* a "speaker" (or "teacher") than the composer who wrote the score, or even the individual musicians whose passionate artistry (or alternatively, dispassionate instrumentalism) conveys the sensory stimuli. Or conversely, one might wonder why the conductor is *less* an audience for the composer than those sitting (or standing) in the concert hall.

Although cases could be made for various speaker-audience relationships, Barenboim takes on the teaching task of interpretation—of not only the composer's score but also his/her depth (or superficiality), motives, and historical (and contemporary) relevance, among other meanings. His sense of exploratory interpretation resonates in response to Edward Said's question as to whether Barenboim studies text prior to his performances:

> I don't. I have no images whatsoever. . . . I always try to find the true expression of it in the music on its own—and very often, if I find what, to me, seems the true sense of the music, it goes hand in hand with the text; and if it doesn't fit, then something is wrong. . . . I think that if one studies the text first and then sees how the music matches, it will match, because it was meant to, but then you don't get the same depth of musical expression as when you try to study that separately. (Barenboim and Said 2002, 50)

In rhetorical terms, Barenboim's ideas suggest that a conductor endeavors to interpret the composer's discourse, and in so doing, she or he has the liberty to deal with the ambiguity and subjectivity in the composer's work. But at an even more fundamental level (apart from the complexity of the composer's discourse), the conductor, at least from Barenboim's perspective, is left to interpret the elements of musicality in the composer's score, such as tonality, tempo, spacing—as well as changes in these qualities and how (im)perceptible those changes may be to the ear.

Rhetorically, such an endeavor could be understood simply as "the interpretation of data." Perelman and Olbrechts-Tyetca suggest that a set of data can be interpreted in numerous ways (1969, 120–123). In the case of particular conductors, it would appear that one's ethnicity, life experiences, and sense of professional obligation could account for distinctive interpretations.

As the (October 10, 1998) dialogue focuses on the relationship between the conductor (as speaker through interpretation) to the audience, concern surfaces about the authenticity of the conductor's voice with respect to expectations. Specifically, Edward Said asks Conductor Barenboim, "To what extent do you, as a performer, pay attention to the audience, in the sense that you're trying to address them?" (Barenboim and Said 2002, 76) Barenboim responds:

> The day you decide to become a conductor, you have to do away with the natural instinct to want to be liked. The minute you have something individual to say, by definition, it will strike consonance in some and dissonance in others. I think that only mediocrity gets an uncontroversial reaction. And controversial has become almost a swear word in today's world, you know, "He's controversial." (2002, 77)

From a rhetorical standpoint, both the question and the answer relate squarely to fundamentals in the *framework* of argumentation; indeed, Barenboim's claim that, as a conductor, he has "something individual to say" attests that his statements qualify as "argumentation" as distinct from less provocative "demonstrations" that allow members of the audience to make what they will of his expressions (see TNR 1969, 13–14). Instead, Barenboim's work constitutes "argumentation [that] aims at gaining adherence of minds, and, by the very fact, assumes the existence of an intellectual contact" (14). But the conductor's response raises more sensitive questions that are central to the framework of argumentation, namely: How does the conductor as a speaker construct her or his notion of "the audience?" (19–23) And how (if at all) does the speaker adapt to that audience? (23–26)

First Barenboim's conception of audience characterizes people who are drawn in by the accessibility of music (relative to other artistic forms) but who have limited capacity to understand it (2002, 24). Thus, he strives to orchestrate the artistic passions of musicians to lead the audience through a discovery process that will awaken people by appealing to their innate curiosities. That discovery experience, according to the conductor, involves telling audiences stories, and often those stories emphasize the fluidity of life and actions. He tells his friend Edward Said, "I believe in the fluidity of life. I believe in the fluidity of thought. We go through periods where we need to feed ourselves through the creation of others. And then there are periods where one has the need to isolate oneself from that. This way to process is the paradoxical fluctuation (2002, 72–73). The audience of Barenboim's construction would be willing to negotiate fluidity and fluctuation along with him.

Second, as the quote above suggests, Barenboim generally resists inclinations to "adjust to the audience," but acknowledges that on occasion the paradoxical nature of musical performance requires him to do so. In stressing the importance of courage in authentic conducting, Barenboim (as does Said) distinguishes the artist from the politician: "What is the difference between a politician and an artist? A politician can only do good if he masters the art of compromise . . . whereas the artist's expression is only determined by his total refusal to compromise in anything— the element of courage" (2002, 60). But he is aware that audiences expect imitation of what they have heard before; he responds to Said, "[S]ome way you vacillate between imitation . . . and the anxiety of influence you mentioned. Basically you vacillate between the two poles. What you are saying is the very nature of paradox, isn't it?" (67–68)

As a teaching maestro, Barenboim speaks to his audience in ways that stress the fluidity, transitional quality, and becomingness of music to be conducted years, decades, or centuries after it was composed. As for becomingness, Barenboim refers to Wilhelm Furtwängler, a 1920s German conductor he admired as a youth and still seeks to emulate: "Furtwängler understood the music philosophically, he understood that music is not about statements or about being. It's about becoming. It's not the statement or the phrase that is really important, but how you get there and how you leave it and how you make the transition to the next phase" (2002, 21). In terms of rhetorical strategy, such education depends upon demonstrating the incompatibility between the (expectation of a) formal, programmed statement and the organic spontaneity of the performance as discovery of meaning (see TNR 1969, 193–197). Discovery is not at the conductor's command, as Barenboim suggests here: "Sound is ephemeral. It goes by. One of the reasons sound is so expressive is that it's not here at your beck and call. You can't draw the curtain and see it again like a painting or open it like a book" (Barenboim and Said 2002, 23).

The Agonist and the Taboo

The speaker of the Israeli Knesset refused to take part in a ceremony that bestowed that nation's prestigious Wolf Prize on Daniel Barenboim on May 9, 2004. An arts columnist for the *Jerusalem Post* reports, "Speaker Reuven Rivlin refused to take part, having been 'personally offended as a Jew by Barenboim's provocative act' at the 2001 Israel Festival" (Fonseca-Wollheim 2004). The conductor's "provocative act" entailed his performance of Richard Wagner's *Prelude to Tristan and Isolde*, an event precipitating wide debate in Israel and elsewhere concerning the propriety of performing the works of this anti-Semitic, German composer to "a country of Holocaust survivors." Although apologetic to those offended, Barenboim largely attributed the debate to agendas intent on politicizing the Holocaust (Fonseca-Wollheim 2004).

Barenboim's attraction was to Wagner the *interpreter of music*, not to Wagner the *man*, as this dialogue with his friend Edward Said clearly points out:

> *DB*: Well, I think it's obvious that Wagner's anti-Semitic views and writings are monstrous. There's no way around that. And I must say that if I, in a naïvely sentimental way, try to think which of the great composers of the past I would love to spend twenty-four hours with if I could, Wagner does not come to mind . . .

> *ES*: You wouldn't invite him to dinner.

> *DB*: Wagner? I might invite him to dinner for study purposes, but not for enjoyment.

> *ES*: Put a glass wall between you.

> *DB*: But in other words, the person, Wagner, is absolutely appalling, despicable, and, in a way, very difficult to put together with the music he wrote, which so often has exactly the opposite kind of feelings. (2002, 97–98)

So what is it about Wagner's musical expression that compels Daniel Barenboim, a conductor from the Jewish faith, to confront the scorn of Jewish audiences for performing the works of this "appalling, despicable" composer? This is precisely the question that animates Said's and Barenboim's conversation before a Columbia University audience on October 7, 1995. In essence, Barenboim speaks to the "thick" gravitas (not his terms) of Wagner's musical personality that stands out in reaction to the superficiality of earlier composers. For example, with respect to Wagner's continually changing meter, Barenboim relates that "what Wagner really maintains is that unless you have the ability to guide the music in [a contextually deep] way, you are not able to express all that is in it, and therefore you remain on the surface. He was diametrically opposed to a metronomic way of interpreting music" (2002, 81).

Put another way, Wagner's statements *expand* rather than *reduce* the art, not only in breaking from the order and stability of conventional forms but also in infusing political context into it. Wagner's discourse, in rhetorical terms, changes the "argument" of musicality by moving the locus (or value orientation) from attention to meter as a quantifiable issue to a locus on quality that focuses on "uniqueness" and "concrete values" (TNR 1969, 89). Barenboim discusses several interpretive techniques that Wagner used to weave uniqueness into his contextual expression— changing tempos in a imperceptible manner in a way that emphasizes the "continuity of sound" (2002, 83), adding "color" and "weight" to harmonies, and exploiting acoustics that venues offer. Barenboim's attention to a venue directs conversation to the provocative topic of Bayreuth, Wagner's orchestra pit that drew visitors from the Third Reich, including Hitler himself.

Yet beyond the technical issues of meter, harmony, and acoustics, Barenboim refers to the "pure intuition and feeling" within Wagner's music inherent in what the conductor describes as the "monumentality" of Wagner's music—"something bombastic, loud, uncouth, not very refined or subtle, in the colors and in the balance" of expression. This monumentality becomes provocative in supporting Wagner's narratives or stories that can be complex and tragic within the bounds of German culture and political regimes. In this regard, Barenboim recalls the skills of his mentor Wilhelm Furtwängler in capturing the essence of Wagner's narratives, such as in Wagner's *Die Meistersinger*:

I think that Furtwängler was an artist who had a great understanding of the tragic element of music—I mean tragic in the mythological sense, i.e., you must journey to hell before you can achieve catharsis, the climax, or whatever you're looking for. There was in Furtwängler's work an ever-present search for ground or the underground, a sort of archeological expedition. (2002, 84)

Nonetheless, Barenboim's explanations for his fascination of the color, acoustics, and monumentality in Wagner's music appear not to resolve perplexity about why a Jewish conductor focuses on the works of such a clearly anti-Semitic composer. Several attendees in the audience of Said's and Barenboim's conversation on Wagner's work on October 7, 1995, raised questions that pressed the conductor further for clarification on this issue, including these three:

Q: [After your father forbade you to play for the Berlin Philharmonic at Furtwängler's invitation], [w]as there a moment for you, obviously with the passage of time, the change in the creation of a democratic government in Germany after the war, where you were able to make that step [perform Wagner]? Was it a clear moment or was it simply something that happened? (2002, 105)

DB: I . . . became more acquainted with certain aspects of Israeli thought in relation to Germany and Austria and a lot of details, which I found not really thought-out, like for instance the fact that there were diplomatic relations established between Israel and Austria very early on, and not with Germany. I don't think Austria was any milder in its way of looking at Jewish extermination. . . . And from that I made up my mind that I wanted to go and play in Germany and try and see how it felt. (105–106)

Q: [Although I am a great admirer of your musicianship], [h]owever your production of *Das Rheingold* . . . had the most appalling anti-Semitism in it that I have ever encountered. . . . I couldn't understand how a Jewish conductor could take part in such a production. (106)

DB: I can only tell you that if the violence of the action offended you, I'm sorry, and you have every right to have this kind of sentiment. The rest is your pure interpretation and imagination. . . . Never was there an intention to make a Jewish character out of [the opera's characters].

Therefore, I'm afraid I have to tell you this: it really says more about how you saw it rather than what it really was. (106–107)

Q: In the process of becoming the leading Jewish Wagnerite, conducting in Bayreuth, have you ever felt embittered, angry, or awkward? (108)

DB: Well, first of all, I don't consider myself a leading Wagnerite or the leading Jewish conductor or the leading anything, I don't really think of myself in those terms. . . . I think one has to be really very clear—and I think as a Jew I can say that—one has to be very clear how one deals with one's enemies and with the people who hate us and who have hated us over the centuries. You can either come to terms with them or you can continue to have no contact with them, but I'm not in favor of accepting only what is in our favor from them [reparations, automobile imports, etc.] and otherwise criticizing them and having nothing to do with them. (108–109)

Yet Barenboim had answered questions such as these previously in an indirect but convincing manner by articulating where he "feels at home." The book *Parallels and Paradoxes* begins with moderator Ara Guzelimian (Director and Artistic Advisor at Carnegie Hall) asking Barenboim and Said, "I want to begin by asking each of you: Where are you at home? Do you ever feel at home? Do you find yourself in perpetual motion?" (2002, 3) Barenboim responds:

Wherever I can play the piano—preferably with a reasonably good instrument—or wherever I travel with the orchestras that I lead, the Chicago Symphony Orchestra, and the Staatsoper from Berlin, I feel at home. I feel at home in a certain way in Jerusalem, but I think this is a little bit unreal, a poetic idea with which I grew up. . . . In the 1950s, Tel Avivians looked to Jerusalem for everything they couldn't find in their own city: spirituality, intellectual and cultural curiosity. Unfortunately, all those things seem to be disappearing now due to the lack of tolerance shown by some of the extreme populations in Jerusalem. (Guzelimian 2002, 47)

A student of Goethe and German culture, Edward Said expresses similar sentiments in telling Barenboim:

[Y]ou act as an interpreter, as an artist not concerned so much with the articulation of the self as with the articulation of other selves. That's a challenge. The interesting thing about Goethe . . . is that art, for Goethe especially, was all about a voyage to the other and not a concentration on oneself, which is very much a minority view today. (Barenboim and Said 2002, 48–49)

Said continues suggesting that quarrels over what American society *is* and *is not* trouble him greatly as departures from the "deeply attractive aspects of America" as a "society in a continual state of flux." He adds:

It seems to me, therefore, that places like the university and the orchestra—those places in the arts and sciences where one's life is given over to an ideal—should be places of exploration rather than of simple affirmation and consolidation, which are really not at all, in my opinion, in conformity with the history of this society and this country. (2002, 49)

But to Guzelimian's original question, Barenboim's concluding statement speaks for his friend Edward Said as well. After commenting upon how he has found himself displaced in the music of Wagner, Stravinsky, and Beethoven, the conductor concludes:

If you have a sense of belonging—this feeling of home, harmonically speaking—and if you're able to establish this as a composer, and as a musician, then you will always get this feeling of being in no-man's-land, of being displaced, yet always finding a way home. Music provides the possibility, on the one hand, to escape from life and, on the other hand, to understand it much better than in any other disciplines. Music says, "Excuse me, this is human life." (2002, 56)

These exchanges suggest that, in response to Guzelimian's query as to *where is home*, both Barenboim and Said break the link between the notion of "home" and some geographic or cultural "place." Instead, they find "home" in ideals, and in venues that support those ideals (e.g., orchestras and universities), which enable them to sojourn outside of themselves, into other selves, and then back home. Clearly Barenboim and his friend speak authentically about what grounds them, rather than about strategy in pursuit of agendas. The musical home for Daniel Barenboim is within ideas and discovery rather than in geographical space or one's own culture. As Said suggests, the contemporary audience finds such a home in music difficult to comprehend.

Steward of Inter-Cultural Performance

In response to Edward Said's complaints about the troubling aspects of American society (discussed above), Daniel Barenboim asks his friend, "How can you explain that, on one hand, globalization makes everything the same . . . yet political conflicts and national politics are deeper and between smaller units than ever before. Why is that?" (Guzelimian 2002, 49–50) Said responds:

> Well, there are two reasons. The first is the reaction *against* global homogenization. . . . Second is the legacy of empires. In the case of the British, whenever they were forced to leave a place, they divided it up. It happened in India. It happened in Palestine. It happened in Cypress. It happened in Ireland. The idea of *partition* as a quick way of solving the problem of multiple nationalities. It's like someone telling you, "OK, the way to learn a musical piece is to divide it into tinier and tinier units." (50; italics in original)

Said's comments about political partitioning take on particular salience historically in Germany during the 1930s; during this period Jewish artists were forcibly partitioned to pursue exclusively Jewish works of art before exclusively Jewish audiences. In *The Inextinguishable Symphony*, a prominent commentator on classical music relates the sensitive story of his parents' experiences as performers in the "Kubu," the *Kulturbund Deutscher Juden* (Cultural Federation of German Jews) formed in 1933; two years later, the government mandated a change of name to the more derisive title *Jüdischer Kulturbund*, i.e., Jewish Cultural Federation (Goldsmith 2000, 51–67).

Four months before the Kubu organized (and a few days after Adolph Hitler became chancellor of Germany), the Jewish conductor Otto Klemperer, a distinguished figure of operatic performance in Germany, came under fire for performing of Wagner's *Tannhäuser* at the Berlin Staatsoper (State Opera). Goldsmith relates,

> The performance of *Tannhäuser* was attacked the next day by critics seeking to curry favor with the new chancellor, who was known to

venerate Wagner and whose close associate Joseph Goebbels had already declared, "the Jew does not understand Wagner's music." Reviewers called the new production an affront to the memory of the great composer and demanded the dismissal of those responsible for this "bastardization." (2000, 41)

In July 1933, the organizer of the Kubu submitted a "letter of understanding" to Hans Hinkel, Goebbel's assistant with official authority over Jewish culture, which proposed rules for partitioning musical expression by Jews from German society:

1. Members [of the Kubu] must be Jewish, and only Jews will be allowed to attend performances.
2. No single-performance tickets may be purchased at the box-office; admission to all event shall be via season subscription.
3. The programs must be approved by the Prussian Theater Commission or a government office named by the Commission at least one month in advance.
4. Each member of the Kulturbund pays the same monthly subscription rate, and no extra charges will be raised for individual events.
5. No advertisements or announcements of Kulturbund activities are to be allowed in the general press. They shall be restricted to Jewish newspapers only. (Goldsmith 2000, 57)

Hinkel approved this proposal, and Jewish musical experience in Germany was so partitioned.

Criticisms of Daniel Barenboim's work that brings Wagner's music to contemporary Jewish audiences take on particular irony in the historical context of the Kubu's partition. Certainly not one who partitions or divides people, Barenboim serves as a conductor and educator who uses music to integrate cultural experiences. In partnership with Edward Said, Barenboim founded the West-Eastern Divan Orchestra in 1999 for youths from Israel and other nations in the Middle East from Palestinian, Jordanian, Lebanese, Egyptian, Syrian, and Iranian backgrounds. The orchestra takes its name (*divan* means "the other") from an anthology of poetry by Goethe, whose work Said pursued through his career; it represents hope for eventual peace between Israel and Palestine. Barenboim says this about the youth orchestra, currently based in Seville, Spain:

The Divan is not a love story, and it is not a peace story. It has very flatteringly been described as a project for peace. It isn't. It's not going to bring peace, whether you play well or not so well. The Divan was conceived as a project against ignorance. I'm not trying to convert the Arab members of the Divan to the Israeli point of view, and I am not trying to convince the Israelis to the Arab point of view. . . . But I want to—and unfortunately I am alone in this now that Edward died a few years ago—and I'm trying to create a platform where the two sides can disagree and not resort to knives. (Vulliamy 2008)

The West-Eastern Divan Orchestra offers opportunities for musical training and performance; however, it also serves as a venue for discourse about the troubled Middle East wherein young people engage in deliberation as speakers and audiences. Barenboim connects performance skill with deliberative ability in this way: " Great music is the result of concentrated listening—every musician listening intently to the voice of the composer and to each other. Harmony in personal or international relations can also only exist by listening, each party opening its ears to the other's narrative or point of view" (Naumann n.d., 2). It follows then that, through their associations with peers, young orchestra members confront a basic element of effective argumentation, negotiating "the contact of minds" (TNR 1969, 14–17).

So in large part, active listening to someone else involves self-deliberation, the discourse of oneself as speaker and audience. Reactions from orchestra members about their inter-personal relationships with peers reflect self-deliberation; a flutist from Israel comments, "We try to go to the extremes in dialogue, we try to go to new places in our imagination, and this project creates a platform for us to do so" (Naumann n.d., 6). Verbalizing a similar view, a cellist from Lebanon explains,

> With my personal background, I had a long way to go to achieve moderation. My most deep-seated feelings and bitter memories fight a constant war with my rational thoughts. As we drove through the Israeli checkpoints to the concert in Ramallah, to make music with Israelis for the common goal of freedom in Palestine—that was just too much. I couldn't even process all my feelings at the time. (6)

This musician's comments about situating "deep-seated feelings" into specific contexts suggest that experience in the orchestra precipitates reasoning that moderates thinking in abstractions and absolutes to allow for the specifics of concrete circumstances.

A Lebanese violinist makes this statement: "It's something important that people need to understand—we are not always in the mentality that I am Palestinian or Israeli or Lebanese, and that this is what I have to represent all the time. Sometimes, I am just me—a human being" (Naumann n.d., 6). The violinist from Lebanon observes, "We can't change the world with a few notes—not in Korea, not in the Middle East. But it's super-exciting—we can't be more than a symbol, and yet that's already a lot" (Naumann n.d., 6).

Most recently, Daniel Barenboim has championed a new project in conjunction with the youth orchestra—to establish the Barenboim-Said Academy in Berlin—that will combine music training with a liberal arts education for up to a hundred students. The Academy will also include a 700-seat concert hall. Scheduled to open in 2015, the Academy is built upon what was previously the weapons depot in the Staatsoper. The Federal Government of Germany has contributed more than 50 percent of the Euro 35 million needed for construction. When asked "Why are you founding your Academy in Germany rather than somewhere in the Middle East," Barenboim responded that Berlin is now regarded as "the music capital of the world" and the instability in the Middle East precludes locating the Academy there. Then his explanation shifts to his aspirations for the Academy, which in turn suggest that location may be a secondary issue:

> Perhaps you can think of the Academy as an unusual, even an unheard of attempt to support a political development by means of music. The goal of this political development is mutual understanding. Music is a universal language, and the word "enemy" is not in its vocabulary. You see, I played in Ramallah for the first time for 200 Palestinian children, a girl came up to me, and I asked her, "Are you happy I'm here?" I'll never forget her answer, "Yes, really happy. You are the first thing I've ever seen from Israel that wasn't a soldier or a tank." That's the way it was—she couldn't imagine Israelis as anything but uniformed objects, "things" or military vehicles. (Naumann, n.d., 10)

For Barenboim, inter-cultural performance, dialogue, and learning leads to international harmony.

Presumably, the contrast between Daniel Barenboim "the harmonizer" and Sheriff Joe Arpaio (discussed next)—an entrepreneur who capitalizes politically through his tough treatment of undocumented Latinos—is stark, to say the least. For both rhetors, life's work revolves around perceptions of the world either as it *is* or *should be*. Barenboim offers an example of a consummate professional who is intentional in incorporating human rights advocacy into creative work. Sheriff Arpaio appears to approach moral work through a forensic rhetoric that typically distinguishes between those who are "worthy" and others who are not.

JOE ARPAIO, THE ENTREPRENEURIAL RHETOR

Joe Arpaio, perhaps the best-known county sheriff in the United States, has served as Sheriff of Maricopa County (that includes greater Phoenix, Arizona) since 1992. As a controversial and divisive figure, Arpaio self-identifies as a tough-talking, abrasive law enforcer and as an author (with the help of co-writers) of books entitled *America's Toughest Sheriff: How We Can Win the War against Crime* (1996) and *Joe's Law: America's Toughest Sheriff Takes on Illegal Integration, Drugs, and Everything Else That Threatens America* (2008). The provocative persona that Arpaio projects, along with the shrill resonance of his ideas, afford him top billing in the broadcast media as a sought-after news personality. In fact, he was the focus of three episodes of the Fox-TV reality show *Smile . . . You're Under Arrest* in 2008 and 2009.

No doubt for some, Joe Arpaio's rhetoric is merely that of a repressive bully who draws upon his popularity to abuse power, often at the expense of vulnerable minorities such as undocumented Hispanics. Whether or not this is the case, Arpaio's opportunities for provocative advocacy arise as a multitude of discourses (such as American patriotism, federal governance, victimization, and ethical obligation, among others) converge—or in some cases, collide. Those advocacy opportunities in fact abound within the unique institutional structure of American governance, the office of county sheriff, that offers sheriffs such as Arpaio considerable autonomy in comparison with most public officials. This sketch comprises the following discussions: "Self-Reflection in 'the Institution of One,'" "The 'Institution of One' as Norms Entrepreneur," and "A Local Pragmatist amid Constructed Abstractions."

Self-Identity in the "Institution of One"

Generally, self-reflection associates with virtue in evaluating one's personal life or, if engaged in public service, in one's professional obligations to the community and its institutions. Thus, it is understandable that Sheriff Joe Arpaio engages in a discourse of self-evaluation in his reference to "Operation Intercept," a Nixon-era federal program to stop the flow of illegal drugs over the US-Mexico border in *Joe's Law* (2008). Turning his attention from the merits of "Operation Intercept" to his overall perspective of Hispanic immigration, Arpaio reflects on his family's history as Italian immigrants as a point of reference—drawing upon six points of comparison that disparage Latino border movement (three of which appear below):

> Again, I must state that I have compassion for the people trying to cross the border in search of better lives. My parents came to this country from Italy. But they came legally, just like millions of others who left their homes to find new opportunities, new freedoms, and new futures. . . . [However,] My parents left Italy and basically never expected to return, unlike the illegal Mexican immigrants . . . [and] My parents came to America legally. That was the norm for our entire history. No other group except the Mexicans, and other Hispanics as well, has broken the immigration laws in such astonishing numbers. (2008, 45–46)

In most public service settings, one's personal narratives and ideological orientation are, or at least should be, restrained by the obligation to serve the *office*. In essence, the abstraction of "office" stands apart from, or above, the person who holds it (Dobel 1999, 8–11). In other words, the individual serves as a temporary trustee of that public office rather than as the *personification* of it. But the anachronistic institutional characteristics of the county sheriff in US governance affords incumbents particularly wide discretion, if not autonomy, which could in turn enable personal narratives to shape public policy. In most cases, the county sheriff serves as an *elected* administrator of a state constitutional office—in effect, "an institution of one"—wielding far more autonomy than his or her counterpart, an *appointed* police chief whose discretion is bounded within an administrative structure. Many trace the origin of the sheriff as an institution to the function of the rural "reeve" in medieval England (reminiscent of the Sheriff of Nottingham in the Robin Hood sagas) to "keep the peace" in the countryside.

This institutional narrative of antiquity and autonomy co-exists with more technical and scholarly discourses of complexity concerning the dynamics of governance in the US federal system. Where exactly county government "fits" in the intergovernmental system has persisted over the years as a puzzle for scholars of American federalism. In an edited book on county government published in the mid-1990s, two experts speak to the "changing role of counties in the intergovernmental system":

> Of all the units of government in the United States, few have experienced as much change as county governments. Generally, one finds a considerable strengthening of their authority, responsibilities, structure, and operation. Much of the impetus for change has come in response to pressures generated by increased urbanization and suburbanization and by the growth of regional problems. (Berman and Salant 1996, 19)

These scholars go on to highlight county officials' lack of influence in the federal system, particularly in response to the fiscal burdens that the US Congress and the state legislatures impose upon them as "mandates" whereby local jurisdictions are "mandated" to absorb the costs of new programs: "Counties have a long-standing image of passivity with regard to exercising authority—the good soldiers—unwilling to seek out new responsibilities and powers, challenge state authority, or even use the powers they have without clear expressions of state approval" (22). More recent assessments of intergovernmental problems essentially revisit the issue of local government influence, although in more contemporary contexts. For example, two intergovernmental system experts articulate fifteen "big questions" about intergovernmental relations, at least two of which relate to the issue of limited county influence:

- Should local governments have a more prominent seat at the intergovernmental table? [and]
- How has the "state" of state–local relations changed, and what actions might be taken to improve these relationships? (Kincaid and Stenberg 2011, 197; 200)

However in sharp contrast to the passivity of their colleagues in other county offices, sheriffs—although they too are affected by mandates and other fiscal constraints—appear bolder in invoking their own authorities and, in doing so, can draw upon any number of discourse narratives and argumentative strategies to bolster their institutional authority. As a case in point, a sheriff could build a narrative derived from what the "oath of office" means to him or her as a justification for policies and actions.

Furthermore, any *two* sheriffs could interpret that oath differently and in ways that rationalize divergent ideas about public service and law enforcement. For example, Joe Arpaio drew a clear comparison between his perspective on the "oath of office" and that of his friend and colleague Richard Mack, the former sheriff of Graham County (Arizona), as both appeared on *Freedom Watch*, a Fox Network television news program that was hosted (prior to its cancellation) by libertarian Andrew Napolitano (no relation for former governor Janet Napolitano), a former justice on the Arizona Supreme Court. As sheriff of a rural county east of Phoenix, Mack gained notoriety during his term in office by refusing to enforce gun laws that he believed to be unconstitutional. Understanding his oath as directed *only to the Constitution of the United States*, Mack founded the Constitutional Sheriffs and Peace Officers Association with a mission to "unite all public servants and sheriffs, to keep their word to uphold, defend, protect, preserve, and obey the Constitution of the United States of America" (CSPOA website). As evident in the introduction to his (self-published) book *The County Sheriff: America's Last Hope* (2009), Mack's interpretation of the oath as preserving individual freedom animates his call to (in)action against perceived usurpations of liberty:

> This book is written to and for every citizen, each police officer, every peace officer, and especially every sheriff in America; that all of us come to an understanding that the sheriff indeed has the authority, the power, and the duty to end "venal and oppressive government." The conclusion is thus unescapable; the *COUNTY SHERIFF* is our nation's *LAST LINE OF DEFENSE*, for the preservation and return to, fundamental and individual liberty. Sheriff, you are the people's **last hope**. . . . This principle is what makes the position of sheriff such a high and noble office. (2009, 2; italics, upper-case, and bold face in original)

The back cover of Mack's book includes Joe Arpaio's endorsement that concludes:

> This book should be read by every citizen, police officer, and especially each sheriff of these United States, that we may become united in our service to the American people and dedicated to the preservation of those precious freedoms that so many have fought and died for. To uphold and defend the US Constitution is our primary duty and our sworn responsibility.

Nonetheless, exchanges between the two sheriffs on Judge Napolitano's June 26, 2010, *Freedom Watch*—in the heat of national debate concerning Arizona's strict immigration statutes—revealed significant differences in their respective views on the oath of office with particular implications for the enforcement of immigration laws in Hispanic communities. Judge Napoalitano introduces Arpaio as "brutally tough on lawbreakers" and as one who considers illegal immigrants as "law-breakers"; by contrast, this television host characterizes Richard Mack as not at all clear as to the legal status of immigrants under the US Constitution.

To Napolitano's question of whether police should stop likely immigrants and demand them to produce documents of citizenship status, Richard Mack voiced his belief that laws or actions that involve random stops to "check papers" . . . "violate the Constitution and strike of Nazi Germany." Joe Arpaio replied to this question by stating that his officers ask for papers "only pursuant to our duties" in the course of other policing activities such as traffic violation stops—"when laws are passed, they need to be enforced, and that's what I do. . . . We have the right to ask—I don't see what the big deal is."

But while attempting to smooth over this difference with Arpaio, Mack makes an especially provocative statement:

> We are to never blindly enforce all laws that the legislature throws at us. If it violates the Constitution, I'm not going to enforce it. And we do have a moral responsibility to look at the Constitution or the constitutionality of every law that the legislature puts out. And this may have been a knee-jerk reaction and response to the ineptness of our federal government to address this [immigration] problem. *This is their problem.* [Italics added to reflect this speaker's emphatic inflection.]

Arpaio responds,

All this [immigration enforcement] has to do with politics; the Mexican government is doing nothing—I was director there for four years in Mexico City [with the US Drug Enforcement Administration]. *It's all politics.* But as far as I'm concerned, I took an oath of office to defend *all the laws*, all the laws Richard, and I'm doing it. If they don't like the laws, change [them]. [Italics added to reflect speaker's inflection.]

Short of "weighing in" on the relative merits of these two perspectives on oath of office, it is helpful here to trace how one influential scholar in the subfield of public ethics understands the significance of "oath of office" as it relates to moral obligation. For John Rohr, through their oath of office, public officials are obliged to adopt ethical norms derived from the salient values of the *regime* (or the polity); *regime values* then "refer to the values of that political entity that was brought into being by the ratification of the Constitution that created the present American republic . . . that can be discovered in the public law of the regime" (1989, 68).

Rohr's stipulations in reference to the Arpaio-Mack exchange appear to cut both ways. On one hand, his reference to "the public law of the regime" seems appropriately interpreted as an accumulation of (local, state, and federal) laws brought about both through constitutional processes and other policy-making activities that the Constitution endows— thus validating Arpaio's oath to *all the laws*. But Rohr goes on to say that "the oath of office provides the bureaucrat the basis of a moral community that our pluralism would otherwise prevent. It rescues pluralism from a downward plunge into an inharmonious mélange of ill-assorted fragmented and presents it anew as an ordered dialogue of interesting viewpoints (1989, 70). Thus, despite his narrow view of public law limited to (an originalist's view of) the US Constitution, Richard Mack reflects on his oath of office in a manner that prioritizes social well-being.

But from a rhetorical standpoint, the sheriffs' differences may reflect not so much on goals (or "ends") *per se* (Arpaio and Mack likely both value "personal liberty" in the abstract) but rather pit Mack's "end" of freedom against Arpaio's "means" as an instrumental enforcer of "all laws." If this is so, it follows that the latter's commitment to *all laws* assures his stance as a speaker with a multiplicity of audiences relating to a variety of laws and alternative implementation strategies (such as forcing all prisoners to wear pink underwear). By contrast, Mack's audience is generally limited to those who share his abstract and idealistic principles of constitutional governance that are far removed from the complexities of contemporary discourses on American federalism discussed above.

Sheriff Arpaio's disparaging comments about "politics" coupled with his instrumental narrative as an enforcer of "all laws" ("If they don't like the laws, change [them].") implies a perceived detachment from politics as a policy-neutral administrator. However, policy analysts recognize the subjective nature of rule implementation within communities. Focusing on how rules and laws actually work in the "polis" (or community), Deborah Stone first elaborates upon the give-and-take nature of rule-formulation in legislatures. But from there, she proceeds to characterize the political nature of rule implementation:

> Writing rules is just the beginning. No rule or set of rules, even the Constitution, is written once and for all. Rules acquire their meanings and their effects as they are applied, enforced, challenged, and revised. . . . In the polis, formal rules are enforced and observed according to informal *rules of thumb*. Officials charged with enforcing rules rarely follow through on all the violations they observe or mete out penalties exactly in accordance with the formal rules. Rather, they develop informal, perhaps only intuitive, guidelines about the seriousness and blameworthiness of violations, and seek to fit the punishment to the crime in a way that matches their own sense of justice. (1997, 298)

Certainly, the institutional character of the sheriff's office (as an "institution of one" described above) serves to insulate it from the "administrative politics" of resource competition and interference that affect other local agencies. Nonetheless, Arpaio's national stature—in large part embellished by his books, frequent broadcast media appearances, and voluminous press coverage—gives testimony to his ability to *influence opinion* as an advocate of particular institutional viewpoints and norms, especially when Arpaio finds himself in conflict with other public (often federal) authorities. This became especially apparent in March of 2014 when a federal district judge skewered the sheriff and his deputy for mischaracterizing and ridiculing his court order to stop profiling Latinos in training sessions. The deputy had called the court order "ludicrous and absurd—this tells you how ludicrous this crap is." Calling both back into court the judge asked them, "Do you believe you're in good-faith compliance with the order if in trainings you mischaracterize the order?" The deputy responded, "I'm ashamed of the things I said. I mischaracterized your order, there is no doubt about that. I had gotten some facts incorrect" (Santos 2014, A18).

The term *political entrepreneur*—used by some scholars to denote one who successfully accumulates political capital in public office as analogous to financial capital in private business (see Frant 1996)—appears to fit Arpaio well, even (and perhaps *especially* when scolded by a federal judge). Yet from a human rights perspective, there is reason for concern about how the influence of such an entrepreneur becomes manifested in rule-of-thumb law enforcement practices and the emergence of professional norms premised upon intuitive notions of "blameworthiness of violations" and by inference upon the (un)worthiness of certain people.

"THE INSTITUTION OF ONE" AS NORMS ENTREPRENEUR

From a rhetorical standpoint, political entrepreneurs profit by persuading their audiences about "reality," or "the way things really are" as opposed to how they appear or alternatively how they are in comparison to how others "misrepresent" them (see TNR 1969, 416–417). Such efforts become politically powerful to the extent they "call attention to issues or even 'create' issues by using language that names, interprets, and dramatizes them" (Finnemore and Sikkink 1998, 897). Policy analyst Deborah Stone maintains that calling attention to, or "creating," issues in the political realm typically enables speakers to "inform" their audiences as to the nature of "problems" that warrant rectification and/or policy "solutions" to alleviate them. Stone asserts that contemporary political activists (e.g., entrepreneurs) frequently rely upon narratives (or stories)—either existing stories that serve as frames of reference or new ones they can formulate—as effective means of persuasion. Specifically, she "introduces the concept of stories—good old-fashioned stories with heroes and villains and moments of triumph. Like speaking prose, we all know the language of stories, but it is so deeply embedded in our political discourse that we are usually unaware of its presence" (1997, 134–135). But for rhetoricians, persuasion through story-telling (or narration) is an age-old technique, one that calls attention to the speaker's liberty to select supportive story-lines (see Perelman and Olbrechts-Tyteca 1969, 116).

In examining the techniques of global advocacy, international relations experts key in on entrepreneurial skills to promote new norms (or shared ideas about appropriate standards of behavior) that presumably lead to better or more human societal outcomes (such as the curtailment of female genital cutting—see Easton, Monkman, and Miles 2003). In their work on "international norm dynamics and political change," Finnemore and Sikkink explain how "activists work hard to frame their issues in ways that make persuasive connections between existing norms and emergent norms" (1998, 901). Their observation that "new frames resonate with broader public understandings and are adopted as new ways of talking about and understanding issues" appears to reiterate the power of narratives (as the rhetoricians point out) and policy stories in moving audiences to consider new or revised grasps of appropriate behaviors for themselves or for the "other" (e.g., the Syrian asylum seeker in Lebanon or the undocumented Latino in Maricopa County, Arizona). Finnemore and Sikkink make a subtle distinction between *norms* and *institutions* in that norms constitute "single standards of behavior, whereas institutions emphasize the way in which behavioral rules are structured together and interrelate (a 'collection of practices and rules')" (891). Thus, nongovernmental organizations (NGOs), legislatures, and public agencies among other authoritative entities can be understood as collections of appropriate practices and behaviors.

So does Joe Arpaio qualify as a *norms entrepreneur* as well as a political entrepreneur? Clearly readers of his books encounter any number of accounts (narrations, stories) that anchor his professional opinions within his experiences; he is an accomplished story-teller to be sure. Beyond this, a strong case for Arpaio as a norms entrepreneur (or at least as a "norms revisionist" improvising further upon currently resonant political narratives) rests on an easily documented claim that a good number of his stories justify his judgments of *what people deserve*. His inmates, for example, *deserve* pink underwear, green bologna, and chain gangs because "criminals should never live better in jail than they do on the outside" (2008, 93). Sometimes this principle of unabashed un-deservedness flies in the face of federal regulations, as Arpaio relates:

We have been tough but we have been right over and over, despite all the obstacles and skeptics and the often vicious political dirty fighting, and we keep going, keep working, and keep moving forward. (Note: I would have cut off all television, but we discovered, to our general amazement, that there is a federal law on the books that *requires* cable TV in jails. So I put back the Disney Channel and the Weather Channel. I was ready when a reporter asked me why the Weather Channel. "So they will know how hot it's gonna be while they are working on my chain gang.") (2008, 99)

On the subject of hot weather during the Phoenix summers, Arpaio often compares the plights of his inmates coping with 135-degree temperatures in his jails with those of US soldiers in Iraq who have *broken no rules.*

As a norms entrepreneur, Sheriff Arpaio appears adept at (in Finnemore and Sikkink's terms) "calling attention to issues" in ways that capitalize upon existing narratives. Dishing up *what people deserve* embellishes upon a *narrative of worthiness* found prevalent among those in public service who directly interact with the public. In their penetrating study of "street-level bureaucrats" (those on the "frontlines of public agencies" such as "cops, teachers, and counselors"), Maynard-Moody and Musheno ask individuals who serve in each of these three capacities to offer verbatim stories of significant (that is, particularly threatening, risky, frustrating, or simply disgusting) events that shed light on the nature of their work. Subsequently, these researchers published *Cops, Teachers, Counselors* (2003) as a compendium of these self-told stories. Some of these stories reflect the worthiness narrative in response to the implicit question as to "who is worthy"—due special consideration—as distinct from the "unworthy" who should confront the full force of the law.

One such story "Watching the Prostitute from a Distance" is told by a police officer serving an urban area in the Midwest; he begins—

I ran into a prostitute named [Angela], and she's thirty-nine years old, she's a white female, and she has no teeth. And she's a chronic alcoholic, and not only that, she's pregnant. . . . I was watching her from a distance to see if she gets picked up for prostitution. She didn't get picked up, but she ended up going to a Circle K. While she was there, she decided she didn't like the shirt she was wearing and she was going to change it. She wasn't wearing a bra or anything . . . [so] I arrested her and brought her to jail [for indecent exposure], and I pretty

much talked her into blowing the Breathalyzer. She did and she blew a
.225, which is over twice the legal limit (2003, 77)

In his story-telling, the officer vents his frustration over his unsuccessful efforts to convince Angela to "do the right thing," admit herself into
an available pilot program to treat alcohol abuse. As the officer's story
unfolds, the reader is led to the inference that Angela is indeed among the
unworthy, not (or no longer) deserving of special consideration. Any
doubt about this is dashed further into the story; he relates that as he was
administering the test, Angela revealed that since learning of the pregnan-
cy "she was doing good because she was cutting down." The officer
admits, "That right there caused me a lot of problems, especially because
I have a seven-month-old baby. That just really bothers me. My wife
didn't touch a single sip of alcohol, didn't take medications or anything,
just because she didn't want any possible thing wrong with the baby"
(78).

This particular story is especially revealing in the way it compares the
narrative of (un)worthiness to self-identity (i.e., the story-teller as a father
of a newborn and husband to an expectant mother who observed all
precautions). This comparison is similar to the assertion that undocumented Mexicans are unworthy, especially in reference to Sheriff Arpaio's family members who *legally* emigrated from Italy. In *Cops, Teachers, Counselors*, Maynard-Moody and Musheno distinguish the roles of
their story-telling front-line bureaucrats from their bosses (or "state
agents") whose official policy-making function might lead them to dis-
courage or sanction the unusual or bizarre accounts of "service delivery"
in these stories. By contrast, Joe Arpaio, a top-administrator or "state-
agent" in himself, leads by story-telling example.

Yet beyond discourses of worthiness, Joe Arpaio capitalizes as well on
the *Latino threat narrative* that Leo Chavez explains in his book *The
Latino Threat* (2008). Chavez's initial paragraph in his introduction sets
the tone of this powerful narrative that has persisted in the US over recent
decades:

On March 24, 2009, Pat Buchanan stated on MSNBC: "Mexico is the
greatest foreign policy crisis I think America faces in the next 20, 30
years. Who is going to care, 30 years from now whether a Sunni or a
Shia is in Baghdad or who's ruling in Kabul? We're going to have 135
million Hispanics in the United States by 2050, heavily concentrated

in the Southwest. The question is whether we're going to survive as a country." Buchanan's apocalyptic pronouncement went beyond immigrants to warn about the threat posed by their children and subsequent generations (2).

Central to Chavez's thesis is a contention that runs parallel to Finnemore and Sikkink's explanation of *norms development*—that ideas about "Latinos as threats" and "illegal aliens" are *socially constructed*, often molded by enterprising norms entrepreneurs. Chavez punctuates his discussion of how the Latino threat narrative was developed in the late twentieth century with front-page images of well-respected US periodicals with disparaging captions that contribute to the myths about Hispanics under construction: "OUR ILLEGAL ALIEN PROBLEM" (*American Legion Magazine*, December 1974); "WELCOME TO AMEXICA" (*Time* special edition, June 11, 2001); and "HISPANIC NATION: Hispanics are an immigrant group like no other. Their huge numbers are changing old ideas about assimilation. Is America ready?" (*Business Week*, March 15, 2004).

The media are centrally complicit in the construction of the Latino threat narrative, according to Chavez, in creating *spectacles* relating to "events or public performances that receive an inordinate volume of media attention and public opinion" (2008, 8). Yet it follows that individuals involved in such events who command media attention are complicit as well in the narrative's development. Chavez identifies how media coverage of a particular event in the *Los Angeles Times* that breathes conspiracy to re-conquer parts of the US Southwest into the Latino threat narrative:

In May 2012, the US Justice Department sued Sheriff Joe Arpaio . . . for "racially profiling Latinos, abusing them in his jails and retaliating against his critics." These alleged unconstitutional behaviors on Sheriff Arpaio's part were directed toward Latino citizens and immigrants alike, Arpaio has achieved a level of notoriety rarely bestowed on a county sheriff . . . [Referring to the distinction between his "legal" Italian relatives and illegal Mexicans, Arpaio is quoted]: Latinos are "[a] growing movement among not only Mexican nationals but also Mexican-Americans [who] contend that the United States stole the territory that is now California, Arizona, and Texas . . . [and their massive immigration] will guarantee the *reconquista* of these lands,

returning them to Mexico (Chavez 2008, 44, quoting Serrano and Castellanos 2012, A14, and Arpaio 2008, 48)

Thus, Joe Arpaio multi-tasks in contributing to the Latino threat narrative: in engaging in provocative professional behaviors, in (so doing)
setting the stage for media spectacles, and in lecturing on the "real"
motives of Latino people—in essence, a vertically integrated norms entrepreneur.

A Local Pragmatist amid Constructed Abstractions

Argumentation needs to start somewhere, and for Richard Mack—Sheriff
Arpaio's friend and colleague—a sheriff's *oath to the Constitution* (as
discussed above) serves as the starting (and perhaps ending) point that
secures his argument that the *county sheriff* [is] *America's last hope*. The
seeming grandiosity and romanticism of this title, which permeate
through his short book, depend more heavily on abstractions than on
concrete circumstances. From such a vantage point, the extensive governance discourses about the (concrete) problems of twentieth- and now
twenty-first centuries about inter-governmental and inter-agency relationships in the American federal system are of little interest. In fact, the
abstract assertion of *the Constitution* can serve as the sheriff's guide to
the moral high ground leads to a subsequent abstraction that most other
public officials and agencies (particularly those at other levels of governments—most notably, the Internal Revenue Service) are actually the "real
criminals" who usurp people's freedom (Mack 2009, 27–29).

Perelman and Olbrechts-Tyteca suggest that, in analyzing argumentation, it is helpful to understand "abstraction" and "concreteness" not as
mutually exclusive but as complementary, since most speakers rely on
both to greater and lesser extents (1969, 77). As compared with Richard
Mack, who frequently reasons in idealistic abstractions, Sheriff Arpaio
appears more inclined to dwell on concrete situations—although in some
cases, concrete circumstances attributed to abstractions of failure on
someone else's part, such as federal immigration officials who "don't do
their jobs." Thus, assertion of the "failure abstraction" justifies the utility
of taking matters into one's own hands to rectify a concrete situation.

It would be understandable if most of Arpaio's readers regard the
sheriff as the quintessential pragmatist and as one who deals with the hard

realities of concrete situations. Chapter titles such as "How to Start Your Own Posse" (1996, 121–144); "More Ways to Take on Immigration, from the Posse to ICE" (2008, 41–68); and "Thinking outside the Box" (2008, 87–110) appear to characterize a pragmatic utilitarian whose defense of ethically-suspect utility (that is, the position that ends justify means) find vindication in the concrete realities of local law enforcement.

But can "pragmatism" be framed as an *abstraction in itself* in ways that offer speakers prerogatives in how they define "concrete reality" and/ or particular "values" that justify recourses (whether *actually* pragmatic or not)? Perelman and Olbrechts-Tyteca suggest this is possible in two of their commentaries in *The New Rhetoric*. First, in their discussion of "the pragmatic argument," they argue *both* that means can be justified by good consequences and that those consequences reinforce the truth of the abstract value pursued (1969, 268). Second, they call attention to the strategy of "dissociative definitions" whereby "[d]issociation is an instrument of quasi-logical argumentation. It is also an instrument of the dissociation of contexts, more especially whenever it claims to furnish the real true meaning of the concept as opposed to its customary or apparent usage" (1969, 444). Thus, discourses could introduce new and different definitions for either "concrete realities" or for what is "valued" in ways that elicit emotive support from audiences in the "pragmatic nature" (an abstraction) of the problem.

In one of his especially poignant narratives, Sheriff Arpaio defines "concrete reality" in a way that justifies using women chain gangs in a way that promotes the "value of self-reflection" among these (otherwise unworthy) women:

I inaugurated a male chain gang, followed by the world's first female chain gang. . . . The female chain gang, fifteen in all, assembled at six in the morning. Padlocked together at the ankle, they are driven by van to a county cemetery, a modern potter's field. . . . A priest is waiting. So are the caskets, ordinarily more than one, containing the corpses of those who . . . [are] unknown and unmourned. Smaller coffins hold the bodies of children or babies. Some of the women, particularly those who are mothers themselves, cry as the priest offers a prayer and the unadorned casket is lowered into the ground. . . . If burying a forgotten infant abandoned by its mother, bereft of love, does not compel a person to take stock of one's own path, then I cannot imagine what would. (2008, 96–97)

By contrast, another of Arpaio's discourses extols (i.e., defines or reinforces) the value of "volunteerism" in the United States in order to justify enlisting the help of the posse to promote effective law enforcement given the "concrete reality" of inadequate resources:

> Volunteerism is a vital part of America's heritage, and we volunteer to help one another, to build and sometimes rebuild America. . . . I quickly determined that the resources available to me, in personnel and matériel, were inadequate to handle all of these issues and needs. I had to call upon outside assets and assistance, and I turned to a tried-and-true answer: the posse. (2008, 112–113)

Are these arguments reflective of a "can do" pragmatist at work, a skilled rhetorician who works through the motif of abstract pragmatism to justify his actions, or a bit of both?

In summary, there are compelling reasons to characterize Sheriff Joe Arpaio as an exemplary advocate, notwithstanding the substance of his advocacy discourses, who operates within the institutional framework of local government with extremely wide discretion. In reference to the archaic institution of county sheriff (as discussed above), Arpaio offers a revealing comment:

> It's almost embarrassing to admit, but when I first ran for office, I stated that the sheriff should be an appointed, not elected, position. It didn't take a month in office before I realized that that might be the stupidest thing I've ever said because it wouldn't have taken a month for my boss . . . to fire me and get rid of a headache before it pounded away and his undoubtedly grander plans and ambitions. . . . I answer directly not to one boss but to 4 million bosses. (2008, 99–100)

That said, the case is made herein that Joe Arpaio's public presence as sheriff can be described as an "institution of one" (rather than of four million) that provides a platform for his efforts as a political entrepreneur capable of developing norms—particularly those affecting human rights.

The final sketch focuses on Lucius Banda, a vocal artist in the African nation of Malawi who legitimized popular music to promote political awareness among the poor. This discussion parallels that of Daniel Barenboim; both use art to foster understanding by encouraging their audiences to come to terms with difficult histories to promote better futures.

LUCIUS BANDA, SINGER AND "SOLDIER FOR THE POOR" IN MALAWI

Through his vocation as a vocal artist and composer of popular music, Lucius Banda has ascended as an icon in Malawi through his protests of social injustice. An especially impoverished, landlocked nation in Sub-Saharan Africa, Malawi has a population of 15 million, just exceeding that of Illinois; 39 percent of that population (in 2011) lives below the national poverty line. Many of the poor depend upon subsistence agriculture in rural areas. In terms of its physical features, Malawi is shaped as a "finger" of about 500 miles (with a 365 mile border along Lake Malawi to the east), but its width (at the most distant points) is less than 100 miles.

As for its governance, Malawi emerged from British colonial rule in 1963 as an independent nation. The first of Malawi's five presidents, Hastings Kamuzu Banda (no relation to Lucius Banda or the fourth president, Joyce Banda—first or middle names are used here to avoid confusion) situated himself constitutionally in a one-party system as "president for life" until a 1993 constitutional referendum provided for open election processes. Early in his singing career, Lucius directed his protests in song toward Kamuzu's dictatorial regime. Of the five presidents, only one (Joyce Banda) has demonstrably supported human rights and other democratic reforms. However, she assumed office as vice president following the death of Bingu Mutherika (known for his abusive domestic policies) in 2012 but was defeated by Mutherika's brother Peter in the 2014 national election.

For the past three decades, Lucius Banda's efforts to institute popular music as a medium of political dialogue and protest for the masses in Malawian society have contended with government measures censoring his material and banning his performances. This sketch includes the following discussions: "Singer Protesting 'Babylon,'" "Singer Protesting More of the Same," and "Singer Participating from the Inside Out."

Singer Protesting "Babylon"

"Wounds," one of Lucius Banda's early songs, protests the stark political oppression under Kamuzu Banda, Malawi's first president, who was in power for some four decades, first as a top administrator (under British rule of the Nyasaland Protectorate) and then as president from 1964 to 1993. Kamuzu Banda spent much of his adult life in London as a practicing physician. After returning to the Protectorate in 1953, Kamuzu's role as leader of the newly created Malawi Congress Party (MCP) led to his six-month imprisonment during a state of emergency imposed by colonial authorities. That party apparatus subsequently placed Kamuzu in power indefinitely, as "president for life," in a one-party system.

For the most part Lucius's performative rhetoric against the Kamuzu Banda regime is sung retrospectively given the personal danger confronted by those who expressed dissent. Lucius relies on a biblical reference to "Babylon" as a metaphor for the repression of the first president's regime. English literature scholar Reuben Chirambo explains:

> Lucius Banda evokes Babylon to allude to the Israelites' experience of captivity in Babylon in the Bible. He uses it to define the oppressive political system in Malawi under Kamuzu Banda and the MCP. His song "Down Babylon" is dedicated "to all families that have lost their loved ones through this system (of Babylon)." In describing Banda's Malawi as Babylon, Lucius Banda views Malawians as the captives of a dictator (2002, 106).

Much of the civil repression endured under Kamuzu Banda's rule tied in with his call for "unity and solidarity." Citizens were subjected to conservative dress codes (prohibiting slacks and shorts for women) and to bans against kissing in public (and censorship of movies showing it). On a broader scale, "unity and solidarity" justified Banda's initiative to establish Chichewa, a language widely spoken in Banda's home (Central) region as the nation's official language. Language scholar Gregory Kamwendo explains the situation:

> Unity and singularity were key values in the authoritarian regime of Kamuzu Banda: one party (Malawi Congress Party); one leader (Life President Kamuzu Banda); one language (Chichewa); and one nation (Malawi). . . . Recognizing that language is one of the key markers of ethno-linguistic identity, the Banda regime . . . began the process of developing and promoting Chichewa at the expense of other indigenous languages. (2002, 140)

Kamuzu's repressive rule over culture extended to control over music as well. Chirambo relates that under Babylon's rule, traditional music, as well as associated dancing, had been appropriated by the regime as a control mechanism and as a political strategy (2002, 103). Regarding the former, the regime's Malawi Broadcast Corporation (MCB) controlled all cultural programming on the nation's only radio station that broadcasted only traditional (as opposed to popular) music. In terms of the latter, Banda exploited dance (as a traditional art form) by calling upon women (including female civil servants) to engage in "praise dancing" on behalf of Kamuzu at political rallies and ceremonial events. A document on development progress in Malawi refers to gender exploitation associated with praise dancing:

> Women were used politically at three levels in the Banda period. They gave public expression to the personal aggrandisement of the president by the composition and public performance of praise-songs and dances. Every woman was compelled to participate as a sign of loyalty, putting on wraps and dresses with the president's face on them. . . . And they were pressured into providing sexual favours to party leaders and functionaries, particularly when they were centrally encamped for days during party functions. . . . One can point to several married women who have benefited their families in this way, either by keeping their husbands in prestigious jobs, or by obtaining business contracts to supply goods or services to the government. (Booth et al. 2006, 11)

Here dancers engage in performative rhetoric that confers legitimacy on political leaders; such symbolism is especially meaningful in matrilineal areas, for example the Central Region of Malawi.

It was amid this background of cultural repression that Lucius Banda introduced popular music as a means of expressing political protest. Chirambo explains that through his popular music, Lucius had the capacity to challenge the truth and legitimacy of the regime's voice, especially its stories about the poor. Subsequently, his songs connected with a wide range of political, social, and economic issues (2002, 104). After Kamuzu was deposed from power (through a successful 1993 referendum that established a multi-party system), Lucius released his noted song "Down Babylon," which castigated Kamuzu in lyrics of the forensic genre—in essence, an indictment put to music.

While the MCP and civil service connected with the regime were institutionally repressive, Kamuzu personally spearheaded acts of political repression that included (1) removing four cabinet ministers who proposed limiting his powers (known as the "Cabinet Crisis" of 1964), causing others to resign in protest, and (2) having three ministers (who supported a multi-party system) found dead at a "traffic accident" scene, even though all three had tent pins piercing their skulls (see Chirambo 2002, 206). Lucius sings about the spirits of those murdered in the staged accident in "Mizumu." He also decried Kamuzu's corrupt acts in extracting national funds that he allegedly deposited in his own personal bank accounts in Britain. Lucius's song "Mabala" speaks to these corrupt actions amid social injustice. Through his work Lucius Banda created space for open political dialogue in Malawian society, and in so doing he led the way for other artists to follow.

Banda's retrospection through the medium of popular music allows him to assume the critical functions both of (1) exposing historical events that account for heightened injustice and (2) evaluating the ethical implications of the injuries that politicians such as Kamuza have inflicted upon Malawian society. Chirambo comments:

> Lucius Banda dwells on the past for reasons that are obviously different from those of the politicians now in power. For Lucius Banda, talking about the past is a way of coming to terms with horrors that have not been fully explained or accounted for. He is trying to explain the little that he knows or has experience of. He relates to it as a victim as well as someone who has had the opportunity to recount such an experience on behalf of others. Also, he thinks revealing the past helps people to appreciate the present democratic dispensation so that no one takes it for granted. (2002, 109)

Singer Protesting More of the Same

Bakili Muluzi's rise to power as Malawi's second president must be understood in the context of mounting opposition to Kamuzu Banda in the early 1990s. An unholy coalition of businessmen (marginalized under Kamuzu) joined forces with silenced (in some cases, imprisoned) intellectual activists and prominent defectors from Banda's MCP (such as Muluzi himself). Ideologically diverse, the group coalesced around its opposition to the president-for-life. But as Danielle Resnick notes, strident opposition arose as well from outside the business and political ranks, specifically among church leaders and the international donor community in reaction to Banda's assaults on human rights. In response, Banda agreed to hold a constitutional referendum in 1993 to establish a multi-party system. That measure carried with strong support, and subsequently Muluzi was elected as the United Democratic Front (UDF) candidate (Resnick 2013).

If Kamuzu Banda typified a ruler whose power was based on autocratic patronage that demanded constituent payments, Bakili Muluzi exemplified a pluralist patrimonial leader who bestowed promises of access and future benefits. Malawian historian John Lwanda relates that even prior to Muluzi's election, the new United Democratic Front (UDF) Party had built a patronage system based on pluralism:

> By the Referendum in June 1993, the UDF and AFORD [the opposition party from the Northern Region] had become confident highly organised movements with horizontal and vertical networks of patronage. They were also able to attract defectors from, and lose members to, the MCP. The role of money in these shifts is important: the MCP paid defectors, while the opposition groups "promised money tomorrow." As the MCP stranglehold loosened, opposition movements attracted more MCP members with these promises—evidence of the lack of significant ideological differences between the parties. (2006, 536)

As Lwanda implies, Muluzi's UDF had, to a certain extent, dislodged Kamuzu's political autocracy, but it was more committed to dividing up the spoils of the treasury than including the masses of poor in the Malawian economy. Lwanda characterizes Muluzi as "the master political technician" whose previous experiences in the MCP leadership afforded him advantages over rivals within the UDF:

> By July 1995, like Banda before him, Muluzi had gained complete control of formal governmental, diplomatic and parastatal appointments, as well as the informal sugar distribution quotas. He was also well on his way to becoming Africa's "third-richest president" . . . in 2002, what Banda had owned in metaphor, Muluzi owned in reality by 2001. (2006, 539)

Thus Lucius Banda became disillusioned by the new regime's penchant for siphoning off resources to maintain its corrupt patronage system at the expense of (deteriorating) public institutions (particularly related to education and public security) and circumstances of the poor.

Rather than the economy improving for the poor under Muluzi, it significantly worsened. Lucius attributed this downturn to economic liberalization—that is, the demands that Western donor organizations place upon development aid. Among other adverse effects, the conditionalities devalue currency in ways that disadvantage farmers needing to buy exported fertilizer and public institutions having to purchase supplies (e.g., hospitals buying medicine). Lucius implicates these international organizations as contributors to Malawian poverty in his song "Take Over," which indicts the IMF and World Bank for exacerbating, rather than alleviating, poverty in Malawi.

But Muluzi and his associates had enough political savvy to beat these development organizations at their own "free market" games. Specifically, Lwanda illustrates how the Muluzi regime exploited an IMF/World Bank privatization program: "To maximise the ruling party elite's business interests, the Muluzi regime exploited the IMF/World Bank privatisation programme. The government allowed parastatals [government industries] to deteriorate through poor management and siphoning off of funds and then floated them for sale, with Muluzi and his associates the usual beneficiaries" (2002, 539–540).

Lucius's disappointment with the corruption and greed of the Muluzi regime led him to turn away from civilian politicians in general—even though he would later join their ranks (as discussed below). He expresses this contempt for Muluzi in the song "Njira Zawo."

As Chirambo points out, Lucius vents his frustrations in two songs mentioned above:

"Take Over" is a call to get rid of civilian politicians. He says, "Soldiers take over,/Rastas [Rastafarians] take over,/People take over." The suggestion for take over should be seen in the context of what he says about the army in "Cease Fire." There he claims that in Africa "men in black suits and red neckties (civilian politicians) have failed while savages in camouflages (soldiers) respect economic equality." Although he refers to soldiers as savages, they are viewed in a better light than civilian politicians. (2002, 113)

Noting that the army generals are as alienated by civilian politicians as he, Lucius broaches the prospect of a military government as perhaps the best hope for the economic futures of Malawi's unemployed and idle youth (113).

In broad strokes, Lucius Banda chronicles Malawi's history in songs that focus upon a continuing pattern of abusive national leadership. Nonetheless, he recognizes appeals to history as double-edged swords that regimes can brandish as a political tactic. For example, Chirambo points out that Muluzi appropriated history in such a way as to blame all of Malawi's problems on Kamuzu Banda's past failures:

> Such failures are blamed on the systems and traditions that the MCP left behind or what they did wrong. Also, to a large extent, members of the UDF government would like to exonerate themselves from the mistakes of the MCP. By insisting on the undemocratic behaviour of the MCP in the past, they are not only laying a claim to democracy, but legitimising themselves as champions of democracy. This is also instrumental to keeping the MCP away from the possibilities of coming back to power. The past atrocities are used to suggest that the MCP will never change. This assures the UDF of remaining in power. (2002, 109)

Yet Chirambo goes on to explain that Lucius primarily illustrates the past as prelude to a "new political dispensation" to usher in an ethos of social justice (109).

Singer Working from the Inside Out

Although his early protests through song have characterized Lucius Banda as a confrontational figure assailing ruling regimes from the outside, Lucius over the years has become collaborative in working *with* political leaders and *in* party and government positions. As Chirambo relates, Lucius appears to understand the dialectic of confrontation and collaboration as a strategy of advocating empowerment of the poor in democratic processes:

> As pragmatic action, Lucius Banda's music tries to promote awareness in the audience, particularly the masses, of the shared interests they have in preserving the unity of their country and fighting the forces of disunity, for example. Although some may see confrontation as an extreme mode of action, in a democracy it is useful for "enlisting

support for a political agenda, . . . for publicizing a political issue, for drawing citizens into active participation in public life, (and) for galvanizing action for specific action on specific issues," they are legitimate goals and reasonable means, which democratic societies provide for and uphold. (2002, 118, quoting Mattern 1998, 33)

Lucius's activism took a pragmatic turn in his 2006 election to the national Parliament as a candidate of the UDF, the party (founded by Muluzi and others) that he had castigated for its corrupt patronage system some fifteen years earlier. After assuming office, Lucius was convicted of falsifying his academic credential and subsequently imprisoned for several months. In fact Lucius assumed the role of UDF leader in 2014, when the incumbent accepted a cabinet position amid revelation of "Cashgate," a massive scandal wherein high-ranking public officials stole millions of US dollars from government coffers.

Lucius's notoriety as a performer fuels his overwhelming support from district constituents. He currently wields that political clout as a party leader to attack President Peter Mutharika (whose brother was in power when Lucius had been jailed) for restricting a new generation of artists for engaging in political protest. A newspaper journalist reports on Lucius's criticism of President Mutharika's state of the nation address as follows:

Renowned musician who is also Member of Parliament for Balaka North, Lucius Banda, has said that President Mutharika's address . . . lacked content to support local artists . . . "There was no mention of arts in the President's statement. Can Ministry of Finance please start subventing [copywriting] so that it can effectively fight piracy which is giving artists a nightmare," argued Banda. (Malawi24 [reporter] 2014)

In his 2014 campaign for re-election to Parliament, Lucius accounted for his overwhelming political support in this way: "I have lived here all my life. I came here some forty-four years ago, that is since I was born. I speak the language of my people and my people let me know who I am. That is my strength" (Tewesa 2014, 104).

CONCLUSION

As performing artists and rights activists, Daniel Barenboim and Lucius Banda speak to their audiences through music in different ways to pursue varying agendas. Barenboim, for example, regards opera and symphonic music as universal discourses that can soothe the wounds of historical oppression and cultivate intercultural dialogue between victims and perpetrators. The Maestro trusts that he can interpret the works of composers—especially those who remain provocative and perhaps despised (such as Wagner)—in spontaneous ways that fall upon "fresh ears" rather than in a manner that reinforces stereotypes. On the other hand, Lucius Banda champions the genre of popular music (prohibited or censored by past regimes) to speak to fellow Malawians in their "lived language." Through his lyrics, Banda urges his audience to remember the nation's political history that systematically oppressed the poor masses; for Banda, such a collective consciousness can support a better future for young Malawians.

As a speaker, Sheriff Joe Arpaio is at no loss for narratives—either those based on *abstractions* (e.g., "the law," "[un]worthiness," and "the Latino threat") or on *concrete* "realities" (the practical values of a citizen posse to help round up criminals and pink underwear to humiliate prisoners) that enhance his standing among constituents. Although the sheriff engages in a rhetoric of human development purporting to help prisoners find themselves in his custody, his "official" actions speak more emphatically of political entrepreneurship fueled by exploiting the circumstances of the vulnerable in his community.

7

DIALECTICAL HUMAN RIGHTS ADVOCACY

Twentieth-century theologian Karl Barth reportedly encouraged the faithful to keep a newspaper in one hand and a Bible in the other to live meaningfully in the world.[1] Thus, Barth appears to have been a pragma-dialectician with a particular inclination to size up the moral vernacular in terms of universal (if not eternal) norms.

Nonetheless Barth's advice to keep the newspaper close at hand served well as a recruiting strategy in selecting exemplars for this study. Three exemplars in fact arose from the pages of the *New York Times* (condemned by some in our polarized society for defiling the culture), while numerous others were considered but did not "make the cut" (in most cases due to unavailability of supporting materials). Additionally, the daily "read" offered up myriad examples of agenda-driven narratives (as characterized by Deborah Stone, 1997), argumentative strategies (TNR), and moral vernaculars laced with an ethics of memory (Margalit 2002; Hauser 2008) that all affect the human condition.

One morning, for example, the editorial page presented a letter from a psychiatrist (one day after the suicide of a beloved entertainer) strenuous-ly complaining about how "demon talk" narratives subvert enlightened discourses on mental health (Pies 2014, A20). An editorial entitled "The Myth of the 'Student-Athlete' is Laid to Rest" appeared on that same page; it tied the origins of that narrative to fears that the alternative designation "student-*employee*" would have subjected universities to worker compensation payments. And while this book was in progress, the

morning paper reported on far too many situations wherein actions causing massive human misery and strife were justified through moral vernaculars; Hauser's and Margalit's conceptualizations *alone* would have suf-
ficed well enough *absent* daily accounts of human despair unfolding in
real time.

This closing chapter takes on three tasks intended to cull meaning
from our study of various rhetorical exemplars. A first involves comparing the exemplars as within the parameters of the analytical questions
posed at the conclusion of chapter 2—readers are encouraged to reflect
on any number of other revealing comparisons.[2] The second takes an
anthropological turn as it examines interfaces between cultures and institutions that bear upon human rights advocacy. A third addresses a concern raised earlier as to whether human rights advocates are obliged to
acquire certain virtues in their callings. This chapter (and book) closes
with some last thoughts about what (if anything) *rhetoric* "is all about" in
the study of human rights advocacy.

COMPARING THE RHETORICAL EXEMPLARS

In large part efforts in this book to examine the rhetoric of human rights
advocates, or alternatively antagonists obstructing rights-causes, follow
the lead of cultural anthropologists such as Clifford Geertz who study
behaviors and actions as meaningful within particular contexts. Such inquiry confronts an intriguing paradox in that the very explicit articulation
of human rights principles (often expressed within international documents) reverberates within particular contexts in which those "principles"
may take on any number of meanings. Chapter 2 addressed this paradox
as it distinguished between "thin" and "thick" explanations as related to
ethical and institutional rhetoric. That discussion concluded with five
questions that serve as criteria to compare the rhetorical exemplars discussed in chapters 3 through 6.

I. Among the various types of audience, from which does
the rhetorical exemplar seek adherence?

In categorizing this study's rhetorical exemplars by types of audiences
addressed, table 7.1 shows that most speakers intend to reach more than

one of the audiences recognized by Perelman and Olbrechts-Tyteca (1969). The three exceptions—Joe Arpaio, James Rhodes, and Geert Wilders—direct their appeals only to particular audiences, presumably their political constituencies that support messages that are antagonistic toward human rights. Moving from left to right in table 7.1 it appears that, of the two rhetors most engaged in self-deliberation, the human rights advocate (Anderson) achieves success in working through cognitive dissonance (in her discernment of an appropriate morality for humanitarian workers) while the antagonist (Johnson) cannot escape his psychological distress encountered in attempting to justify his prosecution of the Vietnam War.

Among the five exemplars who "argue before a single hearer" (TNR 1969, 35–40), rights antagonists seek approval from others—Truman and Eisenhower with Johnson, Deng Xiaoping with Li Ximing, and the ordinary Hutu listener with Rwanda Radio. By contrast, advocates *confront* their hearers—carpet-masters with Masih; and Putin and Kyrill with Pussy Riot. While all exemplars speak to *particular audiences*, antagonists appear more inclined to reinforce or solidify particular moral vernaculars while rights advocates challenge them. Lastly, it is noteworthy that only advocates in this study seek out universal audiences.

2. Is the rhetorical exemplar's argumentation monologic or dialogic in nature?

Dialogic argumentation interacts with audiences, at least in terms of mental or emotional assent if not through actual participation; by contrast, monologic speech seeks adherence on the merits of the argument put

Table 7.1.   Type of Audience Addressed

	Self	Single Hearer	Particular	Universal
Antagonist	LBJ/Vietnam	LBJ/Vietnam Li Ximing Rwanda Radio	Arpaio Rhodes Rwanda Radio Wilders	
Advocate	Anderson	Anderson Masih Pussy Riot	Banda Barenboim LBJ (Great Society) Pussy Riot	Anderson Assange Barenboim Masih Pussy Riot

forward. Table 7.2 shows that only Governor James Rhodes stands out as an exclusively monological speaker who lays out his justification (in his press conference in Kent, Ohio, on May 3, 1970) for his prior decision to request National Guard intervention—as he had on numerous other occasions—in response to student protests at Kent State University. The evidence suggests that Rhodes had more interest in profiting from evident public sentiment against anti-war protestors than in securing support for his action.

Yet the distinction between exemplars who predominantly engage in dialogic discourse and others who intersperse the two modes of argumentation is not so clear. Perhaps there is reason here to distinguish speakers who advance *proposals* to a particular audience (as dialogic) from those who more generally adorn their appeals for adherence with *artful diplomacy* (as both monologic and dialogic discourse) that couches the argument in symbolic deference to the audience (as with the rhetorical technique of *aporia*—"asking" those in the audience how *they* would proceed—discussed in chapter 4). Exemplars who more directly advance proposals include—Lyndon Johnson (to US citizens that it is essential to "stay the course" in Vietnam), Li Ximing (who proposes to Deng Xiaoping that Beijing municipal officials can control student protestors), Mary B. Anderson (to fellow humanitarian workers that "listening" and self-deliberation are necessary for peace-building), and Iqbal Masih before his BLLB involvement (to his young peers that they must question the circumstances of their inbondedness).

By contrast, other rhetors become "diplomats" who take care to couch their arguments as "in the interests" of their audiences, for example:

Table 7.2.   Nature of Speaker's Argumentation

	Monologic	*Dialogic*	*Both*
Antagonists	Rhodes	Li Ximing LBJ/Vietnam	Arpaio Rwanda Radio Wilders
Advocates		Anderson LBJ/Great Society Masih *(before BLLF)*	Assange Banda Barenboim Masih *(through BLLF)* Pussy Riot

- *Joe Arpaio* ("law and order" toughness—particularly in reference to "the Latino threat"—is in the interests of Arizona citizens),
- *Rwanda Radio* (killing Tutsis is in the Rwandan national interest),
- *Geert Wilders* (stopping Islam is in the Dutch national interest),
- *Julian Assange* (transparency that uncovers government and business secrets is in the interests of citizens in democratic societies),
- *Lucius Banda* (Malawians need to acknowledge past political repression to find future well-being),
- *Daniel Barenboim* (music is an international language that can bring healing to victims of oppression and torture),
- *Pussy Riot* (Putin's and Kyrill's nationalistic agendas are not in the interest of Russian citizens), and
- *Iqbal Masih* through his BLLB involvement (that the carpet industry violates Pakistani law and thus enslaves children).

3. Does the rhetorical exemplar incorporate a "thick" ethics of memory or a "thin" morality of universality within her or his argumentation?

As table 7.3 suggests, Iqbal Masih's appeal for children's liberation from bonded servitude stands out as the only argumentative discourse in this study that relies solely on a universal standard of rights and obligations—Pakistan's history and economic circumstances (for example, the nation's reliance on a global market for hand-made carpets) do not register as mitigating factors in Iqbal's appeal. Further, his call for liberation directly corresponds to "children's rights" as articulated in the Universal Declaration of Human Rights pertaining to the economic exploitation of children (notwithstanding industry discourses that dispute whether such labor exploits or abuses children).

Beyond Iqbal Masih, four rhetorical exemplars (three rights antagonists and one advocate) construct the logics of their argumentation within Margalit's understanding of memory within the community and (presumably) Hauser's thick moral vernacular. Among the antagonists, Rwanda Radio contrived and exploited a national "history" that frames Tutsis as a traditional external threat to Rwandans; Lyndon Johnson appeals to a moral vernacular that is fearful of the spread of Communism in his assertion that a US defeat in Vietnam would enable Communists to control southeast Asia; and Geert Wilders advances narratives that portray Islam

Table 7.3.   Nature of Morality (or Ethics) within Argumentation

	Thin Morality* of Universality	Thick Ethics* of Memory	Both
Antagonists		Hate Radio LBJ/Vietnam Wilders	Arpaio Li Ximing Rhodes
Advocates	Masih	Banda	Anderson Assange Barenboim LBJ/Great Society Pussy Riot

°Avishai Margalit makes the distinction between "morality" and "ethics" in *The Ethics of Memory* (2002). Although these differences are explained in chapter 2, they simply connote two standards of behavioral expectations—"morality" with universal imperatives and "ethics" with community obligations (within a particular moral vernacular).

as a scourge that will precipitate the downfalls of Dutch and European societies. On the other hand, Lucius Banda's relies specifically on his portrayal of political oppression *within Malawi's history* as a means of mobilizing the poor to struggle for political and economic justice.

However the majority of exemplars in this study appear to be "astute dialecticians" who can integrate some "thin" (if not universal) sense of categorical obligation within a "thick" vernacular tradition either to obstruct or encourage rights-related initiatives. As for antagonists, Joe Arpaio combines his appeal for "thin" law-and-order with the "thick" tradition of can-do patriotism in the American West. Li Ximing affirms his municipality's "thin" hierarchical obligation to the central party to conserve the "thick" revolutionary spirit of the party and nation. Governor James Rhodes dispatches the Ohio National Guard to uphold the "thin" law in concert with a "thick" political culture that regards protest (especially on the part of "privileged" college students) as an affront to Midwestern values.

Most of the rights advocates as well demonstrate their capabilities of inter-relating some "thin" sense of fairness or justice within a "thick" vernacular memory of experience. Mary B. Anderson appeals to her humanitarian colleagues to study "thick" vernacular contexts and then work within them to foster justice with security. Julian Assange and his WikiLeaks associates essentially play off the "thick" democratic traditions of limited government against the incompatible realities of "security" institutions that routinely usurp citizens' rights. Daniel Barenboim uses his skills of symphonic interpretation to convey the essences of particular vernaculars (such as Wagner's pre–World War II Germany) to promote inter-cultural understandings that can bring the adversaries of history into agonistic discourses. Lyndon Johnson found middle ground between a "thick" way of living in the US South that excluded participation by people of color and a fundamentally "thin" sense of electoral fairness in his efforts to advance a "Great Society" with unlimited opportunity. Lastly, Pussy Riot both confronted and appealed to the conservators of "thick" political and ecclesiastical traditions in Russian society (as other noted dissidents before it had) to honor fundamental individual rights.

4. How (if at all) do Hauser's two types of moral vernacular affect antagonists vis-à-vis advocates' discourses?

The implication here is that rights antagonists may vary in how they rely upon thin or thick moral vernaculars (or perhaps intermingle them)—as might human rights advocates. Table 7.4 shows distinct affects, differentiating among antagonists in terms of those whose discourses are based on "thin" official vernaculars from the discourses of others based upon "thick" particular vernaculars (shown along the top). On the other hand, it also distinguishes among rights advocates who have *not* suffered rights abuse but justify their rights discourses on "thin" principle as distinct from those advocates who *have* in fact personally suffered and who base their discourses on "thick" experience within particular settings.

Table 7.4 indicates that three rights antagonists (Joe Arpaio, Li Ximing, and James Rhodes) advance "thin" vernaculars of "official duties," in each case to enforce the "law" or the "peace." However the case sketches for each (in chapters 3 through 6) imply that these "thin" justifications "played into" (or resonated positively within) the "thick" moral vernacular of (respectively) nativist anti-Latino sentiments, the spirit of the Communist revolution in China, and Midwestern US values against radical protest. Three other antagonist exemplars justify their rhetoric on "thick vernaculars": Lyndon Johnson's that marshaled national patriotism calling for victory in Vietnam, Radio Rwanda's that emerged from (a distorted account of) Rwandan history, and Geert Wilders's that fed into a nativist xenophobia.

Table 7.4.   Exemplar's Rhetoric as Thin or Thick Vernacular

Antagonists	"Thin" Official Rhetoric	"Thick" Vernacular Rhetoric
	Arpaio	LBJ
	Li Ximing	Radio Rwanda
	Rhodes	Wilders
Advocates	Anderson	Banda
	Assange	Masih
	Barenboim	Pussy Riot
	LBJ	
	Did Not Suffer HR Abuse "Thin"	Suffered HR Abuse "Thick"

Advocates who have not suffered actual abuse include Mary B. Anderson (who champions the "thin" principle of discernment through self-reflection and "listening"), Julian Assange (whose discourses advance the universal principle of transparency), Daniel Barenboim (who advocates through the "thin" universality of music), and Lyndon Johnson (promoting the "thin" principle of fairness in his Great Society rhetoric). Of these four, Daniel Barenboim's "thin" messages through music are directed toward a "thick" vernacular of Jewish experience and memory. Three other advocates (Lucius Banda, Iqbal Masih, and Pussy Riot) speak of their personal experiences of rights abuse in terms of (respective) moral vernaculars: Banda was imprisoned for his "protest" performance by a political regime in Malawi—as was Pussy Riot in Russia—and Iqbal Masih was forced into bonded child labor to promote the profitable carpet industry in Pakistan.

5. Does the rhetorical exemplar address the future or merely the past and/or present?

In terms of symbolism, change agents such as policy reformers or other activists (including our rhetorical exemplars) either explicitly or implicitly position themselves within a temporal orientation that emphasizes the past, present, future, or some inter-relationship between them. Policy theorist Deborah Stone asserts that activists may temporally define their concerns in terms of particular *narrative structures* that generally begin as "*Once upon a time*" things were good, bad, or whatever but then changed . . . consistent with the rhetor's argument (Stone 1997, 139).

Table 7.5 categorizes exemplars' temporal orientations by differentiating those whose arguments reflect discernible futures from others who speak primarily of the past or present.

Three rights-antagonists in this study (Joe Arpaio, Li Ximing, and James Rhodes) appear to speak in terms of current circumstances calling for action without significant concern for the future. Each of these individuals functions as a policymaker, and two of them operate within a short US election cycle—as became evident as James Rhodes (unsuccessfully) competed for a US Senate seat in a primary election exactly one day after the Kent State shootings. As a local Communist Party leader, Li Ximing seized the opportunity that surfaced in the near term to enhance his own image and that of his colleagues in the Beijing municipal bureaucracy in the eyes of Deng Xiaoping and Central Party officials.

However the picture is somewhat murky in regard to the temporal orientations of Julian Assange and Pussy Riot, neither of whom appear significantly attentive to the long-term implications of their actions. As described by his friends and WikiLeaks associates, Assange takes on the persona of a self-absorbed utopian who worries little about the current exigencies of running the WikiLeaks operation and concerns himself even less with tomorrow's problems. Pussy Riot performers appear as *anything but utopians* but as ready and willing to protest authoritarian abuses as they occur on a moment's notice.

Three of the exemplar antagonists (Lyndon Johnson, Rwanda Radio, and Geert Wilders) *do* in fact look into the future, but they visualize it as "gloom and doom" if their rhetorical warnings go unheeded—whether to win decisively in Vietnam, eradicate all Tutsis, or deport all Muslims. By

Table 7.5.   Temporal Orientation of Exemplar's Rhetoric

	Past and/or Present Only	*Future*
Antagonists	Arpaio Li Ximing Rhodes	LBJ/Vietnam Rwanda Radio Wilders
Advocates		Anderson Assange Banda Barenboim LBJ/Great Society Masih Pussy Riot

contrast, future-oriented rights advocates project varying degrees of optimism, although none as pronounced as Lyndon Johnson's enchantment associated with the advent of a Great Society. Nonetheless Iqbal Masih promised his friends that freedom from bonded labor would open up unlimited futures. Mary B. Anderson and Daniel Barenboim shared a more restrained confidence that (varying modes of) listening could bring adversaries together. Lastly, Lucius Banda asserts that if his fellow Malawians learn from the repression of the past, they can experience better futures.

CULTURAL CATEGORIES, RHETORIC, AND INSTITUTIONAL BOUNDARIES

This inquiry into the rhetoric of human rights advocacy is largely premised on Gerald Hauser's assertion that since human rights conversation is often expressed as "thin" universal principles, it loses significance (or is patently rejected) in the "thickness" of particular cultural vernaculars (2008). As indicated in chapter 2, Hauser's concern for "thick" vernaculars takes on special significance within anthropological contexts of "cultural categories" that serve to protect a society from various "dangers." Following the work of anthropologist Mary Douglas and political scientist Aaron Wildavsky (1982) for example, Hauser's vernaculars can be understood as collective risk management strategies whereby shared allegiances to categories of cultural "purity" offer hedges against harms. A familiar example of such a cultural category can be found in the book of Leviticus, which promotes cultural hygiene through dietary restrictions (Douglas 1966/2002, 51–71); yet other categories or "risk hedges" can apply to topics (e.g., such as gendered relationships or youths' rites of passage) of interest to human rights advocates.

If the anthropologist's notion of risk management adds texture to Hauser's thick vernacular, it makes sense that (1) ruling elites (or guardians—see Sen 1999, 31–33) accrue authority in ensuring the continuity of categorical "purity" through a system of order and (2) anomalies to system and order are thought to "contaminate" the culture. In *Purity and Danger*, Douglas refers to cultural contamination as "dirt" that threatens the cultural order:

If we can abstract pathogenicity and hygiene from our notion of dirt, we are left with the old definition of dirt as matter out of place. This is a very suggestive approach. It implies two conditions: a set of ordered relations and a contravention of that order. Dirt then, is never a unique, isolated event. Where there is dirt there is a system. Dirt is the by-product of a systematic ordering and classification of matter, in so far as ordering involves rejecting inappropriate elements. (1966/2002, 44)

The implications for human rights advocacy, especially as expressed in the thin universal vernacular, seem fairly clear; rights-talk is likely perceived as presenting "dirty" anomalies that paradoxically tilt "the moral high ground" toward elites who oversee the cultural categories of "purity" (and who would likely qualify as "rights *antagonists*" in this study). This paradox of rights advocacy lending legitimacy to *antagonists* becomes evident in table 7.6. First, the table shows that exemplars designated as *rights antagonists* in this study can logically claim the responsibility for protecting cultural "purity" from those who would defile it. Second, it indicates that the messages of some rights advocates (specifically, Xu Quinxian, Iqbal Masih, Pussy Riot, Daniel Barenboim, and Lucius Banda) could be interpreted as "dirt" that degrades cultural values.

Daniel Barenboim's rights-advocacy through the universal medium of music warrants particular attention in reference to what some behavioral scientists call "cultural trauma"; such a condition persists after a horrendous event that etches into an intergenerational memory that may take on global (diasporic) significance. (Such trauma may relate as well to the effects of Rwandan "Hate Radio" in chapter 3 and Geert Wilders's "Islamophobia" in chapter 5.) Researchers Lazar and Litvak-Hirsch cite the works of others who have studied this condition: "These authors suggested that cultural trauma could be conceived as an event, which may be in the making and, apart from commemorating past physical destruction, could signify any attack upon the essential and vulnerable elements of the collective culture, such as its core symbols (language, religion, history, etc.)" (2009, 184). In *The Ethics of Memory*, Avishai Margalit addresses the issue of trauma stemming from the Holocaust, concluding that:

Trauma, like a covered stain, still has effects. It makes the traumatized person react *disproportionately* to a present trigger on the strength of the injury from the past. Or it displaces that which brought the trauma about with a different object that is somehow associated with the ob-

Table 7.6. Rhetorical Exemplars Protecting or Defiling the "Purity" of Cultural Categories

	Cultural "Purity" Protected by:	Cultural "Purity" Defiled by:
Anderson	Listening to viewpoints	
Rwanda Radio	*Rwanda Radio calling for the killing of Tutsis on behalf of government*	
LSU—Tiananmen Protests	*Rhodes's/Li Ximing's resort to military action against student protests*	Anomaly of Xu Qinxian's defiance of superiors
Masih		Anomaly of Iqbal Masih's confrontation with Pakistan's culture of bonded child labor
Pussy Riot	*Putin's and Kyrill's invocation of church orthodoxy as integral to traditional Russian nationalism*	Pussy Riot's invasion of sacred space in Church of the Saviour
Johnson—Vietnam	*Johnson's invocation of US moral authority over international affairs*	
Johnson—Great Society		Johnson's Great Society rhetoric that threated the Southern culture of segregation
Assange	Counter-Claims : US Government's obligation to provide security --or-- Assange's assertion of transparency as fundamental in a democracy	[Assange] [US Government]
Wilders	*Wilder's campaign against the Islamification of Dutch society*	
Barenboim		Anomaly of Barenboim breaking the taboo of performing Wagner's music to a Jewish audience
Arpaio	*Arpaio's upholding of "the law" in the midst of the "Latino threat"*	
Banda	*Kamazu Banda through his "One Malawi" policies of cultural purity*	Anomaly of Lucius Banda's political protest through popular music idiom

Italics denote behaviors or actions of exemplar antagonists.

ject of the past. These are two manifestations of reliving the past. (2002, 126; italics added)

Thus it may be little surprise that Israel's president Reuven Rivlin, personally outraged at Barenboim having been awarded the prestigious Wolf Prize, articulates a "rhetoric of fear" in reaction to the anomaly of the Maestro's efforts interpreting the works of a despised composer (Richard Wagner) for a Jewish audience. But perhaps Barenboim engages in a rhetoric of hope to evoke a reaction to his performances of Wagner's music, *proportional* to that of *any* audience, which could be taken as an indicator of cultural confidence.

As mentioned in chapter 2, Michael Mulkay's account of "the great embryo debate" in the UK House of Commons regarding the use of human embryos in the new reproductive technologies (NRTs) offers a context for recognizing a "rhetoric of fear" that prophesies cultural harm on the scale of Nazi eugenics (1993, 728). Here certain church leaders and parliamentarians engaged in such discourses to protect the moral categories of cultural "purity" from NRT "contamination." But as Bloomfield and Vurdubakis suggest, these categories encumber the human rights claims of those whose lives are most directly affected by the debate:

> As one 46-year-old woman, pregnant after receiving donor eggs and in vitro fertilization treatment, put it: "I think it's absurd that people would say a woman can't have a child at any age. I don't think we can make rules about this." In other words, not only is such treatment seen as a matter of individual choice—as opposed to societal regulation—but the implication is that any notion of a natural age-dependent boundary delimiting the period when women can have babies is to be resisted; and if the technology in question confounds social categories then these will have to be revised. (1995, 542)

As mentioned above, Mulkay's ideas about a "rhetoric of fear" center around accusations of "boundary (or cultural category) transgressions that lead to cultural contamination" (Bloomfield and Vurdubakis 1995, 536–538). Here the speaker's intent is to instill anxiety in the audience by articulating the "dire" consequences of the violation. Perelman and Olbrechts-Tyteca generally recognize such a strategy of using consequentialist argumentation to arouse emotion, which can be particularly persuasive if hearers are inclined toward superstition (1969, 267). As chapter 3 relates, a farmer who was convicted for his involvement in the Rwanda Genocide testifies to the influence of consequentialist argumentation in the rhetoric of fear broadcasted by the RTLM: "[The radio was] always telling people that if the [Tutsi] RPF comes, it will return Rwanda to feudalism, that it would bring oppression. We didn't know the RPF. We believed what the government told us" (Berkeley 1994, 18).

Yet Mulkay also identifies other discursive techniques for raising anxiety found in "the great embryo debate" that particular rhetorical exemplars in this study use as well. For example, he suggests that rhetors of fear sometimes project a "frightening vision" of moral decline and social disruption (1993, 728). In this regard, the Joe Arpaio sketch in chapter 6 refers to how well-regarded publications sensationalized the "threat" of Latino immigration with issue titles such as—"OUR ILLEGAL ALIEN PROBLEM" (*American Legion Magazine*, December 1974); "WEL-COME TO AMEXICA" (*Time* special edition, June 11, 2001); and "HIS-PANIC NATION: Hispanics are an immigrant group like no other. Their huge numbers are changing old ideas about assimilation. Is America ready?" (*Business Week*, March 15, 2004) (Chavez 2008, 28–38).

Opponents of NRTs also "misus[ed] language and invent[ed] new terms to mislead ordinary people" (Mulkay 1993, 729). Presumably Geert Wilders's production of the provocative film *Fitna* qualifies as rhetoric of fear that "invents . . . to mislead" in a most dramatic fashion. As related in chapter 5, the film associates a few particularly hostile passages from the Koran with incendiary visuals (such as the 9/11 destruction of the World Trade Center towers) for Western audiences. Such a misleading project relates to a way of exploiting sacred texts that religionist Tim Beal associates with "Mark Twain's drugstore":

> In an essay fragment called "Bible Teaching and Religious Practice," Mark Twain suggested that the Bible is like a drugstore. In it you can find both poison and cure. The Bible was used [to justify the Salem witch trials and to condemn them, slavery in the United States, and other human atrocities]. . . . For many, the Bible is a source of power and liberation. For many others, it is a source of wounds and oppression. When we read it honestly, as I think Twain did, it's hard to deny that it is a source of both, and the two are often inextricably inter-mixed. . . . The voices are in tension. (2011, 155; 159)

Although the Koran's polyvocality supported Wilders's rhetoric of fear, it ultimately led some Islamic women to engage a global dialogue that clarified their identities as members of a faith community and citizens of recently adopted nations.

Alternatively, Michael Mulkay observes some from the scientific community and church leaders—professing theological views *other* than those of colleagues so stridently opposed to the NRTs—who spoke in terms of a "rhetoric of hope." These participants in "the great embryo debate" were eventually successful in securing legislation that permitted the use of human embryos in NRT procedures within 14 days of conception. For Mulkay, the "rhetoric of hope" signifies "boundary repair work" rather than boundary transgression; in other words, the strategy involves appealing for modifications that would *support* (rather than oppose or confront) the principle of the cultural category. In the context of the embryo debate, NRT proponents did not contest the "sanctity of life" principle but instead argued that the NRTs could advance it by pre-empting human defects that diminish that sanctity (1993, 725).

Bloomfield and Vurdubakis note that advocacy expressed through rhetoric of hope needs to be grounded in realism rather than naïveté that can be readily challenged, as shown in this testimony:

> We have been warned not to be starry-eyed about science. Let me warn the house not to be starry-eyed about nature. Nature gave us death by smallpox and medical research gave us vaccination. Nature gave us disability inflicted by polio and medical research gave us immunisation. . . . Nature gave us kidney failure and medical research has given people the chance of life through transplant. . . . Those of us who have not suffered infertility or faced the misery of miscarriage and who are blessed with healthy children are fortunate. But thousands of other people are not so fortunate. . . . To allow them hope, I hope the house will join me in voting for embryo research. (1993, 725)

Given that rhetoric of hope is more often based on reason than belief (Mulkay 1993, 736), its formulation requires considerably more effort and time than does a rhetoric of fear. In his article that likens the arguments of NRT advocates with those of Galileo, Mulkay (1995) outlines some critical considerations in formulating such arguments, for example:

- Keep the principle (within the cultural category) but work around the edges of that principle (508)—as Iqbal Masih did in emphasizing the existence of a legal prohibition against bonded child labor in Pakistan.
- Settle for persuasion rather than conviction (509)—a vital distinction that the rhetoricians make (see TNR 1969, 26–30)—as Lyndon Johnson *persuaded* White Southerners to support the Great Society effort to extend political equality to people of color; and
- Avoid "factual absolutism" whereby one refuses to consider the adversary's arguments (510)—as Mary B. Anderson advocates in listening to the arguments of belligerents in conflict and as Julian Assange ignores in his bellicose confrontations with critics.

Whether the rhetoric surrounding the great embryo debate in Britain corresponds directly to human rights advocacy in particular contexts (such as those in chapters 3 through 6) is open to interpretation. Nonetheless, Mulkay's observations concerning the patient and laborious "edgework" of scientists and some religious leaders speak to the level of commitment required to support a rhetoric of hope that (to a limited extent) advances the benefits of NRTs in Britain. Mulkay's accounts here appear somewhat parallel to Peter Easton and colleagues' evaluative review of the NGO Tostan's efforts to offer adult education to Senegalese women that subsequently led to "social change from the bottom-up" (2003)—as discussed in chapter 2. Advocates in both cases took precautions *not* to confront the relevant cultural categories head-on but rather to facilitate boundary restoration (or "repair work") so as to honor the authentic principles of culture and amend them in ways that engender better lives.

The British and Senegalese contexts of a rhetoric of hope support two generalizations that should inform the advocacy of human rights. First, the restorative "edgework" of rights discourses are apt to be heard in *dialectical environments* wherein

> arguments are made; alternative positions on the issue will arise (in which that arguer may make reference to the argument of others); objections will be lodged; criticisms will be directed at the arguments of others. This argumentative material (objections, criticisms, alternative positions) collects around the issue and constitutes the dialectical environment that surrounds that particular issue. (Johnson 2013, 540)

Presumably, Mary B. Anderson coaches her humanitarian colleagues (as discussed in chapter 3) to become able pragma-dialecticians (to use Ralph Johnson's term) to support a rhetoric of hope in contexts of war and conflict. To assert that human rights advocates should become skillful pragma-dialecticians does *not* imply they should pursue graduate-level training in philosophy or political theory. But it *does* mean that human rights advocates must become conversant with (borrowing from scholars of public ethics[3]) "vulgar dialectics." As vulgar dialecticians, rights advocates hopefully become committed to the patience and perseverance needed to understand the counter-logics of a dialectical environment and a respect for the integrity of a culture.

Second, it should become apparent to rights advocates that the pragma-dialectical work needed to support a rhetoric of hope commits them to an extended time horizon. Proponents in the embryo debate persevered for eight years until the UK House of Commons adopted a measure to permit the therapeutic use of human embryos in existence for not longer than 14 days. The sensitivity of time becomes especially salient in comparing the rhetorical exemplars in this book, which is organized around four types of moral situations—two of which (*crisis* and *confrontation* respectively in chapters 3 and 4) are episodic while the others (*project* and *work* in chapters 5 and 6) involve longer-term processes. Clearly, pragma-dialectical "edgework" appears extremely difficult to engage in moral crises (such as the Rwanda genocide, wherein the rhetoric of fear is so shrilly amplified) and in confrontations that pit "factual" absolutes against each other. Contexts of moral process (that is, *projects* and *work*) appear better suited for pragma-dialectic advocacy, but rights rhetoric in crisis and confrontational situations may be more advisedly directed toward transnational audiences (see Keck and Sikkink 1998).

Lastly, what can be said of institutions within a moral vernacular in terms of either integrating cultural "purity" into implementable action or soft-pedaling it in preference for administrative norms such as rule of law or procedural fairness? Although it bears directly upon bureaucratic measures that assist or obstruct people in claiming rights, the question appears both multi-faceted and nuanced. Primarily, the issue centers on *boundaries*, which "define systems and determine the relationships within and between systems" (Schneider 1987, 379) and on the extent to which these boundaries are porous or impermeable. Again in the contexts of moral vernaculars and human rights, the boundary question amounts to how much discretion bureaucrats or other institutional officials may exercise in relation to policy elites who protect cultural "purity" in the moral vernacular. (Recall that in chapter 1, Zhejiang bureaucrats were arrested because they "said the wrong things" [Ingersoll and Adams 1986, 364] in their interactions with Sanjiang Church members.)

So who within the institution or beyond it negotiates (or imposes) boundaries and how? A thin perspective on institutions implies that technically competent decision makers manage boundaries from within. A thicker view anticipates that elites can manipulate organization symbols and myths from "behind the scene" to (re-)establish boundaries. For example, presumably *thin* managerial vernaculars may take on significance in *thick* institutional discourse as a symbol, the "anti-myth" myth that supports some version of "legitimacy" in the institution or regime (see Ingersoll and Adams 1986, 364). Here Geertz's *winks upon winks upon winks* corresponds to *technical rationality upon moral vernacular upon "legitimacy."*

With the exceptions of the military leaders (Sylvester Del Corso and Xu Qinxian) in the Kent State and Tiananmen Square student protests, none of the rhetorical exemplars in this study qualifies as an unelected bureaucrat (or comparable official) administratively buffered from moral vernaculars; however, passing mention is made in various sketches of others who are so situated. Nonetheless, table 7.7 considers how (where pertinent) exemplars or others affect institutional boundaries either by directly managing relationships between the societal environment and the institution or by manipulating symbols through their rhetoric and actions. Taken together, these observations shed light upon organizational (in)capability to promote or obstruct human rights advocacy.

On the whole, table 7.7 shows that exemplar advocates of human rights endeavor to buffer institutions from the cultural influences of the moral vernacular, while antagonists strive to "open the borders" so that these cultural influences permeate how institutions operate. Although Joe Arpaio's rhetorical appeals to "the law" fall under the "boundary impermeability" column, his "law and order" discourses may tie in more closely with entrepreneurial opportunity to shore up his constituency than with principle.

Although each entry in table 7.7 signifies a particular strategy advancing or jettisoning human rights advocacy, four warrant particular elaboration. While Julian Assange's advocacy for the thin principle of transpa-

Table 7.7.   Institutional Boundaries as Affected by Exemplars

	Boundary Impermeability	Boundary Porousness
Managing Boundaries	Arpaio appeals to "the law." Assange champions transparency to insulate agencies from national security vernaculars. Dutch and EU bureaucrats facilitate Muslim migration [in Wilders sketch].	
Manipulating Symbols to Affect Boundaries	Barenboim performs to insulate audiences from vernaculars of memory. Iqbal Masih acts dramatically to emphasize the contradiction to existing law.	Arpaio appeals to "the law" to accommodate moral vernacular. Banda performs to connect poor Malawians with history of repression. Del Corso, Rhodes, and Li Ximing speak to accommodate anti-protest moral vernacular. LBJ appeals to national pride for "staying the course" in Vietnam. Radio Rwanda manipulates symbols for government. Wilders uses "Henk and Ingrid' narrative and *Fitna* to inflame xenophobism.

rency aligns with the limited government ideal, it confronts a deluge of bureaucratic opposition bolstered by a moral vernacular of security in a post-9/11 era. In his campaign against the "Islamification" of the Netherlands, Geert Wilders castigates government officials (much as Alabama Governor George Wallace stigmatized "pointy-headed bureaucrats" in the 1970s) for enabling Muslin immigration. While other state administrators sought to buffer themselves from Governor Rhodes's ventures to exploit student unrest, Ohio Adjutant General Sylvester Del Corso went out of his way to keep his National Guard's boundary open to accommodate the Governor's policy agenda. Yet in subsequent federal court testimony, Del Corso in effect conceded that such boundary erosion led to irresponsible soldiering that cost four people their lives. Regarding the other student protest case, Li Ximing both manages boundaries and ma-

nipulates Communist Party symbols to position Beijing's municipal institutions advantageously in the context of Tiananmen Square disobedience.

HOPE RHETORIC, DIALECTICS, AND VIRTUE

Bertolt Brecht's Galileo serves as the proverbial cat with more than one
life. In his "second life" (i.e., Brecht's second version of the play refer-
enced in chapter 4), Galileo's *cowardice* offers Brecht the ammunition he
needs to rail against the spinelessness of the scientific community to stop
the development of the atomic bomb in (then) present time. However in
his *first* life, Galileo emerges from Brecht's 1938 version as a *courageous
hero*, brave enough to conceal "the truth" under his coat from authorities,
as faithful Communist workers had to do in pre–World War II Germany.
Indeed theater critic Eric Bentley wonders if Brecht's project to associate
Galileo with the Marxist ideological cause reflects the playwright's guilt
for shying away from active involvement in the cause (1966, 37).

To a lesser extent, George Bernard Shaw plays "fast-and-loose" with
history as well in over-dramatizing Joan of Arc's prosecutorial antagonists in *Saint Joan* (discussed in the lead-in to chapter 3) contemporarily
as Joan was about to be canonized—in reality, Joan may have not been so
interesting as the character Shaw develops (Bentley 1966, 11–14; Wisenthal 1988, 44-45). Presumably Brecht, Shaw, and other playwrights extend moral witness to their causes through their art; nonetheless, the
question arises as to whether their uses (or abuses) of history disqualify
them as "legitimate" witnesses. Speaking about Brecht, Bentley explains
the conundrum as follows:

> To a historian it would seem bizarre to suggest that he should reverse a
> judgment he had made on something in the seventeenth century on
> account of something that had happened in the twentieth. To a drama-
> tist, however, the question would mainly be whether a subject which
> had suggested itself because it resembled something in the twentieth
> century would still be usable when asked to resemble something quite
> different in the twentieth century. (1966, 16)

One of Brecht's critics refers to the playwright's use of "dissemblance" where no resemblance appears as his polished "art of dissemblance" (Calabro 1990). Presumably, the rhetoricians touch on the "art of

dissemblance" as the argumentative strategy of "'appearance-reality' pair[ing]": "When a stick is partially immersed in water, it seems curved when one looks at it and straight when one touches it, but *in reality* it cannot be both curved and straight. . . . [T]he effect of determining reality is to dissociate those appearances that are deceptive from those that correspond to reality" (TNR 1969, 416; italics in original).

Among the rhetorical exemplars in this study, a few of those categorized as *antagonists* of human rights appear proficient in the art of dissemblance. Extremist Rwandan Radio (RTLM) *genocidaires* likened Tutsis to external enemies even though Tutsis were in fact internal stakeholders. Similarly, Ohio Governor James Rhodes associated student anti-war protesters with "the strongest, well-trained, militant revolutionary group that has ever assembled in America" even though most of them hailed from such "subversive" places as Elyria, Tallmadge, and Ashtabula in Ohio. Geert Wilders "connected" human rights activists with indifference to the "plight" of Islamic women under Sharia law ("likely" to take root in the Netherlands with high rates of Muslim integration).

But what can be said of human rights *advocates* (if appropriately designated as such) who include dissemblance, or at least wild leaps of "resemblance," in their advocacy rhetoric? For example, can Julian Assange draw on the imagery in the book of Revelation as an analogy to the false pretenses behind government secrecy as in his reference to "the Four Horsemen of the Info-Apocalypse: child pornography, terrorism, money laundering, and the war on some drugs?" Taken within the entirety of this sketch included in chapter 5, these questions center upon whether Assange and other cypher-punk brawlers looking for fights with banks, the Church of Scientology, and government agencies can cultivate and preserve the moral integrity expected from rhetors of hope. As his once-colleague Daniel Domscheit-Berg implies, Assange appears to lack the diplomatic finesse of a pragma-dialectician:

> For Julian in particular, principles were more important than anything else. When one of our sources discovered a misconfiguration on the website of Senator Norm Coleman of Minnesota and sent us the publicly visible data, Julian wanted to publish not only the names of Coleman's campaign supporters but their exact credit card details, including security codes, as well. (2011, 28)

If Julian Assange *does* pass as a human rights advocate with (at least the potential to engage) a rhetoric of hope, he can be aptly regarded as a morally ambiguous individual (among many of us) with much to learn about the dialectical edge-work of making hope real.

Nonetheless, it follows that rights-advocates, no matter how morally "upright" or ambiguous in themselves, typically engage a rhetoric of hope to address *morally ambiguous circumstances*. Both of the Lyndon Johnson sketches are revealing here: The "war president" in chapter 4, clearly a morally ambiguous actor, at first confronts ambiguous accounts of military action in the Gulf of Tonkin and blames the North Vietnamese for sinking the US vessel. Yet after more accurate information surfaced disputing his claim, the morally ambiguous president (according to Press Secretary George Reedy 1982) stuck all the more to his story to rally support at home. By contrast, the enchantment president in chapter 5 appears as a resolute, principled moral actor using his political (perhaps pragma-dialectical) skills to advance a rhetoric of hope for people of color amid the moral ambiguity of a white Southern way of life at odds with constitutional principles. Thus, it can be said that (1) Julian Assange the cypher-punk leader *is no Mary B. Anderson* the reflective peacemaker, (2) Lyndon Johnson the war president *is no Lyndon Johnson* the enchantment president, and (3) we all have our strengths and weaknesses.

Hope takes on different meanings within thick ethics and thin morality (or ethics—see note 1 in chapter 2). For philosopher Avishai Margalit, hope within the thick memory of the community's precariousness allows the *moral witness* to grasp on to a distant possibility of restoration and wholeness:

> The hope with which I credit moral witness is a rather sober hope: that is in another place or another time there exists, or will exist, a moral community that will listen to their testimony. What is so heroic about this hope is the fact that people who are subjected to evil regimes intent on destroying the fabric of their moral community easily come to see the regime as invincible and indestructible and stop believing in the very possibility of a moral possibility. . . . The belief, under such conditions calls for a veritable leap of faith. But then the moral witness does not have to have the assured confidence of a sleepwalker that is manifested by religious witness. (2002, 155)

Gerald Hauser expresses a similar notion of *hope* within thick moral vernaculars that stresses the imperative of maintaining community identity apart from an oppressive regime—for example, the hope kept alive by the Polish Catholic Church in the face of the Communist state (2008, 445). In our study, both Daniel Barenboim and Lucius Banda fit well within Margalit's and Hauser's notions of moral witness committed to keeping memory alive that can lead to an eventual restoration of community. In particular, Barenboim told a music critic, "I don't feel myself as a missionary in this matter, but by not playing Wagner, one is giving Hitler a posthumous victory" (Oestreich 2014, C6).

Hauser argues however that in the context of thin morality, *hope* is understood in connection with various projects to achieve *moral perfection*. Succinctly stated, the thick hope of moving the concrete *is* to what can realistically *be* gives way to the thin universal abstraction of *ought*:

> The ideals of moral perfectionism, however, are hard to live by, especially when trouble hits. Their abstract righteousness offers a language of anti-politics that inspires rhetorical neutrality toward national interests in order to privilege the inherent worth of every human regardless of national origin, belief, or creed. This rhetorical position is problematic when your nation is under attack. It is difficult to criticize your government when you can be assailed for being unpatriotic. (2008, 448)

Despite his pugnacious discourses, Julian Assange advances a rhetoric of hope for individual privacy and institutional transparency in this thin sense of moral perfectionism.

But Margalit's moral witness (particularly within the thick vernacular of Jewish experience) does not necessarily rise to constant moral perfection. In what amounts to more than a play on words, Margalit examines conceivable situations that could lead a person of moral integrity *not to witness* or to temporally *abandon that integrity* to witness to the community in a more profound way—the latter reflects the moral ambiguity of the individual and the latter of the situation (2002, 159–162). Although martyrdom takes on symbolic potency, witness and advocacy are primarily the callings of the living. All of this implies that, although rights-advocates may need some sort of moral foundation for guidance and support, any ethical ladder is bound to wobble given the ambiguous nature of rights advocacy (see Bailey 1964, 238).

Clearly recognizing the moral ambiguity of humanitarian work, Mary B. Anderson helps her colleagues instill "mental attitudes" and "moral qualities" (as administrative theorist Stephen K. Bailey recommends to public officials; 1964)—in essence, *virtues* to support work in the face of ambiguity. In contrast to rule-based ethical foundations (such as those derived from historical imperatives—see MacIntyre 1984, 35–75), a virtue ethic speaks to mental attitudes and moral qualities in the "here and now"—that is, in functioning communities of endeavor such as within Anderson's humanitarian cohort.

Both Anderson's writings and field work focus on rights-advocacy as *praxis* of ideals and virtuous humanitarian vocation dealing with obstacles to peace-building. In particular, one of her books—*Do No Harm* (1999)—illustrates the tensions and complementarities between a deontological, rule-based moral obligation and the virtue ethics of fortitude in persevering amid opposing forces. The title of that book directly refers to a Kantian imperative, but her substance more often addresses the pragmatics of *doing* no harm. Thus, Mary B. Anderson would easily meet Ralph Johnson's criteria of a pragma-dialectician (2013) who is directed both by deontological ideals and a virtue ethics as appropriate in practice.

British urban planner Robert Upton characterizes the tension and complementarity between deontological obligation and virtue ethics in terms of a universal ideal as *concept* as compared with its *conception* in the context of the planner's (praxis) conundrum of advancing sustainable development:

> Sustainable development is so powerful because in the Brundtland formulation it is expressed at the level of deontological intensity that previous generations associated with the Ten Commandments. . . . What seems to me to be self-evident is that the problems associated with the "conception" of sustainable development cannot in practice be "worked through" on a deontological basis. By which I mean that establishing the priority of the issue to be addressed is a deontological matter. However, working through the infinite complexity of how "claims" derived in the language or the currency of three different sets of values— the social, economic and environmental perspectives— in specific contexts, should be assessed and mediated is a task that no rule-based approach could ever manage satisfactorily. (2002, 261–262)

By analogy, we can appeal to deontological obligation as a foundation for particular human rights but rely on the virtue of fortitude in advocating and applying them in context.

WHAT DOES IT ALL MEAN?

"OK, it's *rhetoric*, so what?" The discerning reader has justification to ask such a pointed question about this book and others like it that probe the relevance of a particular topic (e.g., rhetoric) to a broader endeavor such as human rights advocacy, art appreciation, or rocket science. Hopefully, this book advances persuasive arguments about what *rhetoric is not*: not vacuous "hot air" devoid of substance[4] nor simply splendid oratory and effective speaking (as was the case in classical Greece).

A conventional, somewhat satisfactory response could assert that the topic (in this case, "rhetoric") relates to *myriad* human rights concerns, as evident in *the rhetoric of poverty, of empowerment, of civil society organizations*, and so on, such that *the gates are wide open* for future research (as they most likely are). Such statements have their merits; indeed, several references are made in the previous chapter of the power of *rhetorical analysis* in supporting human rights advocacy. In retrospect, perhaps the term *analysis* (preeminent in the rhetoric of empirical science) appears a bit overstated next to the thick, messy confluences of circumstances in which exemplar advocates and antagonists function. As Deborah Stone notes, inquiry sometimes encounters "complex systems" (a term the late entertainer George Carlin would savor) that overwhelm our ability to systematize things (1997, 195–197)—more often than *sometimes* in the case human rights study. Presumably then, *rhetorical study* serves better in toning down our expectations on inquiry.

A more preferable answer to the question above could assert that rhetoric provides a *framework* or lens for directing attention within the thick messes surrounding human rights advocacy. Frameworks appear especially useful in navigating contexts that are by nature messy but appear even more muddled in the midst of veiled power agendas.

For example, it is well recognized that much rights-advocacy work involves collaboration within networks and taskforces wherein individuals from various nations and organizations interact. Here the differences between (Aristotle's) "old rhetoric" and (Perelman's) "new rhetoric" stand out. Presumably the "old" would focus on the *speaker*'s responsibility to facilitate the meeting of minds through decisively clear oratory. But focusing more on *audience* than *speaker*, the "new rhetoric" prepares advocate-participants to expect political posturing from their "colleagues" who rise to speak "eloquently" to gain adherence in furtherance of their interests. Buzzwords such as *poverty-reduction* and *empowerment* become "fuzzwords," and their exact meanings slip and slide in ways that allow politically savvy word-crafters opportunities to redefine ideas to suit their purposes (Cornwall and Brock 2005; Ghere 2012, 23–41). Needless to say, a great deal of ambiguity abounds in such "collaborative" fora, some of it by design. A rhetorical framework here informs the attentive advocate *not* so much about how less-skillful rhetors inadvertently account for ambiguity but instead how that ambiguity energizes the subtle but critical politics of collaboration.

Beyond this, a rhetorical framework can guide observations of human rights deprivations, and advocates' efforts to address them, along the rather serendipitous and curvilinear contours of thick description. Such an orientation makes particular sense in connection with Gerald Hauser's emphasis on particularistic moral vernaculars, "the language[s] of lived experience" (2008, 445), that filter how human rights messages are received by cultural audiences. At the very least, the framework can serve as a "reality check" for human rights reformers intending "to get at the roots" of rights abuse or "pull it out at the roots." As noted earlier in this chapter, a framework grounded on moral cultural vernaculars could shift human rights discourses from the radical ("roots") rhetoric of *eradication* (note that a radish is a root) to talk "around the edges" of cultural purity.

None of this is to suggest that a focus on rhetoric stands alone as the only way to position the study of rights advocacy where it needs to be—as *praxis of research and experience*; however rhetorical frameworks do this very well. They alert students and researchers of rights advocacy to expect a wild ride through the transformations, contortions, and contradictions that collide when "principles" hit the ground. It has been exhilarating travel.

NOTES

1. The exact source cannot be pinned down according to a Princeton Theological Seminary website "Quotes by Barth." http://www.ptsem.edu/Library/index.aspx?menu1_id=6907&menu2_id=6904&id=8450. Accessed August 25, 2014.

2. For reasons of clarity, these comparisons do not include the military leaders (Sylvester Del Corso and Xu Qinxian) in tables 7.1–7.5.

3. Some public management scholars argue that government officials should become conversant in "vulgar" (practical) ethics rather than worry about abstract philosophic issues (see Mainzer 1991; Frederickson 2010).

4. This "so what" question takes on particular salience given that rhetorical expression has been traditionally discounted as a residue of emotive utterances by logical positivists (i.e., empirical purists).

BIBLIOGRAPHY

Adams, John. *Hallelujah Junction: Composing an American Life*. (New York: Farrar, Straus, and Giroux, 2012).

Alyokhina, Maria, Nadezhda Tolokonnikova, and Ekaterina Samutsevich. *Pussy Riot! A Punk Prayer for Freedom*. (New York: Feminist Press, 2013).

Anderson, Mary B. "Aid: A Mixed Blessing." *Development in Practice* 10 (2000): 495–500.

———. *Do No Harm: How Can Aid Support Peace—or War?* (Boulder, CO: Lynne Rienner, 1999).

———. "To Work, or Not to Work, in 'Tainted' Circumstances: Difficult Choices for Humanitarians." *Social Research* 74 (2007): 201–222.

Anderson, Mary B., Dayna Brown, and Isabella Jean. *Time to Listen: Hearing People on the Receiving End of International Aid*. (Cambridge, MA: Collaborative Learning Projects, 2012).

Anderson, Mary B., and Peter J. Woodrow. *Rising from the Ashes: Development Strategies in Times of Disaster*. (Boulder, CO: Westview Press, 1989).

Apuzzo, Matt, and James Risen. "C.I.A. First Planned Jails Abiding by U.S. Standards." *New York Times*, December 11, 2014; A1.

Argyris, Chris. "Double-loop Learning, Teaching, and Research." *Academy of Management Learning & Education* 1.2 (2002): 206–218.

Arpaio, Joe. *America's Toughest Sheriff: How We Can Win the War against Crime*. (Arlington, TX: The Summit Publishing Group, 1996).

———. *Joe's Law: America's Toughest Sheriff Takes on Illegal Immigration, Drugs and Everything Else That Threatens America*. (New York: AMACOM, 2008).

Assange, Julian. *Cypherpunks: Freedom and Future of the Internet*. (New York: OR Books, 2012).

Astrasheuskaya, Nastassia and Steve Gutterman. "Russian Orthodox Patriarch Rails against Pussy Riot Protest," *Globe and Mail*, September 9, 2012. Accessed March 6, 2014. http://www.theglobeandmail.com/news/world/russian-orthodox-patriarch-rails-against-pussy-riot-protest/article4531669/.

Bailey, Stephen K. "Ethics and the Public Service." *Public Administration Review* 24(1964): 234-243.

Barenboim, Daniel, and Edward W. Said. *Parallels and Paradoxes*. (New York: Pantheon Books, 2002).

Beal, Timothy. "Pussy Riot's Theology." *Chronicle of Higher Education*, September 17, 2012. Accessed March 6, 2014. https://chronicle.com/article/Pussy-Riots-Theology/134398/.

———. *The Rise and Fall of the Bible*. (Boston: Houghton Mifflin, 2011).

Bennett, Jane. *The Enchantment of Modern Life: Attachments, Crossing, and Ethics*. (Princeton, NJ: Princeton University Press, 2001).

Benson, Thomas W. "Conversations with a Ghost: A Postscript." *Today's Speeches* 22 (Summer, 1974): 13–15.

Bentley, Eric. "The Science Fiction of Bertolt Brecht." In *Galileo: A Play by Bertolt Brecht*, ed. Eric Bentley. (New York: Grove Press, 1966), 7–42.

Berger, Peter, and Thomas Luckmann. *The Social Construction of Reality*. (Garden City, NY: Doubleday, 1966).

Berkeley, Bill. "Sounds of Violence." *The New Republic*, August 22 and 29, 1994, 18–19.

Berman, David R., and Tanis J. Salant. "The Changing Role of Counties in the Intergovernmental System." In *The American County: Frontiers of Knowledge*, ed. Donald C. Menzel. (Tuscaloosa: University of Alabama Press, 1996), 19–33.

Beschloss, Michael. *Reaching for Glory*. (New York: Simon and Schuster, 2001).

Blinder, Alan. "Trooper Listens to, and Connects with, a Ferguson Torn by Violent Unrest." *New York Times*, August 16, 2014, A13.

Bloomfield, Brian P., and Theo Vurdubakis. "Disputed Boundaries: New Reproductive Technologies and the Language of Anxiety and Expectation." *Social Studies of Science*. 25 (1995): 533–551.

Booth, David, Diana Cammack, Jane Harringan, Edge Kanyongolo, Mike Mataure, and Naomi Ngwira. *Drivers of Change and Development in Malawi*, Working Paper 261. (London: Overseas Development Institute, 2006).

Brecht, Bertolt. *Galileo*. Ed. Eric Bentley. (New York: Grove Press, 1966).

Brewer, John, and Albert Hunter. *Foundations of Multimethod Research: Synthesizing Styles*. (Thousand Oaks, CA: Sage Publications, 2006.)

Brockreide, Wayne. "Trends in Rhetoric: Blending Criticism and Science." In *The Prospect of Rhetoric*, eds. Lloyd Bitzer and Edwin Black. (Englewood Cliff, NJ: Prentice Hall, 1971), 124–125.

Brooks, David. "The Republic of Fear." *New York Times*, March 25, 2014, A27.

Burks, Don M. "Psychological Egoism and the Rhetorical Tradition." *Communication Monograms* 33 (1966): 400–418.

Byham, Lois McNamara. "Rhetoric as Epistemic: A Reexamination." In *Rhetoric 78*, eds. Robert Brown and Martin Steinman. (Minneapolis: University of Minnesota Center for Advanced Studies in Language, Style, and Literary Theory, 1973), 22–23.

Calabro, Tony. *Bertolt Brecht's Art of Dissemblance*. (Wakefield, NH: Longwood Academic, 1990).

Carroll, Lewis. *Alice's Adventures in Wonderland*. (Garden City, NY: Doubleday Classics, 1960).

Cannon, Kati G. *Katie's Canon: Womanism and the Soul of the Black Community*. (New York: Continuum, 1995).

Castle, Stephen. "TV Message by Snowden Says Privacy Still Matters." *New York Times*, December 25, 2013. Accessed March 12, 2014. http://www.nytimes.com/2013/12/26/world/europe/snowden-christmas-message-privacy.html?_r=0.

Chalk, Frank. "Scott Straus. The Order of Genocide: Race, Power and War in Rwanda." *African Studies Review* 50 (2007): 181–183.

Chambers, Robert. *Whose Reality Counts: Putting the Last First*. (Warwickshire, UK: Practical Action Publishing, 1997).

Chavez, Leo. *The Latino Threat: Constructing Immigrants, Citizens, and the Nation*, 2nd ed. (Stanford, CA: Stanford University Press, 2008).

Chirambo, Reuben M. "'Mzimu wa Soldier': Contemporary Popular Music and Politics in Malawi." In *A Democracy of Chameleons*, ed. Harri Englund. (Uppsala SW: Nordic Africa Institute, 2002), 103–122.

Cooper, Terry L., and Jameson W. Doig. "Austin Tobin and Robert Moses: Power, Progress, and Individual Dignity." In *Exemplary Public Administrators*, eds. Terry L. Cooper and N. Dale Wright. (San Francisco: Jossey-Bass, 1992), 80–107.

Cooper, Terry L., and N. Dale Wright, eds. *Exemplary Public Administrators*. (San Francisco: Jossey-Bass, 1992).

Cornwall, Andrea, and Karen Brock. *Beyond Buzzwords:"Poverty Reduction,""Participation" and "Empowerment" in Development Policy* (Programme Paper No. 10). (Geneva: UN Research Institute for Development, 2005).

Cox, Harvey. "Of Ezekiel, Gandhi, and Pussy Riot." *Boston Globe*, August 26, 2012. Accessed March 1, 2014. https://www.bostonglobe.com/opinion/2012/08/25/persecuted-punk-band-pussy-riot-has-parallels-with-ezekiel-gandhi/amWpK80npB6iGOpbzHzLVI/story.html.

Cox, Raymond W., and Sucheta Pyakuryal. "Tacit Knowledge: The Foundation of Information Management." In *Ethics in Public Management*, 2nd ed., eds. H. George Frederickson and Richard K. Ghere. (Armonk, NY: M.E. Sharpe, 2013), 216–242.

Crofts, Andrew. *The Little Hero: One Boy's Fight for Freedom*. London: Vision Paperbacks, 2006.

Crosswhite, James. "Universality in Rhetoric: Perelman's Universal Audience." *Philosophy and Rhetoric* 22 (1989): 157–173.

D'Adamo, Francesco, and Ann Leonon. *Iqbal*. (New York: Atheneum Books, 2003).

Dale, Reidar. "The Logical Framework: An Easy Escape, a Straitjacket, Or a Useful Planning Tool?" *Development in Practice* 13 (2003): 57–70.

Dallaire, Roméo. "The Media Dichotomy." In *The Media and the Rwanda Genocide*, ed. Allan Thompson. (Ottawa, ON: Pluto Press, 2007), 12–19.

Davenport, Thomas H., and Laurence Prusak. *Working Knowledge: How Organizations Manage What They Know*. (Boston: Harvard Business School Press, 1998).

de Bruijn. Hans. *Geert Wilders Speaks Out: The Rhetorical Frames of a European Populist*. (The Hague: Eleven International Publishing, 2011).

Denysenko, Nicholas. "An Appeal to Mary: An Analysis of Pussy Riot's Punk Performance in Moscow." *Journal of the American Academy of Religion* 81 (2013): 1061–1092.

Des Forges, Alison. "Call to Genocide: Radio in Rwanda, 1994." In *The Media and the Rwanda Genocide*, ed. Allan Thompson. (Ottawa, ON: Pluto Press, 2007), 41–54.

Dewey, John. *Theory of the Moral Life*. (New York: Holt, Rinehart and Winston, 1960).

Dobel, J. Patrick. "Paradigms, Traditions, and Keeping the Faith." *Public Administration Review* 61 (2001): 166–171.

———. *Public Integrity*. (Baltimore, MD: Johns Hopkins University Press, 1999).

Domscheit-Berg, Daniel. *Inside WikiLeaks*. (New York: Crown, 2011).

Douglas, Mary. *Purity and Danger*. (London: Routledge, 1966/2002).

Douglas, Mary, and Aaron Wildavsky. *Risk and Culture*. (Berkeley: University of California Press, 1982).

Dreyfus, Suelette, and Julian Assange. *Underground: Tales of Hacking, Madness and Obsession on the Electronic Frontier*. (Edinburgh, UK: Canongate Books, 2012).

Dubnick, Melvin J. "Accountability and the Promise of Performance: In Search of the Mechanisms." *Public Performance and Management Review* 28 (2005): 376–417.

Dubnick, Melvin J., and Ciarán O'Kelly. "Accountability Through Thick and Thin." In *Ethics in Public Management*, eds. H. George Frederickson and Richard K. Ghere. (Armonk, NY: M.E. Sharpe, 2005), 139–164.

Dugdale, Sasha. "Pussy Riot Testimonies," *Modern Poetry in Translation*, Spring 2013. Accessed March 2, 2014. http://www.mptmagazine.com/page/magazine/?pid=154.

du Gay, Paul. *In Praise of Bureaucracy: Weber, Organization, Ethics*. (London, Sage, 2000).

Easton, Peter, Karen Monkman, and Rebecca Miles. "Social Policy From the Bottom Up: Abandoning FGC in Sub-Saharan Africa." *Development in Practice* 13 (2003): 445–58.

Edelman, Murray. *The Symbolic Uses of Politics*. (Urbana: University of Illinois Press, 1964).

Eltahawy, Mona. "Fighting Female Genital Mutilation." *New York Times*, November 17, 2014, A23.

Erlanger, Steven. "Swiss Vote Seen as Challenge to European Integration." *New York Times*, February 11, 2014, A4.

Feldman, Shelley. "Paradoxes of Institutionalisation: The Depoliticisation of Bangladeshi NGOs." *Development in Practice* 13 (2003): 5–26.

Fernando, Udan and Dorothea Hilhorst. "Everyday Practices of Humanitarian Aid: Tsunami Response in Sri Lanka." *Development in Practice* 16 (2006): 292–302.

Finnemore, Martha, and Kathryn Sikkink. "International Norm Dynamics and Political Change." *International Organizations* 52 (1998): 887–917.

Fish, Stanley. "Interpretation and the Pluralist Vision." *Texas Law Review* 60 (1982): 495–503.

Fisher, Walter R. "A Motive View of Communication," *Quarterly Journal of Speech* 56 (1970): 137.

Fletcher, Joseph. *Situation Ethics.* (Louisville, KY: Westminster Press, 1966).

Fonseca-Wollheim, Corinna. "Barenboim Claims His Prize." *Jerusalem Post*, May 5, 2004, Arts 24.

Frankena, William. *Ethics*, 2nd ed. (Englewood Cliffs, NJ: Prentice-Hall, 1973).

Frant, Howard. "High-Powered and Low-Powered Incentives in the Public Sector." *Journal of Public Administration Research and Theory* 6 (1996): 365–381.

Frederickson, H. George. "Searching for Virtue in the Public Life: Revisiting the Vulgar Ethics Thesis." *Public Integrity* 12 (2010): 239–246.

———. *Social Equity and Public Administration.* (Armonk, NY: M. E. Sharpe Press, 2010).

———. *The Spirit of Public Administration.* (San Francisco: Jossey-Bass, 1996).

Frederickson, H. George, and David K. Hart. "The Public Service and the Patriotism of Benevolence." *Public Administration Review* 45 (1985): 547–553.

Fujii, Lee Ann. "Transforming the Moral Landscape: The Diffusion of a Genocidal Norm in Rwanda." *Journal of Genocide Research* 6 (2004), 99–114.

Geertz, Clifford. *The Interpretation of Cultures: Selected Essays.* (New York: Basic Books, 1973).

George-Graves, Nadine. *The Royalty of Vaudeville.* (New York: St. Martin's Press, 2000).

Gessen, Masha. *Words Will Break Cement. The Passion of Pussy Riot.* (New York: Riverhead Books, 2014).

Ghere, Richard K. "Conclusion." In *Ethics in Public Management*, 2nd ed., eds. H. George Frederickson and Richard K. Ghere. (Armonk, NY: M. E. Sharpe, 2013), 361–378.

———. *NGO Leadership and Human Rights.* (Sterling, VA: Kumarian Press, 2012).

Gibson, William. *The Miracle Worker.* http://www.stjohnshigh.org/s/804/images/editor_documents/smith/the_miracle_worker.pdf. Accessed July 26, 2014.

Goldsmith, Martin. *The Inextinguishable Symphony.* (New York: John Wiley and Sons, 2000).

Glikin, Maksim. "Modern Art: Confessions of the Regime." *Vedomosti*, July 26, 2012. Accessed February 28, 2014. http://www.themoscowtimes.com/news/article/what-the-papers-say-july-25-2013/483628.html.

Goodman, Amy. "WikiLeaks Founder Julian Assange on Iraq War Logs, 'Tabloid Journalism' and Why WikiLeaks Is 'Under Siege.'" *Democracy Now! A Daily Independent Global News Hour*, October 26, 2010. http://www.democracynow.org/2010/10/26/wikileaks_founder_julian_assange_on_iraq. Accessed March 11, 2015.

Goodsell, Charles T. *Mission Mystique: Belief Systems in Public Agencies.* (Washington, DC: CQ Press, 2010). http://www.democracynow.org/2010/10/26/wikileaks_founder_julian_assange_on_iraq.

Goodwin, Doris Kearns. *Lyndon Johnson and the American Dream.* (New York: St. Martin's Press, 1991).

Gordon, Michael R. "Meddling Neighbors Undercut Iraq Stability." In *Open Secrets*, ed. Bill Keller. (2011), 74–79.

Govier, Trudy. *The Philosophy of Argument.* (Newport News, VA: Vale Press, 1999).

Gracia, Baltasar. *L'homme de Cour.* (Augsburg, Germany: Paul Kütze, 1710).

Grenberg, Jeanine. *Kant and the Ethics of Humility.* (New York: Cambridge University Press, 2005).

Guzelimian, Ara. "A Dialogue." *Grand Street* 70 (2002): 47.

Hajer, Maarten, and Wytske Versteeg. *Political Rhetoric in the Netherlands: Reframing Crises in the Media.* (Washington, DC: Migration Policy Institute, 2009).

Hantke, Steffen. "*At Stake: Monsters and the Rhetoric of Fear in Public Culture* (Review)." *College Literature* 32 (2005): 186–187.

Hart, David K. "The Moral Exemplar in an Organizational Society." In *Exemplary Public Administrators*, eds. Terry L. Cooper and N. Dale Wright. (San Francisco: Jossey-Bass, 1992), 9–29.

Hart, Roderick P. *The Sound of Leadership*. (Chicago: University of Chicago Press, 1987).

Hashemi, Syed M. "NGO Accountability in Bangladesh: Beneficiaries, Donors, and the State." In *Beyond the Magic Bullet*, eds. Michael Edwards and David Hulme. (West Hartford, CT: Kumarian Press, 1996), 123–131.

Hauser, Gerald A. "The Moral Vernacular of Human Rights Discourse." *Philosophy and Rhetoric* 41 (2008): 440–466.

———. *Vernacular Voices: The Rhetoric of Publics and Public Spheres*. (Columbia: University of South Carolina Press, 1999).

Hayden, Tom. "Closure at Kent State?" *The Nation*, May 15, 2013. http://www.thenation.com/article/174348/closure-kent-state. Accessed July 16, 2014.

Higiro, Jean-Marie V. "Rwandan Private Print Media on the Eve of the Genocide." In *The Media and the Rwanda Genocide*, ed. Allan Thompson. (Ottawa, ON: Pluto Press, 2007), 73–89.

Hilsum, Lindsey. "Reporting Rwanda: The Media and the Aid Agencies." In *The Media and the Rwanda Genocide*, ed. Allan Thompson. (Ottawa, ON: Pluto Press, 2007), 167–187.

Hofstede, Geert. *The Hofstede Centre*. http://geert-hofstede.com/national-culture.html. Accessed May 24, 2014.

Howe, Louis E. "Enchantment, Weak Ontologies, and Administrative Ethics." *Administration and Society* 38 (2006): 422–446.

Ignatieff, Michael. *Human Rights as Politics and Idolatry*. (Princeton: Princeton University Press, 2001).

Ingebretsen, Edward J. *At Stake: Monsters and the Rhetoric of Fear in Public Culture*. (Chicago: University of Chicago Press, 2001).

Ingersoll, Virginia H. and Guy B. Adams. "Beyond Organizational Boundaries: Exploring the Managerial Myth." *Administration and Society* 18 (1986), 360–383.

Jacobs, Andrew, and Chris Buckley. "Tales of Army Discord Show Tiananmen Square in a New Light." *New York Times*, June 3, 2014, A1.

Johnson, Ian. "A Toppled Spire Points to a Church-State Clash in China." *New York Times*, May 30, 2014, A4.

———. *Wild Grass*. (New York: Vintage Books, 2004).

Johnson, Ralph H. "The Role of Audience in Argumentation: From the Perspective of Informal Logic." *Philosophy and Rhetoric* 46 (2013): 533–549.

Johnstone, Christopher L. "Dewey, Ethics, and Rhetoric: Toward a Contemporary Conception of Practical Wisdom." *Philosophy and Rhetoric* 16 (1983): 185–207.

Kamwendo, Gregory H. "Ethnic Revival and Language Associations in the New Malawi: The Chase of Chitumbuka." In *A Democracy of Chameleons*, ed. Harri Englund. (Uppsala, SW: Nordic Africa Institute, 2002), 140–150.

Karim, Mahbubul. "NGOs in Bangladesh: Issues of Legitimacy and Accountability." In *Beyond the Magic Bullet*, eds. Michael Edwards and David Hulme. (West Hartford, CT: Kumarian Press, 1996), 132–141.

Karotki, Siarhei. "Julian Assange Crowned as 'Rock Star of the Year" by Rolling Stone." Theblogismine. December 14, 2010. http://www.theblogismine.com/2010/12/14/julian-assange-crowned-rock-star-of-the-year-by-rolling-stone/. Accessed March 10, 2015.

Kearns, Kevin P. "Ethical Challenges in Nonprofit Organizations: Maintaining Public Trust." In *Ethics in Public Management*, 2nd ed., eds. H. George Frederickson and Richard K. Ghere. (Armonk, NY: M. E. Sharpe, 2013), 265–292.

Keck, Margaret, and Kathryn Sikkink. *Activists beyond Borders: Advocacy Networks in International Politics*. (Ithaca NY: Cornell Press, 1998).

Keller, Bill ed. *Open Secrets: WikiLeaks, War, and American Diplomacy*. (New York: Grove Press, 2011).

Kelner, Joseph. *The Kent State Coverup*. (New York: Harper-Row, 1980).

Kennedy, George. *Aristotle on Rhetoric: A Theory of Civic Discourse*. (New York: Oxford University Press, 1991).

Kincaid, John, and Carl W. Stenberg. "'Big Questions' about Intergovernmental Relations and Management: Who Will Address Them?" *Public Administration Review* 71 (2011): 196–202.

Kishkovsky, Sophia. "Tea and Sympathy with Pussy Riot." *Art Newspaper*, January 15, 2014. Accessed March 3, 2014. http://www.theartnewspaper.com/articles/Tea-and-sympathy-with-Pussy-Riot/31566

Kroc (Joan B.) Institute for Peace and Justice. *Peace Scholar Mary B. Anderson*. February 21, 2012. Accessed April 3, 2014. https://www.sandiego.edu/peacestudies/institutes/ipj/events/eventlist.php?_focus=40647.

Kuklin, Susan. *Iqbal Masih and the Crusaders Against Child Slavery*. (New York: Henry Holt, 1998).

Landler, Mark. "From WikiLemons Clinton Tries to Make Lomonade." In *Open Secrets*, ed. Bill Keller. (2011) 216–218.

Lazar, Alon, and Tal Litvak-Hirsch. "Cultural Trauma as a Potential Symbolic Boundary." *International Journal of Politics, Culture, and Society* 22 (2009): 183–190.

Leach, Fiona and Shashikala Sitaram. "Microfinance and Women's Empowerment: A Lesson from India." *Development in Practice* 12 (2002): 575–588.

Lederman, Josh. "Obama Hails Civil Rights Act." *Dayton Daily News*, April 11, 2014, A5.

Leff, Michael. "Tradition and Agency in Humanistic Rhetoric." *Philosophy and Rhetoric* 36 (2003): 135–147.

Li, Darryl. "Echoes of Violence: Considerations on Radio and Genocide in Rwanda." *Journal of Genocide Research* 6 (2004), 9–27.

Liu, Alan P. "Symbols and Repression at Tiananmen Square." *Political Psychology* 13 (1989), 15–60.

Lwanda, John. "Kwacha: The Violence of Money in Malawi's Politics, 1954-2004." *Journal of Southern Africa Studies* 32 (2006): 525–544.

Lynskey, Dorian. "Pussy Riot: Activists, Not Pin-Ups." *Guardian*, December 20, 2012. Accessed February 22, 2012. http://www.theguardian.com/music/2012/dec/20/pussy-riot-activists-not-pin-ups.

Mack, Richard. *The County Sheriff: America's Last Hope*. (self-published, 2009).

MacIntyre, Alasdair. *After Virtue*, 2nd ed. (Notre Dame, IN: Notre Dame University Press, 1984).

Mackey, Robert. "Ron Paul's Defense of WikiLeaks." In *Open Secrets*, ed. Bill Keller. (2011), 228–229.

Mainzer, Lewis C. "Vulgar Ethics for Public Administration." *Administration and Society* 23 (1991): 3–28.

Malawi24 [reporter], "Mutharika's Speech Sidelined Artists—Lucius Banda," *Malawi24*, June 25, 2014. http://malawi24.com/mutharikas-speech-sidelined-artists-lucius-banda. Accessed July 21, 2014.

Manier, Larry. *The Humanitarian Exercise*. (Bloomfield, CT: Kumarian Press, 2002).

March, James G., and Johan P. Olsen. *Rediscovering Institutions: The Organizational Basis of Politics*. (New York: Free Press, 1989).

Marcuello Servos, Chaime, and Carmen Marcuello. "NGOs, Corporate Social Responsibility, and Social Accountability: Inditex vs. Clean Clothes." *Development in Practice* 17 (2007): 393–403.

Margalit, Avishai. *The Ethics of Memory*. (Cambridge, MA: Harvard University Press, 2002).

Mattern, Mark. "Cajun Music, Cultural Revival: Theorizing Political Action in Popular Music." *Popular Music and Society* 22(1998): 31–47.

Maynard-Moody, Steven W., and Michael C. Musheno. *Cops, Teachers, Counselors: Stories from the Front Lines of Public Service*. (Ann Arbor: University of Michigan Press, 2008).

Meyer, John W. "Social Environments and Organizational Accounting." In *Institutional Environments and Organizations*, eds. W. Richard Scott, John W. Meyer and Associates. (Thousand Oaks, CA: Sage Publications, 1994), 121–136.

Michener, James A. *Kent State: What Happened and Why*. (New York: Random House, 1971).

Miller , Andrew. "Perfect Opposition: On Putin and Pussy Riot," *Public Policy Research* 19 (2012): 205–207.

Miller, Lawrence W., and Lee Seligman. "Is the Audience the Message? A Note on LBJ's Vietnam Statements." *Public Opinion Quarterly* 42 (1978): 71–80.

Misser, François and Yves Jaumain. "Death by Radio." *Index on Censorship*, 23 (1994): 72–74. http://ioc.sagepub.com/content/23/4-5/72. Accessed May 24, 2014.

Morgan, Stephan. *Pussy Riot vs Putin: Revolutionary Russia*. (Self-published, 2013).

Morrison, Sarah. "Imitation and Incitement: An Analysis of Media-driven Behaviour and Criminality." *Internet Journal of Criminology* (2012): 1–31. http://www.internetjournalofcriminology.com/Morrison_Imitation_and_Incitement_IJC_July_2012.pdf. Accessed March 10, 2015.

Mulkay, Michael. "Galileo and the Embryos: Religion and Science in Parliamentary Debate over Research on Human Embryos." *Social Studies of Science* 25 (1995): 499–532.

———. "Rhetorics of Hope and Fear in the Great Embryo Debate." *Social Studies of Science* 23 (1993): 721–742.

Myers, Steven Lee and Patrick Reevell. "Wall of Riot Police Greets Demonstrators at Sentencing of Moscow Protesters." *New York Times*, February 25, 2014, A11.

Nash, N. Richard. *The Rainmaker*. 1966. Commonweal Theater Company. http://www.commonwealtheatre.org/pdfs/Rainmaker_Study_Guide.pdf. Accessed July 26, 2014.

Naumann, Michael. *Barenboim-Said Academy*, Berlin, no date. www.daniel-barenboim-stiftung.org/.../130913%20BSA%20Brochure%2. Accessed May 24, 2014.

New York Times Editorial Board. "The Myth of the 'Student-Athlete' is Laid to Rest." April 14, 2014, A22.

Nordquist, Richard. "What Is Aporia?" *About.Com: Grammar & Composition*, no date. Accessed April 28, 2014. http://grammar.about.com/od/qaaboutrhetoric/f/QAaporia.htm.

Oestreich, James R. "Arabs and Israelis Find Common Ground under a Baton." *New York Times*, August 21, 2014, C6.

Oomen, Barbara. "The Rights for Others: The Contested Homecoming of Rights in the Netherlands." *Netherlands Quarterly of Human Rights* 31 (2013): 41–73.

Paneyakh, Ella. "Extra Jus: This Is Not about Blasphemy." *Vedomosti*, July 26, 2012. Accessed February 28, 2014. http://www.themoscowtimes.com/news/article/what-the-papers-say-july-25-2013/483628.html.

Parkinson, Sarah. *Finding a Way in International Development: Options for Ethical and Effective Work*. (Boulder, CO: Lynne Riener, 2013).

Pauli, Carol. "Killing the Microphone: When Broadcast Freedom Should Yield to Genocide Prevention." *Alabama Law Review* 61 (2010): 665–700.

Payne, Ruby K. *A Framework of Understanding Poverty*, 4th revised ed. (Highlands, TX: aha! Process, 2005).

Perelman, Ch., and L. Olbrechts-Tyteca. *The New Rhetoric: A Treatise on Argumentation*. (Notre Dame, IN: University of Notre Dame Press, 1969).

Perrow, Charles. *Complex Organizations: A Critical Essay*, 3rd ed. (New York: McGraw-Hill, 1986).

Peterson, Scott. "For Iran, WikiLeaks Cables Validate Its Skepticism of Obama's Sincerity." *Christian Science Monitor*, November 30, 2010. Accessed March 12, 2014. http://www.csmonitor.com/World/Middle-East/2010/1130/For-Iran-WikiLeaks-cables-validate-its-skepticism-of-Obama-s-sincerity.

Pies, Ronald. "Enough Talk of 'Demons.'" *New York Times*, April 14, 2014, A22.

Reedy, George. *Lyndon B. Johnson: A Memoir*. (New York: Andrews and McMeel, 1982).

Reilly, Mollie. "John Bolton: Edward Snowden 'Ought to Swing from A Tall Oak Tree.'" *Huffington Post*, December 17, 2013. Accessed March 12, 2014.http://www.huffingtonpost.com/2013/12/17/john-bolton-edward-snowden_n_4461196.html.

Resnick, Danielle. "Two Steps Forward, One Step Back: The Limits of Foreign Aid on Malawi's Democratic Consolidation." In *Democratic Trajectories in Africa: Unraveling the Impact of Foreign Aid*, eds. Danielle Resnick and Nicolas van de Walle. (Oxford, UK: Oxford University Press, 2013), 110–138.

Riak, Abikök. "The Local Capacities for Peace Project: The Sudan Experience." *Development in Practice* 10 (2000): 501–505.

Rohr, John A. *Ethics for Bureaucrats: An Essay on Law and Values*, 2nd ed. (New York: Marcel Dekker, 1989).

Roth, Andrew. "Court Orders House Arrest, and No Internet, for Fierce Critic of Putin." *New York Times*, February 28, 2014, A4.

Roth, Nancy L., Sam B. Sitkin, and Ann House. "Stigma as a Determinant of Legalization." In *The Legalistic Organization*, eds. Sam B. Sitkin and Robert J. Bies. (Thousand Oaks, CA: Sage Publications, 1994), 137–168.

Rubin, Jerry. *DO IT!: Scenarios of the Revolution*. (New York: Simon and Schuster, 1970).

Rubinstein, Richard. *The Cunning of History*. (New York: Harper-Row, 1975).

Sanger, David E., James Glanzer, and Jo Becker. "Around the World, Distress over Iran," in *Open Secrets*, ed. Bill Keller. (2011) 62–70.

Sanger, David E., and Eric Schmidt. "Secret Data Still at Risk of Theft after Snowden." *New York Times*, February 13, 2014, A8.

Santos, Fernanda. "Angry Judge Says Sheriff Defied Order on Latinos." *New York Times*, March 25, 2014, A18.

Savage, Charlie. "Judge Questions Legality of N.S.A. Phone Records." *New York Times*, December 16, 2013. Accessed March 12, 2014. http://www.nytimes.com/2013/12/17/us/politics/federal-judge-rules-against-nsa-phone-data-program.html.

———. "Obama Says N.S.A. Curbs Would Address Worries." *New York Times*, March 26, 2014a, A16.

———. "Republicans Spar on Leaks and Surveillance, Underscoring Partisan Shake-up." *New York Times*, February 4, 2014b. Accessed March 12, 2014. http://www.nytimes.com/2014/02/05/us/politics/republicans-spar-on-leaks-and-surveillance-underscoring-partisan-shake-up.html.

Schneider, Susan C. "Managing Boundaries in Organizations." *Political Psychology* 8 (1987): 379–393.

Scott, Robert. "A Synoptic View of Systems of Western Rhetoric." *Quarterly Journal of Speech* 61 (1975): 440–447.

Scott, W. Richard. *Institutions and Organizations*. (Thousand Oaks, CA: Sage, 1995).

Seal, Lizzie. "Pussy Riot and Feminist Cultural Criminology: A New 'Femininity in Dissent?'" *Contemporary Justice Review* 16 (2013): 293–303.

Selznick, Philip. *Leadership in Administration: A Sociological Interpretation*. (Evanston, IL: Row Patterson, 1957).

Sen, Amartya. *Development as Freedom*. (New York: Anchor Books, 1999).

Serrano, Richard A., and Dalina Castellanos. "Federal Officials Sue Arizona Lawman." *Los Angeles Times*, May 11, 2012, A14.

Shane, Scott. "Yemen Sets Terms of War on Al Qaeda." In *Open Secrets*, ed. Bill Keller. (2011), 80–84.

Shaw, George B. *Saint Joan*. (Gutenberg of Australia, 2002). http://gutenberg.net.au/ebooks02/0200811h.html. Accessed July 26, 2014.

Shevzov, Vera. *Russian Orthodoxy on the Eve of Revolution*. (Oxford, UK: Oxford University Press, 2004).

Smillie, Ian, and John Hailey. *Managing for Change: Leadership, Strategy, and Management in Asian NGOs*. (London: Earthscan, 2002).

Solomon, Martha. "The Rhetoric of Stop ERA: Fatalistic Reaffirmation." *Southern Speech Communication Journal* 44 (1978): 42–59.

Stone, Deborah. *Policy Paradox: The Art of Political Decision Making*. (New York: Norton, 1997).

Straus, Scott. "What Is the Relationship between Hate Radio and Violence? Rethinking Rwanda's 'Radio Machete.'" *Politics and Society* 35 (2007): 609–637.

Tavris, Carol, and Elliot Aronson. *Mistakes Were Made (But Not by Me)*. (Orlando, FL: Harcourt Books, 2007).

Terry, Larry. *Leadership of Public Bureaucracies: The Administrator as Conservator*. (Thousand Oaks, CA: Sage Publications, 1995).

Tewisa, Damian. "Lucius Banda Brings Balaka to a Standstill with a Grand Launch of a Campaign Manifesto." *Malawi Voice*, April 22, 2014. http://www.malawivoice.com/2014/04/22/lucius-banda-brings-balaka-to-a-standstill-with-grand-launch-of-campaign-manifesto. Accessed July 21, 2014.

Thompson, Allan. *The Media and the Rwanda Genocide.* (Ottawa, ON: Pluto Press, 2007).

Tindale, Christopher W. "Rhetorical Argumentation and the Nature of the Audience: Toward an Understanding of Audience— Issues in Argumentation." *Philosophy and Rhetoric* 46 (2013): 508–531.

Uphoff, Norman. "Why NGOs Are Not a Third Sector: A Sectoral Analysis With Some Thoughts on Accountability, Sustainability, and Evaluation." In *Beyond the Magic Bullet,* eds. Michael Edwards and David Hulme. (West Hartford, CT: Kumarian Press, 1996), 23–39.

Upton, Robert. "Planning Praxis: Ethics, Values, and Theory." *The Town Planning Review* 73 (2002): 253–269.

Uvin, Peter. *Human Rights and Development.* (Bloomfield, CT: Kumarian Press, 2004).

vanden Heuvel, Katerina. "Pussy Riot and the Two Russias." *The Nation,* August 2, 2012, 5.

van Velzen, Anna. 2012. "The Construction and Counter-construction of the Muslim Discourse." MA thesis, Utrecht University.

van Zoonen, Liesbet, Farida Vis, and Sabina Mihelj. "YouTube Interactions between Agonism, Antagonism and Dialogue." *New Media Society* 13 (2011): 1283–1300.

Vis, Farida, Liesbet van Zoonen and Sabina Mihelj. "Women Responding to the Anti-Islam Film *Fitna*: Voices and Acts of Citizenship on YouTube." *Feminist Review* 97 (2011): 110–129.

Vokes, Richard. "Charisma, Creativity, and Cosmopolitanism: A Perspective on the Power of the New Radio Broadcasting in Uganda and Rwanda." *Journal of the Royal Anthropological Institute* 13 (2007): 805–824.

Vulliamy, Ed. "Bridging the Gap, Part 2." *The Guardian,* July 12, 2008. http://www.theguardian.com/music/2008/jul/13/classicalmusicandopera.culture. Accessed May 24, 2014.

Wagenvoorde, R. A. 2011. "Dutch Governmental Rhetoric on Good Citizenship and the Implications for Religion." PhD dissertation, University of Groningen.

Wagner, Michelle. "All the Bourgmestre's Men: Making Sense of Genocide in Rwanda." *Africa Today* 45(1998): 25–36.

Walker, Charles. "Rhetoric and Science: Darwin's *Origin of Species.*" *The Journal of Theory Construction and Testing* 14 (2010): 31–32.

Wallace, Tina. *The Aid Chain.* (Warwickshire, UK: Practical Action Publishing, 2007).

White, Lee C. *Government for the People.* (Lanham, MD: Hamilton Books, 2008).

Wildavsky, Aaron. *The Nursing Father: Moses as a Political Leader.* (University: University of Alabama Press, 1984).

Wilders, Geert. *Marked for Death: Islam's War against the West and Me.* (Washington, DC: Regency Publishing, 2012).

Wisenthal, J. L. *Shaw's Sense of History.* (Oxford: Clarendon Press, 1988).

Wolken, Dan. "Pussy Riot Band Members Released after Being Detained in Sochi." *USA Today,* February 18, 2014.

Yardley, Jim. "Spain Seeks to Curb Law Allowing Judges to Pursue Cases Globally." *New York Times,* February 10, 2014, A7.

Yuravlivker, Dror. "'Peace without Conquest': Lyndon Johnson's Speech of April 7, 1965." *Presidential Studies Quarterly* 36 (2006): 457–481.

Zhang, Liang, Andrew J. Nathan, and Perry Link. *The Tiananmen Papers.* (New York: Public Affairs, 2001).

INDEX

abstractions, 162; concreteness and, 204–206, 215; of Wilders, 163, 163–164

accountability, 55–56; charity and, 178; pity related to, 177–178; thin institutional vernaculars and, 29

accusatory discourses, 71–73

accusatory narrative, 71

act-utilitarianism, 55

advocacy, 2–3, 164–165, 192; of Assange, 237–238; exemplary, of Arpaio, 206; of Pussy Riot, 113–114; in rhetorical analysis and empirical inquiry, 18–19; of Rwanda hate radio, 78. *See also* thick and thin advocacy rhetoric

advocacy praxis, 3–4

Afghanistan, 53, 155–156

age factor, 91

Agnew, Spiro, 80

agonism, 170, 171, 183

Agyris, Chris, 51

Alice in Wonderland, 11

Alyokhina, Maria, 106–107, 116–117

America. *See* United States

America's Toughest Sheriff: How We Can Win the War Against Crime (Arpaio), 192

analytical questions, 42–45

analyticity, 74. *See also* Rwanda hate radio

anarchism, 149, 151, 154–155

Anderson, Mary B., 92, 92n1, 240; argumentation morality or ethics for, 222; audience of, 219; as bridge builder, 59–64; as collaborative learner, 50–52; cultural "purity" in, 228, 232; *Do No Harm* by, 52, 53, 54–56, 63, 240; as ethicist, 54–59; for listening, 49; monologic or dialogic argumentation of, 220; as social psychologist, 52–54; temporal orientation in, 225; thin or thick vernacular in, 224; vulgar dialectics and, 233, 243n3

animateurs (radio personalities), 69, 70

Anonymous, 152–153

antagonism, 170–171, 171

antagonists, 219, 220, 221, 222, 223–224, 225, 227, 237; exemplars compared to, 4, 5–6; moral vernacular and, 44; in visual space, 166–171, 169; Wilders as, 163–164, 174

argumentation, 4, 10; audience and, 181–182; of Johnson, Lyndon B., 121, 139–141. *See also* monologic or dialogic argumentation

argumentation morality or ethics, 221–223, 222

Aristotle, 8, 45, 241

Aronson, Elliot, 53, 54

Arpaio, Joe, 7, 179, 206; abstraction and concreteness of, 204–206, 215;

ABOUT THE AUTHOR

Richard K. Ghere is associate professor at the University of Dayton where he is a researcher in the Human Rights Center. His books include *Ethics and Public Management* (1st ed., 2005; 2nd ed., 2013) both co-edited with H. George Frederickson, *NGO Leadership and Human Rights* (2012), and articles on public ethics and public–private partnerships.

CPSIA information can be obtained at www.ICGtesting.com
Printed in the USA
BVOW05*1657120415

395597BV00002B/2/P